Advances in
Spoken Discourse Analysis

Edited by
Malcolm Coulthard

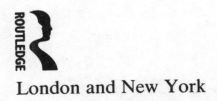

London and New York

First published in 1992 by
Routledge
11 New Fetter Lane, London EC4P 4EE

Simultaneously published in the USA and Canada
by Routledge
29 West 35th Street, New York, NY 10001

Reprinted 1995

Typeset in 10/12 Times by
Florencetype Ltd, Kewstoke, Avon
Printed in Great Britain by
Clays Ltd, St Ives plc

British Library Cataloguing in Publication Data
Advances in spoken discourse analysis.
I. Coulthard, Malcolm.
415

Library of Congress Cataloguing in Publication Data
Advances in spoken discourse analysis / edited by Malcolm Coulthard.
    p. cm.
Includes bibliographical references.
1. Discourse analysis.   I. Coulthard, Malcolm.
P302.A33   1992   91-40402
401'.41–dc 20

ISBN 0–415–06686–7 (hbk)
       0–415–06687–5 (pbk)

Contents

Preface

The aim of this book is to present current Birmingham work in the analysis of Spoken Discourse. The first three 'historical' papers outline the foundation on which the other nine build: Chapter 1 is, with very minor alterations, the central chapter of *Towards an Analysis of Discourse* (Sinclair and Coulthard 1975); Chapter 2 introduces the Brazil description of intonation assumed in all the later chapters; Chapter 3 is a slightly modified version of sections 1 and 3 of *Exchange Structure* (Coulthard and Brazil 1979). In republishing these papers we resisted the very strong temptation to rewrite and update, feeling it was more useful to give readers access to these texts very much in their original form, warts and all, particularly as several of the later articles are developments of or reactions to them.

Many of the other papers are revised, sometimes substantially revised, versions of papers which first appeared in a restricted-circulation University of Birmingham publication, *Discussing Discourse, Papers Presented to David Brazil on his Retirement*. Three papers were specially written for this collection: John Sinclair's 'Priorities in discourse analysis' (Chapter 4), David Brazil's 'Listening to people reading' (Chapter 11), and my own 'Forensic discourse analysis' (Chapter 12).

In order to give the reader easier access to the work of the Birmingham school I have collected all references from the individual articles together at the end of the book and supplemented them with other relevant publications, in order to form a reference bibliography.

Malcolm Coulthard
Birmingham
July 1991

About the authors

David Brazil is a Fellow of the Institute for Advanced Research in the Humanities at the University of Birmingham. The second edition of his *The Communicative Value of Intonation* appeared in 1992.

Malcolm Coulthard is Senior Lecturer in English Language at the University of Birmingham. His recent publications include the two edited volumes 'presented to David Brazil on his retirement', *Talking about Text*, 1986, and *Discussing Discourse*, 1987, and, in Portuguese, *Linguagem e Sexo* and *Tradução: Teoria e Prática*, both published in 1991.

Gill Francis is a Senior Researcher working on corpus-based grammar and attached to the Cobuild project at the University of Birmingham. Among her recent publications are 'Noun group heads and clause structure', *Word*, Aug. 1991, 27–38, 'Aspects of nominal group lexical cohesion', *Interface* 4, 1, 1989, 27–53, and, with A. Kramer-Dahl, 'Grammaticalising the medical case history', in *Essays in Contextual Stylistics*, Routledge, forthcoming.

Martin Hewings is a Lecturer in English to Overseas Students at the University of Birmingham. He is the author of *Pronunciation Tasks*, Cambridge University Press, forthcoming.

Sue Hunston is Lecturer in Applied Linguistics at the University of Surrey. Her 'Text in world and world in text' was published in the *Nottingham Linguistic Circular* in 1985 and 'Evaluation and ideology in scientific English' will appear in *Varieties of Written English*, Vol. 2, Pinter, 1992.

Mike McCarthy is Senior Lecturer in English Language and Director of the Centre for English Language Education at the University of Nottingham. His recent publications include *Vocabulary*, Oxford University Press, 1990, *Discourse Analysis for Language Teachers*, Cambridge University Press, 1991, and, with Ron Carter, *Vocabulary and Language Teaching*, Longman, 1988.

John Sinclair is Professor of Modern English Language at the University of Birmingham and Editor-in-Chief of Cobuild Publications. His recent publications are *The Structure of Teacher Talk*, ELR, 1990, *Corpus, Concordance, Collocation*, Oxford University Press, 1991, and the edited collection *Looking Up*, Collins Cobuild, 1987.

Amy Tsui is a Lecturer in the Department of Curriculum Studies at Hong Kong University. Her studies on conversational analysis, pragmatics and speech act theory have appeared in *Semiotica*, *Language in Society*, the *Journal of Pragmatics* and various conference proceedings.

Dave Willis is a Lecturer in the Centre for English Language Studies at the University of Birmingham. His most recent publications are *The Lexical Syllabus*, Collins Cobuild, 1990 and, with Jane Willis, *The Collins Cobuild English Course, Levels 1, 2 and 3*, 1988–9.

Jane Willis is a Lecturer at the University of Aston in Birmingham. Her latest publication is *First Lessons*, Collins Cobuild, 1990, a task-based ELT course for beginners which is linked to the *Collins Cobuild English Course*.

1 Towards an analysis of discourse

John Sinclair and Malcolm Coulthard

THE DEVELOPMENT OF THE SYSTEM OF ANALYSIS

When we began to investigate the structure of classroom interaction we had no preconceptions about the organization or extent of linguistic patterning in long texts. Obviously lessons are highly structured but our problem was to discover how much of this structure was pedagogical and how much linguistic. It seemed possible that the presence of a linguistic introduction was a clue to the boundary of a linguistic unit, but we quickly realized that this is not a useful criterion. On the first morning of the academic year a headmaster may welcome the new pupils with

> 'Good morning, children, Welcome to Waseley School. This is an important day for you . . .'

thereby introducing them to several years of schooling. When the children then meet their new class teacher she will also welcome them and explain their timetable. They go to their first subject lesson. Here the teacher may introduce the subject and go on to delimit part of it;

> 'This year we are going to study world geography, starting with the continent of Africa. . . . Today I want to look at the rivers of Africa. Let's start with the map. Can you tell us the name of one river, any one?'

Everything the headmaster and teachers have said so far could be considered as introductions to a series of hierarchically ordered units: the whole of the child's secondary education; a year's work; one academic subject; a section of that subject area; a lesson; a part of that lesson; a small interactive episode with one pupil. However, while the language of the introduction to each unit is potentially distinctive, despite overlap, we would not want to suggest that for instance 'a year's work' has any linguistic structure.

The majority of the units we referred to above are pedagogic ones. In order to avoid the danger of confusing pedagogic with linguistic structure we determined to work upwards from the smallest to the largest linguistic units. The research problem with contiguous utterances is primarily a descriptive one; major theoretical problems arise when more extensive units are postulated.

We decided to use a *rank scale* for our descriptive model because of its flexibility. The major advantage of describing new data with a rank scale is that no rank has more importance than any other and thus if, as we did, one discovers new patterning, it is a fairly simple process to create a new rank to handle it.

The basic assumption of a rank scale is that a unit at a given rank, for example, *word*, is made up of one or more units of the rank below, *morpheme*, and combines with other units at the same rank to make one unit at the rank above, *group* (Halliday 1961). The unit at the lowest rank has no structure. For example in grammar 'morpheme' is the smallest unit, and cannot be subdivided into smaller grammatical units. However, if one moves from the *level* of grammar to the level of phonology, morphemes can be shown to be composed of a series of phonemes. Similarly, the smallest unit at the level of discourse will have no structure, although it is composed of words, groups or clauses at the level of grammar.

Each rank above the lowest has a structure which can be expressed in terms of the units next below. Thus, the structure of a clause can be expressed in terms of nominal, verbal, adverbial and prepositional groups. The unit at the highest rank is one which has a structure that can be expressed in terms of lower units, but does not itself form part of the structure of any higher unit. It is for this reason that 'sentence' is regarded as the highest unit of grammar. Paragraphs have no grammatical structure; they consist of a series of sentences of any type in any order. Where there are no grammatical constraints on what an individual can do, variations are usually regarded as 'stylistic'.

We assumed that when, from a linguistic point of view, classroom discourse became an unconstrained string of units, the organization would be fundamentally pedagogic. While we could then make observations on teacher style, further analysis of structure would require another change of level not rank.

We began by looking at adjacent utterances, trying to discover what constituted an appropriate reply to a teacher's question, and how the teacher signalled whether the reply was appropriate or inappropriate.

Initially we felt the need for only two ranks, *utterance* and *exchange*; utterance was defined as everything said by one speaker before another began to speak, and exchange as two or more utterances. However, we quickly experienced difficulties with these categories. The following example has three utterances, but how many exchanges?

T: Can you tell me why do you eat all that food?
    Yes.
P: To keep you strong.

T: To keep you strong. Yes. To keep you strong. Why do you want to be strong?

An obvious boundary occurs in the middle of the teacher's second utterance, which suggests that there is a unit smaller than utterance. Following Bellack *et al.* (1966) we labelled this unit *move*, and wondered for a while whether moves combined to form utterances which in turn combined to form exchanges.

However, the example above is not an isolated one; the vast majority of exchanges have their boundaries within utterances. Thus, although utterance had many points to recommend it as a unit of discourse, not least ease of definition, we reluctantly abandoned it. We now express the structure of exchanges in terms of moves. A typical exchange in the classroom consists of an *initiation* by the teacher, followed by a *response* from the pupil, followed by *feedback*, to the pupil's response from the teacher, as in the above example.

While we were looking at exchanges we noticed that a small set of words – 'right', 'well', 'good', 'OK', 'now', recurred frequently in the speech of all teachers. We realized that these words functioned to indicate boundaries in the lesson, the end of one stage and the beginning of the next. Silverman (personal communication) noted their occurrence in job interviews and Pearce (1973) in broadcast interviews where the function is exactly the same. We labelled them *frame*. Teachers vary in the particular word they favour but a frame occurs invariably at the beginning of a lesson, marking off the settling-down time.

Now,
I want to tell you about a King who lived a long time ago in Ancient Egypt.

An example of a frame within a lesson is:

Energy. Yes.
When you put petrol in the car you're putting another kind of energy in the car from the petrol. So we get energy from petrol and we get energy from food. Two kinds of energy.
Now then,
I want you to take your pen and rub it as hard as you can on something woollen.

We then observed that frames, especially those at the beginning of a lesson, are frequently followed by a special kind of statement, the function of which is to tell the class what is going to happen, see the examples above. These items are not strictly part of the discourse, but rather metastatements about the discourse – we called them *focus*. The boundary elements, frame and focus, were the first positive evidence of the existence of a unit above exchange, which we later labelled *transaction*.

Exchanges combine to form transactions and it seems probable that there will be a number of transaction types, distinguished according to their interactive function, but we cannot isolate them as yet. The unanswered question is whether we will be able to provide structures for transactions or whether the ways in which exchanges are combined to form transactions will prove to be purely a feature of teacher style.

The highest unit of classroom discourse, consisting of one or more transactions, we call *lesson*. This unit may frequently be coextensive with the pedagogical unit *period*, but need not be.

For several months we continued using these four ranks – move, exchange, transaction, lesson – but found that we were experiencing difficulty coding at the lowest rank. For example, to code the following as simply an initiation seemed inadequate.

Now I'm going to show you a word and I want you – anyone who can – to tell me if they can tell me what the word says.
Now it's a bit difficult.
It's upside down for some of you isn't it?
Anyone think they know what it says?
(Hands raised)
Two people. Three people.
Let's see what you think, Martin, what do you think it says?

We then realized that moves too can have a structure and so we needed another rank with which we could describe this structure. This we labelled *act*.

Moves and acts in discourse are very similar to words and morphemes in grammar. By definition, move is the smallest free unit although it has a structure in terms of acts. Just as there are bound morphemes which cannot alone realize words, so there are bound acts which cannot alone realize moves.

We needed to distinguish discourse acts from grammatical structures, or there would be no point in proposing a new level of language description – we would simply be analysing the higher ranks of grammar. Of course if acts did turn out to be arrangements of clauses in a consistent and hierarchical fashion, then they would replace (in speech) our confusing notions of 'sentence' and the higher ranks of what we now call discourse would arrange themselves on top.

The evidence is not conclusive and we need comparative data from other types of discourse. We would argue, however, for a separate level of discourse because, as we show in detail later, grammatical structure is not sufficient to determine which discourse act a particular grammatical unit realizes – one needs to take account of both relevant situational information and position in the discourse.

The lowest rank of the discourse scale overlaps with the top of the grammar scale (see table below). Discourse acts are typically one free clause, plus any subordinate clauses, but there are certain closed classes where we can specify almost all the possible realizations which consist of single words or groups.

There is a similar overlap at the top of the discourse scale with pedagogical structures and we have been constantly aware of the danger of creating a rank for which there is only pedagogical evidence. We have deliberately chosen *lesson*, a word specific to the particular language situation we are investigating, as the label for the top rank. We feel fairly certain that the four lower ranks will be present in other discourses; the fifth may also be, in which case, once we have studied comparative data, we will use the more general label *interaction*.

We see the level of discourse as lying between the levels of *grammar* and *non-linguistic organization*. There is no need to suppose a one-to-one correspondence of units between levels; the levels of phonology and grammar overlap considerably, but have only broad general correspondence. We see the top of our discourse scale, lesson, corresponding roughly to the rank *period* in the non-linguistic level, and the bottom of our scale, act, corresponding roughly to the clause complex in grammar.

Levels and ranks

Non-linguistic organization	Discourse	Grammar
course		
period	LESSON	
topic	TRANSACTION	
	EXCHANGE	
	MOVE	sentence
	ACT	clause
		group
		word
		morpheme

SUMMARY OF THE SYSTEM OF ANALYSIS

This research has been very much text-based. We began with very few preconceptions and the descriptive system has grown and been modified to cope with problems thrown up by the data. The system we have produced is hierarchical and our method of presentation is closely modelled on Halliday's 'Categories of a theory of grammar'. All the terms used, *structure*, *system*, *rank*, *level*, *delicacy*, *realization*, *marked*, *unmarked*, are Halliday's. To permit readers to gain an overall impression, the whole system is first presented at primary delicacy and then given a much more discursive treatment.

Working downwards, each rank is first labelled. Then the elements of structure are named, and the structure is stated in a general way, using shortened forms of the names of elements. Brackets indicate structural options.

The link between one rank and the next below is through *classes*. A class realizes an element of structure, and in this summary classes are both numbered and named. Let us look at one of the tables as an example:

RANK II: Transaction

Elements of structure	Structures	Classes of exchange
Preliminary (P) Medial (M) Terminal (T)	PM (M^2 . . . M^n) (T)	P, T: Boundary (II.1) M: Teaching (II.2)

This table identifies the rank as second from the top of the scale, i.e. transaction. It states that there are three elements of structure, called Preliminary (symbol P), Medial (M), and Terminal (T). In the next column is given a composite statement of the possible structures of this transaction: PM (M^2 . . . M^n) (T). Anything within brackets is optional, so this formula states:

(a) there must be a preliminary move in each transaction,
(b) there must be one medial move, but there may be any number of them,
(c) there can be a terminal move, but not necessarily.

In the third column the elements of transaction structure are associated with the classes of the rank next below, exchange, because each element is realized by a particular class of exchange. Preliminary and terminal exchanges, it is claimed, are selected from the same class of move called Boundary moves, and this is numbered for ease of reference. The element medial is realized by a class of exchange called Teaching. Later tables develop the structure of these exchanges at rank III. There now follows the presentation of the whole rank scale.

RANK I: Lesson

Elements of structure	Structures	Classes
	an unordered series of transactions	

RANK II: Transaction

Elements of structure	Structures	Classes of exchange
Preliminary (P) Medial (M) Terminal (T)	PM (M^2 . . . M^n) (T)	P, T: Boundary (II.1) M: Teaching (II.2)

RANK III: Exchange (Boundary)

Elements of structure	Structures	Classes of move
Frame (Fr) Focus (Fo)	(Fr)(Fo)	Fr: Framing (III.1) Fo: Focusing (III.2)

RANK III: Exchange (Teaching)

Elements of structure	Structures	Classes of move
Initiation (I) Response (R) Feedback (F)	I(R)(F)	I: Opening (III.3) R: Answering (III.4) F: Follow-up (III.5)

RANK IV: Move (Opening)

Elements of structure	Structures	Classes of act

signal (s)
pre-head (pre-h)
head (h)
post-head (post-h)
select (sel)
	(s) (pre-h) h (post-h)
	(sel)
	(sel) (pre-h) h
		s: marker (IV.1)
		pre-h: starter (IV.2)
		h: system operating at h;
		   choice of elicitation,
		   directive, informative,
		   check (IV.3)
		post-h: system operating
		   at post-h; choice
		   from prompt and
		   clue (IV.4)
		sel: ((cue) bid)
		   nomination (IV.5)

RANK IV: Move (Answering)

Elements of structure	Structures	Classes of act

pre-head (pre-h)
head (h)
post-head (post-h)
	(pre-h) h (post-h)	pre-h: acknowledge (IV.6)
		h: system operating at h;
		   choice of reply, react
		   acknowledge (IV.7)
		post-h: comment (IV.8)

RANK IV: Move (Follow-up)

Elements of structure	Structures	Classes of act
pre-head (pre-h) head (h) post-head (post-h)	(pre-h)(h)(post-h)	pre-h: accept (IV.9) h: evaluate (IV.10) post-h: comment (IV.8)

RANK IV: Move (Framing)

Elements of structure	Structures	Classes of act
head (h) qualifier (q)	hq	h; marker (IV.1) q: silent stress (IV.11)

RANK IV: Move (Focusing)

Elements of structure	Structures	Classes of act

signal (s)
pre head (pre-h)
head (h)
post-head (post-h)
	(s) (pre-h) h (post-h)	s: marker (IV.1)
		pre-h: starter (IV.2)
		h: system at h; choice
		   from metastatement or
		   conclusion (IV.12)
		post-h: comment (IV.8)

EXPLANATION OF THE SYSTEM OF ANALYSIS

The previous section presented a downward view showing how units at each rank had structures realized by units at the rank below. The following section begins at the lowest rank and discusses the realization and recognition of acts; succeeding sections then discuss the structures of moves, exchanges, transactions and lessons.

ACTS

The units at the lowest rank of discourse are *acts* and correspond most nearly to the grammatical unit *clause*, but when we describe an item as an act we are doing something very different from when we describe it as a clause. Grammar is concerned with the *formal* properties of an item, discourse with the *functional* properties, with what the speaker is using the item for. The four sentence types, declarative, interrogative, imperative, and moodless, realize twenty-one discourse acts, many of them specialized and some quite probably classroom-specific.

There are three major acts which probably occur in all forms of spoken discourse – *elicitation*, *directive*, and *informative* – and they appear in classroom discourse as the heads of Initiating moves. An elicitation is an act whose function is to request a linguistic response – linguistic, although the response may be a non-verbal surrogate such as a nod or raised hand. A directive is an act whose function is to request a non-linguistic response; within the classroom this means opening books, looking at the blackboard, writing, listening. An informative is, as the name suggests, an act which functions to pass on ideas, facts, opinions, information and to which the appropriate response is simply an acknowledgement that one is listening.

Elicitations, directives and informatives are very frequently realized by interrogatives, imperatives, and declaratives respectively, but there are occasions when this is not so. A native speaker who interpreted 'Is that the mint sauce over there?' or 'Can you tell me the time?' as yes/no questions, 'Have a drink' as a command, or 'I wish you'd go away' as requiring just a murmur of agreement, would find the world a bewildering place full of irritable people. These are examples of the lack of fit which can occur between form and function.

The opportunity for variety arises from the relationship between grammar and discourse. The unmarked form of a directive may be imperative, 'Shut the door', but there are many marked versions, using interrogative, declarative and moodless structures.

can you	shut the door
I wonder if you could	shut the door
would you mind	shutting the door
the door is still open	
the door	

To handle this lack of fit between grammar and discourse we suggest two intermediate areas where distinctive choices can be postulated: situation and tactics. Both of these terms already have various meanings in linguistics, but still seem appropriate to our purpose. *Situation* here includes all relevant factors in the environment, social conventions, and the shared experience of the participants. The criterion of relevance is obviously vague and ill-defined at the moment, though some dignity can be attached to it on the grounds that anyone who considers such factors irrelevant must arrive at a different interpretation of the discourse. Examples of situational features 'considered relevant' and the use to which they are put in the analysis of classroom language will be detailed below.

The other area of distinctive choice, *tactics*, handles the syntagmatic patterns of discourse: the way in which items precede, follow and are related to each other. It is place in the structure of the discourse which finally determines which act a particular grammatical item is realizing, though classification can only be made of items already tagged with features from grammar and situation.

Situation

In situation we use, at present in an *ad hoc* and unsystematized way, knowledge about schools, classrooms, one particular moment in a lesson, to reclassify items already labelled by the grammar. Usually the grammatical types declarative, interrogative, imperative, realize the situational categories *statement*, *question*, *command*, but this is not always so. Of the nine possible combinations – declarative statement, declarative question, declarative command, and so on – there is only one we cannot instance: imperative statement. For ease of reference the situational and grammatical categories are listed in the table below, together with their discourse category equivalents.

Grammatical categories	Situational categories	Discourse categories
declarative	statement	informative
interrogative	question	elicitation
imperative	command	directive

The interrogative, 'What are you laughing at?', can be interpreted either as a question, or as a command to stop laughing. Inside the classroom it is usually the latter. In one of our tapes a teacher plays a recording of a television programme in which there is a psychologist with a 'posh' accent. The teacher wants to explore the children's attitude to accent and the value judgements they base on it. When the recording is finished the teacher begins,

T: What kind of a person do you think he is? Do you – what are you laughing at?
P: Nothing.

The pupil interpreted the teacher's interrogative as a directive to stop laughing, but that was not the teacher's intention. He had rejected his first question because he realized that the pupil's laughter was an indication of her attitude, and if he could get her to explain why she was laughing he would have an excellent opening to the topic. He continues and the pupil realizes her mistake.

T: Pardon?
P: Nothing.
T: You're laughing at nothing, nothing at all?
P: No.
    It's funny really 'cos they don't think as though they were there they might not like it. And it sounds rather a pompous attitude.

The girl's mistake lay in misunderstanding the situation not the sentence, and the example demonstrates the crucial role of situation in the analysis of discourse. We can at the moment make only a rudimentary attempt to deal with situation. We suggest four questions one can ask about the situation and depending on the answers to these questions and the grammatical form of the clause, propose three rules which predict the correct interpretation of teacher utterances most of the time. The questions we ask are

1 If the clause is interrogative is the addressee also the subject of the clause?
2 What actions or activities are physically possible at the time of utterance?
3 What actions or activities are proscribed at the time of utterance?
4 What actions or activities have been prescribed up to the time of utterance?

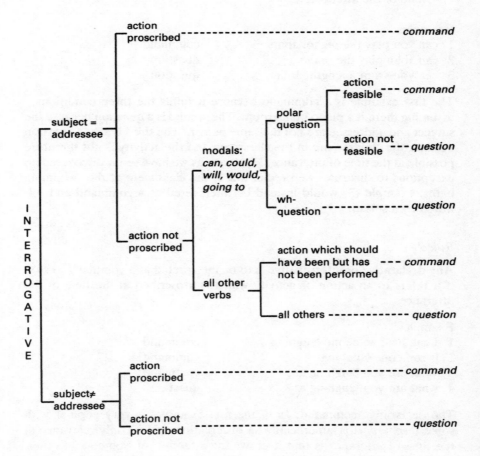

Figure 1: The classification of an interrogative by situation

Using the answers to these questions we can formulate three rules to predict when a declarative or interrogative will be realizing something other than a statement or question. See Figure 1 (p. 11) for a systemic treatment of the classification of interrogatives by means of these rules.

Rule 1

An interrogative clause is to be interpreted as a command to do if it fulfils all the following conditions:

(i) it contains one of the modals 'can', 'could', 'will', 'would' (and some-times 'going to');
(ii) the subject of the clause is also the addressee;
(iii) the predicate describes an action which is physically possible at the time of the utterance.

Examples:
1 can you play the piano, John   command
2 can John play the piano   question
3 can you swim a length, John   question

The first example is a command because it fulfils the three conditions – assuming there is a piano in the room. The second is a question because the subject and addressee are not the same person. The third is also a question because the children are in the classroom and the activity is not therefore possible at the time of utterance. However, as we have so far discovered no exceptions to this rule, we predict that if the class were at the swimming baths, example (3) would instead be interpreted as a command and fol-lowed by a splash.

Rule 2

Any declarative or interrogative is to be interpreted as a command to stop if it refers to an action or activity which is proscribed at the time of the utterance.

Examples:
1 I can hear someone laughing   command
2 is someone laughing   command
3 what are you laughing at   command
4 what are you laughing at   question

The declarative command, as in the first example, is very popular with some teachers. It is superficially an observation, but its only relevance at the time of utterance is that it draws the attention of 'someone' to their laughter, so that they will stop laughing. Examples (2) and (3), though interrogative in form, work in exactly the same way. Example (4) is only interpreted as a question when laughter is not regarded as a forbidden activity.

Rule 3

Any declarative or interrogative is to be interpreted as command to do if it refers to an action or activity which teacher and pupil(s) know ought to have been performed or completed and hasn't been.

Examples:
1 the door is still open   command
2 did you shut the door   command
3 did you shut the door   question

Example (1) states a fact which all relevant participants already know; example (2) is apparently a question to which all participants know the answer. Both serve to draw attention to what hasn't been done in order to cause someone to do it. Example (3) is a question only when the teacher does not know whether the action has been performed or not.

Labov (1970) independently proposed a rule for the interpretation of questions in conversation which is very close to Rule 3 above.

> If A makes a request for information of B about whether an action X has been performed, or at what time T, X will be performed, and the four preconditions below hold, then A will be heard as making an underlying form 'B: do X!'

The preconditions are, that A believes that B believes:

1 X should be done for a purpose Y.
2 B has the ability to do X.
3 B has the obligation to do X.
4 A has the right to tell B to do X.

For us, preconditions (1), (3), and (4) are part of the general teaching situation and do not need to be invoked for the interpretation of a particular utterance.

Tactics

In *grammar* we classify an item by its structure; from the relative position of subject and verb we label a clause declarative, interrogative or imperative. In *situation* we use information about the non-linguistic environment to reclassify items as statement, question or command. We need to know what has happened so far in the classroom, what the classroom contains, what the atmosphere is like, but then, given such detailed information, we can make a situational classification of even an isolated clause. However, the *discourse* value of an item depends on what linguistic items have preceded it, what are expected to follow and what do follow. We handle such sequence relationships in *tactics*.

The definitions of the discourse acts, informative, elicitation and directive, make them sound remarkably similar to statement, question, and command but there are major differences. While elicitations are always realized by questions, directives by commands, and informatives by statements, the relationship is not reciprocal: questions can realize many other acts; indeed, the expression 'rhetorical question' is a recognition of this fact. Statements, questions and commands only realize informatives, elicitations and directives when they are initiating; an elicitation is an initiating question whose function is to gain a verbal response from another speaker. Questions occur at many other places in discourse but then their function is different, and this must be stressed. A question which is not intended to get a reply is realizing a different act from one which is; the speaker is using the question for a different purpose and we must recognize this in our description.

Spoken discourse is produced in real time and our descriptive system attempts to deal with the 'now-coding' aspect of speech. Speakers inevitably make mistakes, or realize that they could have expressed what they intended much better. A teacher may produce a question which he fully intends as an elicitation and then change his mind. Obviously he can't erase what he has said, and he doesn't tell the children to ignore it, but he does signal that the children are not expected to respond as if it were an elicitation. In the 'what are you laughing at' example discussed above, the teacher abruptly changes course in the middle of a question. This is rare and signals to the class that what has gone before should be regarded as if it had never been said, should be deleted completely.

More frequently, as in the example below, the teacher follows one potential informative, directive or elicitation with another, usually more explicit one, signalling paralinguistically, by intonation, absence of pausing or speeding up his speech rate, that he now considers what he has just said to be a *starter*, and thus the pupils are not intended to respond. Starters are acts whose function is to provide information about, or direct attention or thought towards an area, in order to make a correct response to the initiation more likely. Some starters are intended initiations which have been down-graded when the teacher perceived their inadequacy for his purpose:

   T: *What about this one?* This I think is a super one.
        Isobel, can you think what it means?
   P: Does it mean there's been an accident further along the road?

The teacher begins with a question which appears to have been intended as an elicitation. She changes her mind and relegates it to a starter. The following statement is in turn relegated by a second question which then functions as the elicitation.

To recapitulate: while speaking the teacher produces a series of clauses classifiable as statements, questions and commands in *situation*. If the teacher then allows a pupil to respond, these items are seen as initiating, and have the discourse value of informative, elicitation and directive respectively; if the teacher immediately follows one of these clauses with another the first is 'pushed down' to act as a starter.

Thus in any succession of statements, questions, and commands the pupil knows that he usually has only to respond to the final one which alone has an initiating function. This can lead to an incorrect response if the pupil doesn't fully understand what the teacher is saying. In the following example a quoted question is understood as an elicitation.

P: Well, he should take some look at what the man's point of view is.
T: Yes, yes.
    But he wasn't asked that question don't forget. He was merely asked the question '*Why, why are they reacting like this?*'
P: Well, maybe its the way they've been brought up.

At the head of each initiating move by the teacher is one elicitation, directive, or informative. That is to say, a move constitutes a coherent contribution to the interaction which essentially serves one purpose. The purpose is selected from a very small set of available choices. Where a move is made up of more than one act, the other acts are subsidiary to the head, and optional in the structure. The teacher's initiation is typically followed by a responding move from a pupil:

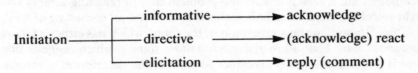

Acknowledge, a verbal or non-verbal signal which confirms that the pupil is listening and understanding; *react* is the performance of whatever action is required by the directive. Acknowledge is also an optional part of the response to a directive, when it serves to let the teacher know that the pupil has heard.

T: John, I wonder if you could open that window.
P: Yes/mm/sure.

The response to an elicitation is a *reply*. Replies are all too often one word moodless items, but they can also be realized by *statements*, as in the example above, 'Well, he should take some look at what the man's point of view is.'; or *questions* like, 'Does it mean there's been an acccident?' in the earlier example. A reply can optionally be followed by *comment*.

Comments serve to exemplify, expand, justify, provide additional information about the head of the move, and can occur in Follow-up and Focusing moves as well as Answering moves. Comments are almost always realized by statements or tag questions:

P: Are the number for le – for the letters?
T: Yes.
     They're – that's the order, one, two, three, four.

A special feature of the classroom situation is that a number of individuals have (been) gathered together for the specific purpose of learning something. They answer questions and follow instructions and they need to know whether they are performing adequately. A teacher rarely asks a question because he wants to know the answer; he asks a question because he wants to know whether the pupil knows. In such a situation the pupils need to know whether their answer was judged correct and thus an act we label *evaluate* is of vital importance. If we think of the following exchange

T: What time is it, Susan?
P: Three o'clock.

The closing item outside the classroom could well be 'Thanks'; inside the classroom, 'Good girl'. In evaluate, the teacher presents his estimation of the pupil's response and creates a basis for proceeding. Evaluate is usually realized by a statement, sometimes by a tag question.

Evaluate is often preceded by *accept*, an act which confirms that the teacher has heard or seen the response and that it was appropriate. It is frequently used when a child's reply is wrong but the teacher wants to encourage him. There is always the problem that in rejecting a reply one might reject the child. Accept is realized by a closed set consisting of 'yes', 'no', 'fine', 'good', or by a repetition of the reply, which has either a falling intonation, tone 1, or a low rising intonation, tone 3, which suggests that there is another answer. (A succinct account of the description of intonation used here is given in Halliday 1970.) Alternatively, following a pupil's wrong answer, one can get an accepting 'yes' with a fall–rise intonation, tone 4, which leads on to a negative evaluation or a *clue* (see below).

In all forms of spoken discourse there are rules about who speaks when (Schegloff and Sacks 1973). Within the classroom the teacher has the right to speak whenever she wants to, and children contribute to the discourse when she allows them to. Teachers differ in the degree of formality they impose on children's contributions, and the rigidity with which they stick to the rule of 'no shouting out'. As noted above, a typical structure as a classroom exchange is a teacher elicitation followed by a pupil reply. However, a teacher elicitation followed by thirty replies would be useless and most teachers have a way of selecting which pupil will reply.

Sometimes teachers *nominate* a child to answer; sometimes children raise their hands or shout 'Miss, Miss', *bidding* to be nominated, to be given permission to speak, and sometimes the teacher gives the children a *cue* to bid, 'hands up'. Cue is a command but not a directive. It is addressed to the class but they do not all raise their hands because the command is to be interpreted as 'Put your hands up if you know.' We can compare this with a real directive, when the whole class is expected to react. In the following extract there are examples of both.

Directive: *All eyes on me.* Put your pencils down. Fold your arms. Hands on your heads. Hands on your shoulders. Hands on your knees. Fold your arms. Look at me.

Cue: *Hands up.* What's that.

Nomination, bid, and cue are all subordinate elements of the teacher's initiating move, and there are two other acts which occur in initiating moves, *clue* and *prompt*. Clue is a statement, question, command, or moodless item, subordinate to the head of the initiation which provides additional information to help the pupil answer the elicitation or comply with the directive. 'Look at the car', in the example below is a clue.

T: What about this one? This I think is a super one. Isobel, can you think what it means?
P: Does it mean there's been an accident further along the road?
T: No.
P: Does it mean double bend ahead?
T: No.
     Look at the car (tilts the picture)

It does not have the status of a directive because its function is not to cause a pupil reaction. If the whole class simply looked at the car the teacher would be very annoyed; the children are to look at the car in the light of the elicitation 'can you think what it means?'

Sometimes elicitations or directives are reinforced by a *prompt*. We said above that elicitations and directives request a response; a prompt suggests that the teacher is not requesting but expecting or even demanding. Prompts are always realized by commands, and a closed set at that. The ones we have discovered so far are 'go on', 'come on', 'hurry up', 'quickly', 'have a guess'.

There are four more acts to introduce: *marker*, *metastatement*, *conclusion*, *loop*. Marker is an item whose sole function is to indicate a boundary in the discourse. It is realized by a very small set of words, 'well', 'OK', 'right', 'now', 'good', 'all right', and can occur at the beginning of opening, focusing and framing moves.

Metastatement is an act occurring in a focusing move, whose function is to state what the discourse is going to be about. In other words it is technically not part of the discourse but a commentary on the discourse.

Such items are not informatives because the teacher is not telling the children something, he is telling them what he is going to tell them. Thus:

> Now,
> *I want to tell you about a king who lived a long time ago . . .*

Conclusion is a special kind of statement which occurs at the end of some transactions and summarizes what has been done. In a way it is the converse of metastatement. Conclusions are marked by 'so' or 'then', and often also a noticeable slowing down in rate of speech.

> *So that then is why the Pharaohs built their pyramids.*
> *So that's the first quiz.*

Sometimes the channel of communication is too noisy and the teacher needs the child to repeat what he has just said. The act he uses we call *loop*; it is realized by 'pardon', 'you what', 'eh', 'again', and functions to take the discourse back to the stage it was at before the pupil spoke. The channel noise cannot be only one-way, but it is significant that no child in any of our tapes ever admits to not having heard something the teacher has said. Thus, we only have examples of teacher loops. Loop can of course be used tactically to draw the attention of the class to something one child has said.

> T: You told me before.
> P: Energy.
> T: *Again*.
> P: Energy.

Finally, at times teachers produce speech acts that are not specifically part of the discourse. We refer to these as *asides*. They include remarks which are unrelated to the discourse, though not to the situation. Often they are muttered under the breath.

> T: *It's freezing in here.*

> T: The Egyptians, and –
> *when I can find my chart. Here it is –*
> Here are some of the symbols they used.

The classes of acts

There now follows a summary description of all the acts, each numbered as they were in the summary of analysis on pp. 6–8. First the label, then the symbol used in coding, and finally the functional definition and characteristic formal features. For the closed class items there is a list of all the examples so far discovered.

Reference Number	Label	Symbol
IV.1	marker	m

Realized by a closed class of items – 'well', 'OK', 'now', 'good', 'right', 'alright'. When a marker is acting as the head of a framing move it has a falling intonation, [1] or [1+], as well as a silent stress. Its function is to mark boundaries in the discourse.

IV.2	starter	s

Realized by a statement, question or command. Its function is to provide information about or direct attention to or thought towards an area in order to make a correct response to the initiation more likely.

IV.3.1	elicitation	el

Realized by a question. Its function is to request a linguistic response.

IV.3.2	check	ch

Realized by a closed class of polar questions concerned with being 'finished' or 'ready', having 'problems' or 'difficulties', being able to 'see' or 'hear'. They are 'real' questions, in that for once the teacher doesn't know the answer. If he does know the answer to, for example, 'have you finished', it is a directive, not a check. The function of checks is to enable the teacher to ascertain whether there are any problems preventing the successful progress of the lesson.

IV.3.3	directive	d

Realized by a command. Its function is to request a non-linguistic response.

IV.3.4	informative	i

Realized by a statement. It differs from other uses of statement in that its sole function is to provide information. The only response is an acknowledgement of attention and understanding.

IV.4.1	prompt	p

Realized by a closed class of items – 'go on', 'come on', 'hurry up', 'quickly', 'have a guess'. Its function is to reinforce a directive or elicitation by suggesting that the teacher is no longer requesting a response but expecting or even demanding one.

IV.4.2	clue	cl

Realized by a statement, question, command, or moodless item. It is subordinate to the head of the initiation and functions by providing additional information which helps the pupil to answer the elicitation or comply with the directive.

IV.5.1   cue   cu
Realized by a closed class of which we so far have only three exponents,
'hands up', 'don't call out', 'is John the only one'. Its sole function is to
evoke an (appropriate) bid.

IV.5.2   bid   b
Realized by a closed class of verbal and non-verbal items – 'Sir', 'Miss',
teacher's name, raised hand, heavy breathing, finger clicking. Its function
is to signal a desire to contribute to the discourse.

IV.5.3   nomination   n
Realized by a closed class consisting of the names of all the pupils, 'you'
with contrastive stress, 'anybody', 'yes', and one or two idiosyncratic items
such as 'who hasn't said anything yet'. The function of nomination is to call
on or give permission to a pupil to contribute to the discourse.

IV.6   acknowledge   ack
Realized by 'yes', 'OK', 'cor', 'mm', 'wow', and certain non-verbal gestures and expressions. Its function is simply to show that the initiation has
been understood, and, if the head was a directive, that the pupil intends to
react.

IV.7.1   reply   rep
Realized by a statement, question or moodless item and non-verbal surro-
gates such as nods. Its function is to provide a linguistic response which is
appropriate to the elicitation.

IV.7.2   react   rea
Realized by a non-linguistic action. Its function is to provide the appropriate non-linguistic response defined by the preceding directive.

IV.8   comment   com
Realized by a statement or tag question. It is subordinate to the head of the
move and its function is to exemplify, expand, justify, provide additional
information. On the written page it is difficult to distinguish from an
informative because the outsider's ideas of relevance are not always the
same. However, teachers signal paralinguistically, by a pause, when they
are beginning a new initiation with an informative as a head; otherwise
they see themselves as commenting.

IV.9   accept   acc
Realized by a closed class of items – 'yes', 'no', 'good', 'fine', and repetition of pupil's reply, all with neutral low fall intonation. Its function is to
indicate that the teacher has heard or seen and that the informative, reply
or react was appropriate.

IV.10 evaluate e

Realized by statements and tag questions, including words and phrases such as 'good', 'interesting', 'team point', commenting on the quality of the reply, react or initiation, also by 'yes', 'no', 'good', 'fine', with a high–fall intonation, and repetition of the pupil's reply with either high–fall (positive), or a rise of any kind (negative evaluation).

IV.11 silent stress ∧

Realized by a pause, of the duration of one or more beats, following a marker. It functions to highlight the marker when it is serving as the head of a boundary exchange indicating a transaction boundary.

IV.12.1 metastatement ms

Realized by a statement which refers to some future time when what is described will occur. Its function is to help the pupils to see the structure of the lesson, to help them understand the purpose of the subsequent exchange, and see where they are going.

IV.12.2 conclusion con

Realized by an anaphoric statement, sometimes marked by slowing of speech rate and usually the lexical items 'so' or 'then'. In a way it is the converse of metastatement. Its function is again to help the pupils understand the structure of the lesson but this time by summarizing what the preceding chunk of discourse was about.

IV.13 loop l

Realized by a closed class of items – 'pardon', 'you what', 'eh', 'again', with rising intonation and a few questions like 'did you say', 'do you mean'. Its function is to return the discourse to the stage it was at before the pupil spoke, from where it can proceed normally.

IV.14 aside z

Realized by statement, question, command, moodless, usually marked by lowering the tone of the voice, and not really addressed to the class. As we noted above, this category covers items we have difficulty in dealing with. It is really instances of the teacher talking to himself: 'It's freezing in here', 'Where did I put my chalk?'

THE STRUCTURE AND CLASSES OF MOVES

Moves are made up of acts, and moves themselves occupy places in the structure of exchanges. In this account the structure of moves is described class by class. As is evident from the tables on pp. 7–8 there are five classes of move which realize two classes of exchange: Boundary exchanges are realized by Framing and Focusing and Teaching exchanges by Opening, Answering, and Follow-up moves.

Each of these moves has a different function. Framing moves are probably a feature of all spoken discourse, but they occur more frequently in classroom discourse because it is carefully structured by one participant. Framing moves are realized by a marker followed by silent stress, 'Right$_\wedge$' 'now$_\wedge$' 'OK$_\wedge$'.

Framing moves are frequently, though not always, followed by focusing moves whose function is to talk about the discourse. Focusing moves represent a change of 'plane'. The teacher stands for a moment outside the discourse and says 'We are going to communicate/have been communicating; this is what our communication was/will be about.' Focusing moves have an optional marker and starter, a compulsory head, realized by a metastatement or a conclusion, and an optional comment. In the examples which follow, the third column contains the structural label of the item, the fourth column the label of the act which occurs at that place in the structure.

Classes of move	Example	Structure of move	Classes of act
Framing	Right	h	marker
	∧	q	silent stress
Focusing	Now,	s	marker
	what we've just done, what we've just done is given some energy to this pen.	h	conclusion

With focusing moves, as with many units in discourse, there are possible ambiguities, and the teacher who focuses 'Today we are going to play rounders' must be careful to continue quickly 'but first we must finish our sums', or the children might interpret his focus as an opening move and rush out of the classroom.

The function of an opening move is to cause others to participate in an exchange. Opening and answering are complementary moves. The purpose of a given opening may be passing on information or directing an action or eliciting a fact. The type of answering move is predetermined because its function is to be an appropriate response in the terms laid down by the opening move.

The structure we provide for opening moves is complicated. Much of this complexity arises from the element *select* which is where the teacher chooses which pupil he wants to respond. Select can be realized by a simple teacher nomination, or by a pupil bid followed by a nomination, or by a teacher cue followed by a bid and a nomination.

It would be possible to suggest that teaching exchanges actually have a structure of five moves, with both bid and nomination as separate moves. The argument for this would be that a new move should begin every time there is a change of speaker. We rejected this alternative, because it would have created as many difficulties as it solved. When a teacher nominated without waiting for a bid, we would have had to regard this as two moves, one consisting of a single word, and at times even embedded inside the other move. Such a solution would also have devalued the concept of move. We prefer to say that a move boundary signals a change in the speaker who is composing/creating the discourse, and therefore that a move boundary is a potential change in the direction of the discourse, whereas a child making a bid must choose from a very limited set of choices. Thus we regard the function of an opening move, with elicitation or directive as head, as not only requesting a reply or reaction but as also deciding who should respond. An opening move ends after the responder has been selected.

Prompt and clue can also occur in a post-head position in opening moves. This means that the structure of a teacher's opening move is,

(signal)   (pre-head)   head   (post-head)   (select)

with brackets showing that all elements except head are optional. The example below has all the elements except signal.

Classes of move	Example	Structure of move	Classes of act
Opening	A group of people used symbols to do their writing. They used pictures instead of as we write in words.	pre-h	starter
	Do you know who those people were?	h	elicitation
	I'm sure you do.	post-h	prompt
	Joan.	sel	nomination

Pupil opening moves have a simpler structure. There are no examples of signal; pre-heads can, but rarely do, occur; post-heads, realized by prompt and clue, by their very nature are not the sort of acts used by pupils. As the pupil must indicate that he wants to speak, select occurs before the head. Sometimes the teacher will allow the pupil to follow his bid with an elicitation or informative, sometimes he/she insists on the nomination. We must emphasize that the pupil has no right to contribute to the discourse, and the teacher can ignore him. In the first example on p. 24 the pupil thinks he has been ignored and goes on bidding.

Answering moves have a simpler structure; a maximum of three elements, pre-head, head, and post-head, and very often only the head occurs. There are three types of head appropriate to the three heads of opening moves. The response appropriate to an informative is simply an acknowledgement that one is listening, and this can be, and usually is in the classroom, non-verbal. Following a directive the head of an answering move is realized by react, but the pupil may also acknowledge verbally that he has heard. Following an elicitation there is a reply, and sometimes a comment as well as we can see in the second example on p. 24.

Classes of move	Example	Structure of move	Classes of act
Opening (pupil)	Sir,	sel	bid
	Sir.	sel	bid
	Can I go to the toilet?	h	elicitation
Answering	Yes.	h	reply
Opening (teacher to another child)	If you've got a printed one you shouldn't have.	h	comment
Opening (pupil)	Sir.	sel	bid
	Can I go to the toilet?	h	elicitation
Opening (pupil)	Sir.	sel	bid
	Please can I go to the toilet?	h	elicitation
Opening	Climb over that way.	h	directive

Classes of move	Example	Structure of move	Classes of act
Opening	Well,	s	marker
	what leads you to believe he's like that?	h	elicitation
Answering	He's rather free to – rather free in criticizing somebody else yet he might not like to be criticized himself.	h	reply
	Criticizing the local councillor, it's not right really.	post-h	comment

Follow-up, the third class of move in teaching exchanges, is an interesting category. Its function is to let the pupil know how well he/she has performed. It is very significant that follow-up occurs not only after a pupil answering move, but also after a pupil opening move when the head is realized by an informative. In other words the teacher often indicates the value of an unelicited contribution from a pupil, usually in terms of relevance to the discourse.

Follow-up has a three-term structure, pre-head, head, post-head, realized by accept, evaluate, and comment respectively.

The act evaluate is seen by all participants as a compulsory element. A teacher can produce a follow-up move which overtly consists of only accept or comment, but evaluation is then implicit (and usually unfavourable).

Classes of move	Example	Structure of move	Classes of act
Opening	Do you know what we mean by accent?	h	Elicitation
Answering	It's the way you talk.	h	reply
Follow-up	The way we talk. This is a very broad comment.	pre-h h	accept evaluate

Very frequently, if the teacher accepts a reply without evaluating, the class offers another reply without any prompting.

THE STRUCTURE AND CLASSES OF EXCHANGES

There are two major classes of exchange, Boundary and Teaching. The function of boundary exchange is, as the name suggests, to signal the beginning or end of what the teacher considers to be a stage in the lesson; teaching exchanges are the individual steps by which the lesson progresses. Boundary exchanges consist of two moves, framing and focusing; often the two occur together, the framing move frequently occurs on its own, the focusing move does so only rarely. A typical boundary exchange is:

Classes of move	Example	Structure of move
Framing	Well∧	marker, silent stress
Focusing	Today . . .	metastatement

The definition of teaching exchange given above is vague, but there are eleven subcategories with specific functions and unique structures. Of the eleven subcategories six are Free exchanges and five are Bound. The function of bound exchanges is fixed because they either have no initiating move, or have an initiating move without a head, which simply serves to reiterate the head of the preceding free initiation.

Free exchanges

The six free exchanges are divided into four groups according to function, and two of the groups are further subdivided according to whether teacher or pupil initiates, because there are different structural possibilities. The four main functions of exchanges are informing, directing, eliciting, and checking, and they are distinguished by the type of act which realizes the head of the initiating move, informative, directive, elicitation and check respectively. The structure of each of these exchanges will now be exemplified.

Each exchange type is given a number and a functional label and the characteristic structure is noted. The structure is expressed in terms of Initiation (I), Response (R) and Feedback (F); moves are coded across the page with three main columns for Opening, Answering and Follow-up, while the narrow columns give the move structure in terms of acts. A single line across the page signifies an exchange boundary, so one reads down the first column until the boundary line, then down the second column and then down the third. Each act begins on a separate line.

I Teacher inform

This exchange is used when the teacher is passing on facts, opinions, ideas, new information to the pupil. Pupils may, but usually do not, make a verbal response to the teacher's initiation. Thus the structure is I(R); there is no feedback.

Opening		Answering	Follow-up
Now,		m	
luckily, the French could read Greek.		i	

II Teacher direct

This category covers all exchanges designed to get the pupil to do but not to say something. Because of the nature of the classroom the response is a compulsory element of structure. This is not to suggest that children always do what they are told to do, but it does imply that the teacher has a right to expect the pupil to do so. Just as anyone can produce an ungrammatical sentence when he feels like it, so a pupil can break the rules of discourse. Feedback is not an essential element of this structure although it frequently occurs. The structure is IR(F).

Opening		Answering		Follow-up
I want you to take your pen and	d	Activity	rea	
I want you to rub it as hard as				
you can on something woollen.				

III Teacher elicit

This category includes all exchanges designed to obtain verbal contributions from pupils. Very frequently a teacher will use a series of elicit exchanges to move the class step by step to a conclusion. Sometimes an elicit is used in isolation in the middle of a series of informs to check that the pupils have remembered a fact. The elicit exchanges which occur inside the classroom have a different function from most occurring outside it. Usually when we ask a question we don't know the answer; very frequently the teacher does know the answer, indeed the pupils may get quite annoyed if he doesn't – after all that is his job!

This fact enables us to explain why feedback is an essential element in an eliciting exchange inside the classroom. Having given their reply the pupils want to know if it was correct. So important is feedback that if it does not occur we feel confident in saying that the teacher has deliberately withheld it for some strategic purpose. It is deviant to withhold feedback continually – we have a tape of one lesson where a teacher, new to the class, and trying to suggest to them that there aren't always right answers, does withhold feedback and eventually reduces the children to silence – they cannot see the point of his questioning. Thus the structure of elicits differs from that of directs in that F is a compulsory element.

Opening		Answering		Follow-up	
What's the name of this cutter?	el	Hacksaw.	rep	The hacksaw.	e
Hands up.	cu			And I'll put that one there.	z
Non-verbal bid	b				
Janet.	n				

IV Pupil elicit

In many classrooms children rarely ask questions and when they do they are mainly of the order 'Do we put the date' or 'Can I go to the lavatory'. Usually the child has to catch the teacher's attention and get permission to speak. (See Sacks 1972 on the ways children get into ordinary conversation.) This permission may not be granted. The initial bid may be countered with a 'not now' or 'just a minute' and the exchange never get off the ground. The crucial difference between teacher and pupil elicits is that the pupil provides no feedback – an evaluation of a teacher reply would be cheeky. Thus the structure is IR.

Opening		Answering		Follow-up
Mrs H.	b	Yes.	rep	
Yes.	n	They're – that's the order, one, two, three, four.	com	
Are the numbers for le – for the letters?				

V Pupil inform

Occasionally pupils offer information which they think is relevant, or interesting – they usually receive an evaluation of its worth and often a comment as well. Thus the structure is IF not I(R) as for teacher informs.

Opening		Answering		Follow-up	
Miss P.	b			Oh yes.	acc
There's some – there's a				You're right.	
letter's missing from that	i			It is. I can't	e
up and down one.				remember	
				what it is.	com

This example has been simplified by the omission of a *repeat* bound exchange, which will be described below on pp. 30–3.

VI Check

At some time in most lessons teachers feel the need to discover how well the children are getting on, whether they can follow what is going on, whether they can hear. To do this they use a checking move which could be regarded as a subcategory of elicit, except that feedback is not essential, because these are real questions to which the teacher does not know the answer. Any evaluation is an evaluation of an activity or state not the response. Thus the structure is IR(F). A broken line between exchanges signifies that the second is bound to the first.

Opening		Answering		Follow-up	
Finished Joan?	ch‹n›	NV	rep	Good girl.	e
And Miri?	n	Yes	rep	Good.	re
Finished?	ch	Yes	rep		

Bound exchanges

Of the five types of bound exchange, four are bound to teacher elicits and one to a teacher direct. As we said above, an exchange is bound either if it has no initiating move, or if the initiating move it does have has no head, but simply consists of nomination, prompt, or clue.

VII Re-initiation (i)

When the teacher gets no response to an elicitation he can start again using the same or a rephrased question, or he can use one or more of the acts prompt, nomination, clue to re-initiate. The original elicitation stands and these items are used as a second attempt to get a reply. This gives a structure of IRI^bRF, where I^b is a bound initiation.

Opening		Answering		Follow-up	
What is 'comprehend'?	el	$\emptyset$			
Nicola?	n	$\emptyset$			
In fact if you get this word you'll comprehend.	c	Find out.	rep	Yes find out	e
NV	b				
David again.	n				

VIII Re-initiation (ii)

When a teacher gets a wrong answer there are two major routes open to him: he can stay with the same child and try by Socratic method to work him round to the right answer or he can stay with the question and move on to another child. This type of re-initiation differs from the previous one in that feedback does occur. It is usually realized by 'Yes', 'No' or a repetition of what the pupil has just said, with a tone 3 intonation indicating incompleteness or a tone 4 intonation indicating reservation. An initiating move is not essential for the bound exchange, but if it does occur it is realized by prompt, nomination, or clue. This gives a structure of $IRF(I^b)RF$.

Opening		Answering		Follow-up	
This I think is a super one.	s	Does it mean there's been an accident further down the road?	rep	No[3]	e
Isobel.	n				
Can you think what it means?	el				
		Does it mean a double bend ahead?	rep	No[3]	e
Look at the car.	cl	Slippery roads?	rep	Yes It means Be careful because the road's very slippery	e

IX Listing

Occasionally teachers withhold evaluation until they get two or three answers. Sometimes they are making sure that more than one person knows the answer, sometimes they have asked a multiple question. In this case the structure is exactly the same as for Re-initiation (ii), $IRF(I^b)RF(I^b)RF$, but the realization of two of the elements is different. I^b is only realized by nomination and the F preceding I^b contains no evaluation.

Opening		Answering		Follow-up	
What's the name of each one of those?	el	Paper clip.	rep	Paper clip.	acc
		Nail.	rep	Nail.	acc
		Nut and bolt.	rep	Nut and bolt [1+]	e

X Reinforce

Very occasionally in the tapes there is a bound exchange following a teacher direct. Bound exchanges occur when the teacher has told the class to do something and one child is slow or reluctant or hasn't fully understood. The structure is IRI^bR, with the I^b realized by a clue, prompt or nomination. In the following example a West Indian boy has misunderstood the directive.

Opening		Answering		Follow-up
I want you to take your pen and I want you to rub it as hard as you can on something woollen.	d	ACTIVITY	rea	
Not in your hair, on your jumper.	cl	ACTIVITY	rea	

XI Repeat

In every communicative situation there will be times when someone does not hear. There are no examples in our tapes of a child admitting to not hearing but teachers do so quite frequently. Thus instead of feedback following the pupil response we get a bound initiation. Of course teachers can and do use this exchange when they have heard but want a reply repeated for other reasons. The structure is IRI^bRF.

Opening		Answering		Follow-up	
What are you laughing at Rebecca?	el {n}	Nothing	rep		
Pardon	loop	Nothing	rep	You're laughing at nothing.	acc

THE STRUCTURE OF TRANSACTIONS

Transactions normally begin with a Preliminary exchange and end with a Final exchange. Within these boundaries a series of medial exchanges occur. Although we have identified eleven types of medial exchanges we cannot yet specify in detail how they are ordered within transactions. We can specify that the first medial exchange in a transaction will normally be selected from the three major teacher-initiated free exchange types – Inform, Direct and Elicit. Following a selection of one of these types, characteristic options occur in the rest of the transaction.

From now on what we say will be much more speculative and we will be talking about ideal types of transaction. We have not yet done sufficient work on transactions to be sure that what we suggest here will stand up to detailed investigation. We provisionally identify three major transaction types, informing, directing, and eliciting. Their basic structures will be outlined below. We do not, however, in an analysis of texts yet feel sufficiently confident in the identification of these structures to make the labelling of these transaction types a major element of coding.

Informing transactions

$$
T \begin{cases} E & - \quad \text{Boundary} \\ E & - \quad \text{T-Inform} \\ (\langle E \rangle)^n & - \quad \text{T-Elicit} \\ (\langle E \rangle)^n & - \quad \text{P-Elicit} \\ E & - \quad \text{Boundary} \end{cases}
$$

(The round brackets indicate that an item is optional, the diamond brackets that it occurs inside the previous item.) During a lengthy informing exchange from the teacher, the pupils do little but acknowledge. However, embedded within an informing transaction may be brief teacher elicitations, used to keep attention or to check that pupils are understanding, and also pupil elicitations on some point raised by the teacher.

Directing transactions

$$
\text{T} \begin{cases}
\text{E} & - & \text{Boundary} \\
\text{E} & - & \text{T-Direct} \\
\text{(E)}^n & - & \text{P-Elicit} \\
\text{(E)}^n_. & - & \text{P-Inform} \\
\text{E} & - & \text{T-Elicit} \\
\text{E} & - & \text{Boundary}
\end{cases}
$$

This structure occurs where a T-Direct exchange stands at the head of a transaction, rather than in a subordinate position. The directive will usually be one requesting pupils to engage in some work on their own, for example working out some cartouches, or writing a sentence in hieroglyphs. When pupils are working separately, they have most opportunity for initiating exchanges. They can make comments on, or ask questions about their task, and ask for evaluation of their work. Characteristically the teacher ends such a transaction with an elicitation asking for the pupils' answers or results.

Eliciting transactions

$$
\text{T} \begin{cases}
\text{E} & - & \text{Boundary} \\
\text{E}^n & - & \text{T-Elicit} \\
\text{E} & - & \text{Boundary}
\end{cases}
$$

When the teacher is asking questions, the pupils contribute continually to the discourse by making verbal responses, but they have little opportunity to initiate exchanges. When a pupil does break out of the usual structure with an elicitation, and this is rare, it does not lead to a series of pupil elicitations. The teacher quickly resumes the initiating role either by refusing an adequate answer as in the first example below, or by taking over the pupil's topic as in the second.

P-Elicit	Sir,	b
	how did this man manage to work out the names of the people?	
T-Reply	Because he was clever, that's how.	rep

P-Elicit	What were Popes?	el
P-Reply	Still have Popes. The Pope's the head of the Catholic Church.	rep
P-Feedback	mm oh.	acc

T-Elicit	Where does he live?	el
P-Reply	Rome.	rep
T-Feedback	Rome yes.	e

| T-Elicit | Do you know which part of Rome . . . | el |

We have so far mentioned only the characteristic places in the structure of transactions at which three teacher-initiated, and two pupil-initiated exchanges can occur. Even more tentatively we can suggest that the teacher-initiated check exchange typically occurs in a directing transaction before the final elicit exchange. The teacher here is usually checking on pupils' progress with the task he directed them to do at the beginning of the transaction.

We can specify no ordering for the bound exchanges. They occur after a T-Direct or T-Elicit exchange, but whether any or all occur, and in what order, is dependent on unpredictable reactions to and involvement with the teacher's presentation of the topic.

THE STRUCTURE OF LESSONS

The lesson is the highest unit of classroom discourse, made up of a series of transactions. If the pupils are responsive and co-operative, the discourse unit 'lesson' may approximate closely to any plan the teacher may have formulated for presenting his chosen topic. He may have decided, for example, to start off by presenting some information, to continue by discovering whether that information has been assimilated, and then to get the pupils to use that information he has presented in their own work. Alternatively a teacher might begin with a series of elicit exchanges, attempting to move the pupils towards conclusions which will later be elaborated in an informing transaction. However, a variety of things can interfere in the working-out of the teacher's plan in actual discourse. The structure of the lesson is affected by such performance features as the teacher's own memory capacity for ordering speech, and, more importantly the need to respond to unpredicted reactions, misunderstandings or contributions on the part of the pupils.

We cannot specify any ordering of transactions into lessons. To do this would require a much larger sample of classroom discourse. We might find, for example, that there are characteristic lesson structures for different subjects, or for different teachers. At the moment, however, we must think of the lesson as a stylistic type, which means that actually there is little point in labelling the lesson as a unit. We could describe the ordering of transactions into lessons in the texts we have, but that ordering varies for each teacher and we can identify no restrictions on the occurrence of different types.

'Towards an analysis of discourse' is a slightly modified version of Chapter 3 of Sinclair and Coulthard (1975) *Towards an Analysis of Discourse*, 14–60.

2 The significance of intonation in discourse

Malcolm Coulthard

INTRODUCTION

Paralinguistic phenomena in general and intonation in particular are areas of language patterning which have received comparatively little attention from linguists who, for differing reasons, have chosen to concentrate on segmental phonology, morphology, syntax and lexis. Although detailed descriptions of intonation do exist and there is a fair measure of agreement about the phonetic and phonological facts, at least of British English, little work has been done on the interactive significance of intonation. Crystal (1969) contents himself with a very detailed description of all the phonological options without attempting to assign significance to them. Halliday (1967) asserts that 'all English intonation contrasts are grammatical' and thus restricts their significance to the language system, while Crystal (1975) argues that the 'vast majority of tones in connected speech carry no meaning' although he does concede that a few do carry attitudinal options like 'absence of emotional involvement'.

Only O'Connor and Arnold set out to describe all intonation choices as interactively meaningful, asserting that a major function of intonation is to express 'the speaker's attitude to the situation in which he is placed' (1973:2). Unfortunately, until there is some set of agreed and mutually exclusive attitudinal labels to match against the intonation choices, an attitudinal description must be impossible; the experiment reported in Crystal (1969:297ff) shows the difficulties native speakers have in matching attitudinal labels with intonation contours, while O'Connor and Arnold's own examples undermine their claim to have managed to do so. For example, they describe the significance of the rise–fall in relation to a number of exemplificatory sentences. In (1), B is said to be 'quietly impressed, perhaps awed' whereas in (2), B is thought to be expressing a 'challenging' or 'censorious' attitude:

1 A: Have you heard about Pat?   B: ^Yes!

2 A: Why don't you like it?   B: I ^do.

In other examples this very same tone choice is said to convey that the speaker is 'impressed, favourably or unfavourably . . . by something not entirely expected'; 'complacent, self-satisfied or smug'; 'disclaiming responsibility, shrugging aside any involvement or refusing to be embroiled'.

It soon becomes evident that some, perhaps much, of the claimed attitudinal meaning is, in fact, being derived from the lexico-grammatical and contextual features of the examples themselves and not from the intonation contour.

Thus, although there is no disagreement that speakers can vary independently tempo, loudness, pitch, and voice quality, and thereby alter aspects of the meaning of their utterances, one must conclude that any systematic relationship between intonation choices and lexical meanings has so far remained undiscovered. Indeed, Labov and Fanshel imply that a search for systematic relationships is misguided when they suggest that the lack of clarity or discreteness in the intonational signals is not 'an unfortunate limitation of this channel, but an essential and important aspect of it' (1977:46). The result is that, in the absence of any satisfying theory to account systematically for the interactional meaning of intonation, those involved in the analysis of spoken interaction have, of necessity, taken only intermittent notice of intonation choices, at those points where they felt they could attach significance to them.

Perhaps the paradigm example of this approach to intonation is the way in which Sinclair and Coulthard (1975) used the co-occurrence of the prosodic features 'high falling intonation' and a 'following silent stress' with 'now', 'well', 'OK', 'right', 'good', to isolate occasions when these lexical items were functioning as *'frames'*, markers of boundary points in the ongoing lesson.

More generally, most analysts have felt able, as native speakers, to recognize, though not necessarily to describe, the intonational features that mark certain declarative clauses as questions and certain words as 'stressed'. Indeed, Jefferson's (1978) transcription system, which sets out to be 'one that will look to the eye how it sounds to the ear' (p. xi), also allows for a 'continuing intonation', and a 'stopping fall', plus three degrees of stress. However, as none of the published transcriptions have an accompanying tape and as only Labov and Fanshel provide fundamental frequency traces, it is impossible to be sure what phonological features particular analysts are focusing on, how consistently they are recognizing and marking them, how much agreement there is between analysts on what constitutes a question-marking intonation or a particular degree of stress, and how far it is the phonological features alone to which they are responding.

Thus, it is evident from the use made so far of intonational information in published work that all those involved in the analysis of verbal interaction would agree with Labov and Fanshel (ibid.:46), that it is at the moment impossible 'to provide a context-free set of interpretations of prosodic cues'.

TOWARDS AN INTERACTIONALLY MOTIVATED
DESCRIPTION OF INTONATION

The description of the way intonation functions in discourse that is outlined below is one on which David Brazil has been working continuously since 1975. The most recent and comprehensive presentation is in Brazil (1992). Brazil does not claim, by any means, to be able to handle the way in which all paralinguistic features carry meaning (nor indeed that they all have interactional meaning), but he does present a workable description of many pitch phenomena which is based on sound and explicit principles.

The first principle is that features which are acoustically on a continuum must be analysed as realizations of a small number of discrete units that 'form a closed set, defined by their mutual oppositions' (Labov and Fanshel, ibid.:42). The second principle is that there is no constant relationship between particular acoustic phenomena and particular analytic categories: it is contrasts and not absolute values which are important. These two principles are not, of course, novel and create no problems theoretically or practically, as analysts of tone languages discovered long ago:

> tone languages have a major characteristic in common: it is the relative height of their tonemes, not their actual pitch which is pertinent to their linguistic analysis . . . the important feature is the relative height of a syllable in relation to preceding and following syllables. A toneme is 'high' only if it is higher than its neighbours in the sentence, not if its frequency of vibrations is high.
>
> (Pike 1948:4)

A third principle is that there is no necessary one-to-one relationship between particular paralinguistic cues and interactional significance: on the one hand, as Bolinger's (1964) 'wave' and 'swell' metaphor suggests, a given pitch choice can at the very least be simultaneously carrying both general information about emotional state and a specific local meaning of the kind described in detail further on in this chapter; on the other hand, certain interactionally significant signals – for instance, request for back-channel support – may be carried by the co-occurrence of a particular pitch choice and a kinesic one, each of which singly conveys a different meaning.

The final principle is to regard intonation as primarily concerned with adding specific interactional significance to lexico-grammatical items and thus enabling the speaker to refine and at times redefine the meaning oppositions given by the language system. It is for this reason that Brazil argues that the intonational divisions that speakers make in their utterances are not grammatically motivated (though for explainable reasons intonation unit boundaries frequently coincide with major grammatical boundaries); rather they are motivated by the need to add moment-by-moment, situationally specific, intonationally conveyed meanings to particular words or group of words.

The description is expressed in terms of pitch choices, though this is almost certainly a simplification. Intensity and durational features regularly co-occur with the pitch choices, and it may well turn out that choices described as being realized by pitch phenomena are being identified by hearers through associated intensity and durational phenomena – we must never forget Lieberman's (1960) experiments on the perception of stress.

Brazil's description sets out to account both for the paradigmatic options available to a speaker at any point in the discourse and for the syntagmatic structures he can build up. He has so far isolated four systems of options, labelled *tone*, *prominence*, *key* and *termination*, all of them realized by pitch phenomena and all potentially realizable in a single syllable. In addition there are four units of structure, syllable, segment, tone unit, and pitch sequence, of which the most important is the tone unit. The four intonation systems all work within and attach meaning to the tone unit; divisions within utterances are seen to be intonationally and not grammatically motivated and, like Laver (1970), Brazil thinks that the tone unit, rather than the clause, is 'the most likely unit of neurolinguistic pre-assembly'.

The structure of the tone unit

The tone unit has the following structure:

(Proclitic segment)   Tonic segment   (Enclitic segment)

As this structure implies, tone units may consist simply of a tonic segment, and many do; indeed, a considerable number consist of no more than the tonic syllable, i.e. the syllable on which there is a major pitch movement, as in (3) below. Tone unit boundaries will be marked by a double slash, //.

3 // GOOD //; // YES //; // ME //; // JOHN //

Most tone units, of course, do consist of more than the minimal tonic segment, and then the question of segmentation arises. With the syllables following the tonic there is, in fact, no analytic problem: even though the pitch movement of the tone may be continued over succeeding syllables; the tonic segment is considered to end with, and the enclitic to begin after, the tonic syllable, as shown in (4).

4 *Tonic segment*   *Enclitic segment*

   // GOOD   ness knows //
   // YES   sir //
   // WE   did //
   // JOHN   ny's coming //

However, while the final boundary of the tonic segment is obviously unproblematic, recognizing where the tonic segment begins is a more difficult matter and depends on an understanding of the concept of *prominent* syllable.

Prominent syllables

Brazil points out that it is not always easy, in the literature of phonology, to be sure what significance is attached to such terms as 'stress', 'accent', 'salience', and 'prominence'. By 'accent' Brazil means the attribute which invariably distinguishes the marked from the unmarked syllables in words like '*cur*tain', 'con*tain*', 're*la*tion', and which distinguishes the lexical items from the others in a sentence like '*Tom* is the *best boy* in the *class*.' The expression 'word accent', although tautologous, may serve as a reminder that accent is an inherent property of the word, which, being inherent, has no possible contrastive significance. When we say 'Tom *is* the best boy in the class' we are not accenting 'is', we are making it 'pitch prominent'. (A full discussion of the fundamental frequency characteristics of prominent syllables can be found in Brazil (1978a), and a briefer but more accessible discussion in Brazil *et al.* (1980). 'Prominence' is thus a property associated with a word by virtue of its function as a constituent of a particular tone unit.

We are now in a position to define the scope of the tonic segment. The tonic segment begins with the first prominent syllable, henceforth called the 'onset', and ends with the last prominent syllable, the 'tonic', which in addition has a pitch movement. (From now on all prominent syllables will be capitalized.) There are thus, by definition, no prominent syllables in the proclitic and enclitic segments, as shown in (5).

5 *Proclitic segment*	*Tonic segment*	*Enclitic segment*
he was	GOing to GO	
that's a	VERy TALL STOR	y
it was a	WED	nesday

Prominence, then, is a linguistic choice available to the speaker which is independent of both the grammatical structure of his utterance and the accents of the citation forms of the constituent words. What then *is* its significance? Let us consider the question/response pair in (6):

6 Q: Which card did you play?
    R: // the QUEEN of HEARTS //

It is easy to see that in the response the word 'of' is the only word that could occupy the place between 'queen' and 'hearts'. If we think of each word as representing a selection from a set of words available at successive slots, then at the slot filled by 'of' there is a set of one. In this respect it can be compared with the slots filled by 'queen' and 'hearts'. The total range of possibilities is presented in (7):

```
7           ace
            two                 hearts
    the      .          of     clubs
             .                 diamonds
            queen              spades
            king
```

We can see that in creating his utterance the speaker had a limited choice of 13 possibilities for the slot occupied by 'queen' and 4 for the slot occupied by 'hearts', but this time the limitation has, as Brazil points out, nothing to do with the working of the language system: there is no linguistic reason why the response should not have been, for instance, the 'prince of tides' or 'the thirteen of lozenges'. What imposes the lexical limitation is an extra-linguistic factor, the conventional composition of a pack of playing cards.

Brazil uses the term *existential paradigm* for that set of possibilities that a speaker can regard as actually available at a given moment in an inter-action. This enables him to distinguish this set of options from the *general paradigm* which is inherent in the language system. It is clear that at the place occupied in examples (6) and (7) by 'of'; the two paradigms coincide: there can be no possibility of selection in the existential paradigm because there is none in the general paradigm.

From examples like these we can deduce that items are marked as prominent in order to indicate to the hearer that the speaker is selecting from a range of oppositions in the existential paradigm. Thus we can invent a context in which 'of' could be situationally selective – for example a correction of a foreigner's 'the queen *in* hearts' would certainly be realized as (8), while contexts in which first 'queen' and then 'hearts' would be non-selective and therefore non-prominent, are exemplified in (9) and (10):

8 // the queen OF hearts //

9 Which heart did you play?
  // the QUEEN of hearts //

10 Which queen did you play?
  // the queen of HEARTS //

In examples (9) and (10) the questioner sets up a context which effectively removes the possibility of choice for one of the items by indicating that he knows either the suit, (9) or the denomination of the card, (10). Thus the answerer's use of 'hearts' in (9) and 'queen' in (10) is not the outcome of his making any kind of selection, a fact which would probably result, in many circumstances, in their being omitted altogether:

11 Which heart did you play?
  // the QUEEN //

12 Which queen did you play?
  // HEARTS //

One may think, in this particular case, of the wide range of options that comprise the general paradigm at each of the two places being reduced by shared card-playing conventions and then further reduced by shared experience of the immediate conversational environment of the response.

The examples used so far suggest that the non-prominent/prominent distinction is very similar to the textually given/textually new distinction, but this is misleading; rather we are concerned with the interactionally given. All interaction proceeds, and can only proceed, on the basis of the existence of a great deal of common ground between the participants: that is, what knowledge speakers (think they) share about the world, about each other's experiences, attitudes and emotions. Common ground is not restricted to shared experience of a particular linguistic interaction up to the moment of utterance; rather it is a product of the interpenetrating biographies of the participants, of which common involvement in a particular ongoing interaction constitutes only a part.

Thus one can imagine a situation in which items are contextually given but not linguistically realized. In a game of cards after one player has, without saying anything, put down the jack of hearts; the next player could quite naturally verbalize

13 // QUEEN of hearts //

using prominence to indicate that the suit is unchanged and contextually derivable.

Tone choices

In discussing the significance of *tonic* pitch movement we will confine ourselves to primary delicacy and the central meaning opposition realized by end-rising and end-falling tones respectively.

All interaction proceeds, and can only proceed, on the basis of the existence of a great deal of *common ground* between the participants. In fact a major difference between interactions between strangers and those between friends lies in the degree of uncertainty about the boundaries of common ground and the amount of time spent exploring these boundaries. 'Common ground' is intended to encompass what knowledge speakers (think they) share about the world, about each other's experience, attitudes and emotions. Thus, it is not restricted to shared experience of a particular linguistic interaction up to the moment of utterance; rather it is a product of the interpenetrating biographies of the participants, of which common involvement in a particular ongoing interaction constitutes only a part.

It was suggested above that the speaker has a major choice between an end-rising *referring* tone, symbol 'r', and an end-falling, *proclaiming tone*, symbol 'p'. Brazil suggests that in choosing to attach a referring tone to a particular part of his message the speaker is marking it as part of the existing common ground, whereas by choosing proclaiming tone he is indicating his expectation that the area of common ground will be enlarged, as a result of the speaker being told something he didn't already know.

In the following examples we can see the effect of altering the tone selections:

14 //r she'll be TWENty //p in AUgust //

15 //p she'll be TWENty //r in AUgust //

In (14) the hearer is told *when* someone will have her twentieth birthday – the tone choice marks that the birthday is a shared topic and that the new information is the date. In (15), by contrast, the date is already known, what is new is *how old* she will be. In each case, the assumed focus of interest is *referred* to and the new assertion is *proclaimed*. It must, however, be stressed that what is referred to may not have been made explicit; in other words referring tone allows a speaker to call on shared knowledge and opinions which have not so far been verbalized in the conversation.

Key choices

In addition to making choices in the tone and prominence systems, a speaker must also, for each and every tone unit, select relative pitch or *key* from a three-term system: high, mid and low. However, unlike Sweet (1906), Brazil does not see mid key as the norm for the speaker's voice; rather key choices are made and recognized with reference to the key of the immediately preceding tone unit. In other words, there are no absolute values for high, mid and low key, even for a particular speaker; in fact, a given high key tone unit may well be at a lower pitch than an earlier mid key one. However, as we noted earlier, the phenomenon of the continually varying reference point is already well attested in analyses of tone languages.

Key choice is realized on the first prominent syllable of the tonic segment and adds a meaning that can be glossed at the most general level as:

High key	contrastive
Mid key	additive
Low key	equative

The way in which these intonational meanings combine with lexico-grammatical ones is discussed in detail in Brazil *et al.* (1980) and Brazil (1985/1992) but can be simply illustrated with the invented examples in (16a, b, c) below, where only key is varied. (In all subsequent examples the double slashes, //, mark the mid key line; items that are in high or low key are printed above or below this not(at)ional line.)

16a // he GAMbled // and LOST //

Here the choice of high key and the consequent contrastive meaning indicate an interaction-bound opposition between 'gambled' and 'lost'; perhaps the 'he' usually wins when he gambles.

16b // he GAMbled // and LOST //

Here the mid key choice and consequent additive meaning simply convey that he both gambled and lost.

16c // he GAMbled // and LOST //

Here the low key and consequent equative meaning, carries 'as you would expect', i.e. there is an interaction-bound equivalence between gambling and losing.

In examples (16a, b, c), we see key being used to indicate relationships between successive tone units in a single utterance, but these same relationships can occur across utterance boundaries. If we begin with the polar options 'yes' and 'no', we quickly realize that they only carry contrastive information, that is they are only in opposition, when they co-occur with high key. In other words, when wishing to convey 'yes not no' or 'no not yes', a speaker must select high key. (To simplify the presentation all the examples used in the presentation of key are assumed to have a falling, proclaiming tone.)

In (17) below, B chooses contrastive high key in (a) to mark the choice of opposite polarity in his response; in (b) he chooses to highlight an agreed polarity, and this apparently unnecessary action is usually interpreted as emphatic, and then in a particular context as 'surprised', 'delighted', 'annoyed', and so on. Much more usual than (b) is (c), while (d) sounds odd because the speaker is heard as simultaneously agreeing and contradicting, or perhaps rather agreeing with something that has not been said; the normal interpretation would be that he had misheard. This contradiction is, in fact, only made evident by the repeated auxiliary, 'will', which carries the polarity. Interestingly, because 'yes' is the unmarked term of the pair if the speaker does not repeat the auxiliary he can choose either 'yes' or 'no', as in (e) or (f), to convey the same interactive meaning of agreement, an option which at times causes confusion even for native speakers.

17 A: // well you WON'T be HOME // before SEVen //

  B: (a)   // YES // I WILL //

     (b)   // NO // I WON'T //

     (c)   // NO // I WON'T //

   *(d)   // YES // I WILL //

     (e)   // NO // (I agree I won't)

     (f)   // YES // (I agree with your assessment)

When the polarity is positive, however, there is only one choice, (18a). In (18b) the co-selection of mid key agreeing intonation with 'no' creates a contextually nonsensical response:

18   // well you'll be HOME // before SEVen //

    (a)   // YES // (I agree I will/with your assessment)
  *(b)   // NO // (I agree I won't)

The examples of high key contrastivity have so far implied that the contrast is a binary one between polar opposites, but this is not necessarily so. In example (19), 'wife' could in some contexts be heard as in contrast with the only other possibility, 'daughter', and therefore as a flattering introduction (i.e. doesn't she look young?),

19 // MEET elIZabeth // johns WIFE //

but given the right context, 'wife' could be heard as contrasting with a whole series of other relations one might, in the context, have assumed Elizabeth to be: John's secretary, sister, sister-in-law, friend, mistress . . . Thus high key marks for the listener that an item is to be heard as contrastive but leaves him to fill out the existential paradigm.

The choice of low key marks an item as equative, as contextually synonymous; thus when the option is co-selected with 'yes' or with a repetition, the utterance does little more than acknowledge receipt of the information, as in (20) and (21).

20 D: Whereabouts in your chest?
  P: On the heart side.
  D: // YES //

21 A: What's the time?
  B: Ten o'clock.
  A. // Ten o'CLOCK //

If a speaker reformulates in low key, he is indicating that he does not feel he is adding any new information, but is simply verbalizing an agreement that the two versions are situationally equivalent in meaning.

22 A: What's the time?
  B: Ten o'clock.
  A: // BEDtime //

23 // HE'S DEAD // and BURied //

By contrast the choice of mid key marks the matter of the tone unit as additionally informing, and thus (24) is slightly odd.

24 // HE'S DEAD // and BURied //

As is (25), from a newscast reporting how a Palestinian terrorist organization had tried to invade Israel by balloon, but had met disaster when the balloon

25 // CRASHED // and BURNED //

This listener, at least, expected a low key for 'burned', indicating 'as you would have expected'.

Pitch concord

It has long been accepted that some polar questions seem to expect or even predict a particular answer like (26a), while others like (26b) appear to allow for either:

26a You'll come, won't you?

26b Will you come?

In fact, all utterances set up expectations at a very general level about what will follow. In order to demonstrate this, we need to discuss *termination*, a second three-term pitch choice made this time at the tonic syllable.

When we look at transcribed texts, we discover a marked tendency for concord between the termination choice of the final tone unit of one utterance and the initial key choice of the next; in other words, it appears that with his termination choice a speaker predicts or asks for a particular key choice and therefore, by implication, a particular meaning from the next speaker. This is easiest to exemplify with questions. In example (26a), the speaker is looking for agreement, i.e. a mid key 'yes', and his utterance is likely, therefore, to end with mid termination, as in (27a), to constrain the required response; (remember that key and termination can be realized in the same syllable).

27a A: // you'll // COME // WON'T you //
    B: // YES // (I agree I will)

A choice of high termination with 'won't you' needs some ingenuity to contextualize because the conflict between the lexico-grammatical markers of a search for agreement and the intonational indication that there is a 'yes/no' choice makes it sound like either a threat or a plea:

27b // you'll COME // WON'T you //

Example (26b), 'will you come', by contrast, quite naturally takes a high termination, looking for a 'yes/no' contrastive answer, as in (28a), although the persuasiveness of (28b) can be explained simply as the intonation choice converting an apparently open request into one looking for agreement:

28a A: // Will you COME //   B: // YES // or // NO //
28b A: // WILL you COME //   B: // YES //

We can see this same phenomenon of pitch concord working in examples (29) and (30), both of them taken from the same doctor/patient interview.

29   D: // its DRY skin // ISn't it //   P: // MM //

30   D: // VERy IRritating you say //   P: // VERy irritating //

The initial key choices in the answers in both (29) and (30) have the meanings we have already discussed, and in both we can see the first speaker asking for or constraining a response of a particular kind by his final termination choice. Thus, in (29), the doctor ends with mid termination because he wants the patient to agree with his observation, while in (30) he wants the patient to exploit the contrastive 'yes not no' meaning of high key to confirm what he has said. Had the doctor stopped at 'skin', in example (29), his question would have had a very different force, and he would again have been heard as asking for confirmation of a fact in doubt; but both the key and the lexical realization of the rest of the utterance show that what is required is agreement with a presumed shared opinion.

The pressure towards pitch concord can, of course, be disregarded; the patient could have responded to the doctor's mid key 'isn't it' with a high key 'yes' or 'mm', but telling the doctor he was correct would, in these circumstances, sound like noncompliant behaviour, suggesting perhaps annoyance at an unnecessary question. In example (31) below the patient solves his dilemma by selecting the predicted agreeing mid key but also lexicalizing the correctness just to make sure.

31   D: // FIVE tiller ROAD // ISn't it //
     P: // THAT'S corRECT // YES //

While high and mid termination place concord constraints on what follows, low termination does not; it marks, in fact, the point at which prospective constraints stop and thus occurs frequently at the boundaries of exchanges, as in:

32   D: Whereabouts in your chest?
     P: On the heart side.
     D: // YES //

33   D: And how long have you had those for?
     P: Well I had them er a week last Wednesday.
     D: // a WEEK last WEDnesday //

It is not unusual in certain types of interaction for even an answer to end with low termination. Example (34) is unremarkable:

34   A: // have you GOT the TIME //
     B: // its THREE o'CLOCK //

In choosing low termination, the second speaker does not preclude the first from making a follow-up move but he certainly does not constrain him to do so as he could have done by high termination. If the first speaker chooses to continue in the same exchange and produce a follow-up, one option is a low key 'thanks', particularly if the exchange has occurred between strangers in the street in Britain, in which case the item would serve simultaneously to acknowledge receipt of the information and to terminate the encounter. (In the United States, one would expect a mid or even high termination 'thanks', allowing for or even constraining, the 'you're welcome', 'sure', 'OK' which almost invariably follows.) If the exchange had occurred during a longish interaction, the acknowledging function could equally well have been realized by 'mm', a repetition, 'three o'clock' or an equative reformulation, 'time to go'.

Form and function

We can now use these observations on the significance of pitch concord to explain one of the major puzzles in discourse analysis: why are some items which are declarative or moodless in form taken to be questioning in function?

Following example (34), we discussed the possibilities for the follow-up; options we did not discuss were those in which the speaker ends in mid or high termination, rather than low. The exchange could have ended as in (34a), and the message would have been 'I take "three o'clock" as equivalent in meaning in this context to "time to go" (indicated by choice of low key), and I assume you will agree' (mid termination predicting mid key 'yes, I agree'):

34a A: Have you got the time?
    B: It's three o'clock.
    A: // TIME to GO //

Another alternative would be (34b), and this time the speaker is heard as both adding the information that he considers 'three o'clock' to be 'time to go' and asking for positive confirmation in the form of a 'yes/no' response.

34b A: // TIME to GO //

We can see the difference that termination choice makes in the following two extracts from a doctor/patient interview: in (35), the repetition with low termination is heard as exchange final; in (36), the repeated item with high termination is heard as eliciting.

35 D: How long have you had these for?
    P: Well I had them a week last Wednesday.
    D: // a WEEK last WEDnesday //
    D: // HOW many atTACKS have you HAD //

36   D: What were you doing at the time?
       P: Coming home in the car.
            I felt a tight pain in the middle of the chest.
       D: // TIGHT pain //
       P: // YOU KNOW // like a – // DULL ACHE //

There are two significant points about these observations: firstly, although the items with mid or high termination are initiating and in some sense questioning, the pitch movement on the tonic is falling, not rising as is frequently claimed in intonation manuals; in other words, it is definitely termination and not tone choice which carries the eliciting function; secondly, it is now possible to identify the function of these items through the phonological criteria which realize them and there is no need to draw on assumptions about speaker's and hearer's knowledge or A-events and B-events, as suggested in Labov (1972).

As philosophers have frequently pointed out, the two major assumptions underlying commands are that the speaker has the right to tell the listener to do x and that the listener is, in the most general sense, willing to do x. From what has been said here about termination choices, key concord, and the meaning of choices in the key system, one would expect commands to end with a mid termination choice, looking for a mid key agreeing 'yes', 'surely', 'certainly'. It is thus quite fascinating to discover that most classroom instructions, even those in a series and to the whole class, when no acknowledgement is possible or expected, also end with mid termination, symbolically predicting the absent agreement:

37   // FOLD your ARMS // LOOK at the WINdow // LOOK at the

       CEILIng // LOOK at the FLOOR // LOOK at the DOOR //

It is also instructive, if not worrying, to realize that when parents and teachers become irritated because their instructions are being ignored, they typically switch to high termination which paradoxically allows for the high key contrastive refusal:

38 Mother: // PUT it DOWN //   Child: // NO i WON'T //

The pitch sequence

We noted earlier that the particular significance of low termination is that it does not place any constraints on a succeeding utterance. When we examine sequences of tone units it becomes useful to regard all the tone units occurring between two successive low terminations as comprising a phonological unit which Brazil has called the 'pitch sequence'.

Pitch sequences are often closely associated with topic: speakers appear to use a drop to low termination to signal that a particular mini-topic is ended. The next pitch sequence may begin in mid or high key; a mid key choice indicates that what follows is additively related, or topically linked, with what has just ended. Thus in (39), the doctor ends one part of his examination and begins another linked one. (Three slashes, ///, indicate a pitch sequence boundary.)

39   D: // IT'S DRY skin // ISn't it //
     P: // MM //
     D: // SCAly // LET'S have a LOOK /// OPen your mouth WIDE //

On other occasions, the next pitch sequence begins in high key and the contrastive meaning serves to mark the beginning of a completely new topic. In fact, if we now generalize, we discover that the frames which Sinclair and Coulthard (1975) isolated on item-specific intonation criteria are actually pitch sequence initial items following low termination, pitch sequence final ones.

40   T: So we get energy from petrol and we get energy from food.

         // TWO kinds of ENergy /// NOW then // . . .

Indeed, once one recognizes them, pitch phenomena appear to be much more important than lexical items in marking boundaries: a re-examination of some of the classroom data shows that at certain points, where on topical grounds one felt a need for a boundary but had accepted that as no frame occurred the teacher had not marked and probably had not intended one, there are boundaries marked by pitch:

41   T: Good girl, energy, yes, you can have a team point; that's a very good word.

         // we USE // we're USing ENergy // we're USing ENergy /// when a CAR // GOES into the GARage // . . .

In other words, the low termination/high key pitch sequence boundary, here occurring between 'energy', and 'when a car', appears to carry the transaction boundary signal.

CONCLUDING REMARKS

My intention in this chapter has been to present a brief (and therefore necessarily partial) introduction to Brazil's intonation system, in order to allow readers to cope more easily with several of the subsequent chapters which draw directly on, and assume a knowledge of, his system. Those who wish to enter more deeply into the system are referred to Brazil (1992).

'The significance of intonation in discourse', is a substantially modified version of 'Intonation and the description of interaction', first published in Coulthard (1987a) *Discussing Discourse*, 63–79.

3 Exchange structure

Malcolm Coulthard and David Brazil

DESCRIPTIVE PROBLEMS

Introduction

Following any piece of research one is faced with the problem of demonstrating the validity and generality of one's findings and of showing that an explanation, based of necessity on a fairly small sample of data, is applicable to similar data collected by other investigators. During the past thirty years this problem has been elegantly solved within traditional linguistics by the development of generative grammars. A linguist can now present and exemplify his findings quite briefly and then encapsulate them in a few abstract rules which will generate all and only acceptable instances of the phenomena. The reader is then able to insert his own lexical items and check the outcomes against his own data or, more usually, his own intuitions and thereby evaluate the description for himself.

By contrast most of the descriptive problems in the analysis of spoken discourse remain to be solved. There has, so far, been no detailed theoretical discussion of the peculiar nature of verbal interaction nor of the components and categories appropriate to describing it – there is no *Discourse Structures* or *Aspects of the Theory of Discourse*. Indeed, it is by no means certain that the kind of generative description that grammarians have used so successfully is an appropriate tool for handling interaction. As a result there are virtually no commonly agreed descriptive categories; it is still not even clear what is the largest structural unit in discourse and descriptions tend to concentrate on fragments.

One notable obstacle to the development of a description of interaction is that speakers seem to have weaker intuitions about permissible sequences of interactive units than they do about permissible sequences of grammatical units. Of course it may be that this is only the case because relatively little work has so far been undertaken on the structure of interaction, but, nevertheless, we have found the safest working assumption to be that, in the co-operatively produced object we call *discourse*, there is no direct equivalent to the concept of *grammaticality*. Indeed, the concept of *com-*

petence, as it has been understood since Chomsky set it in sharp contrast to *performance*, may ultimately be unhelpful in our field.

Utterances do, of course, place constraints upon what will be considered a relevant or related utterance, but a next speaker always has the option of producing an *unrelated* utterance. If he does so, even in so conspicuous a way as by failing to respond to a greeting or by producing a whole string of apparently inconsequential utterances, it seems more appropriate to characterize his behaviour as socially deviant than as linguistically so. This is not to say that interaction has no structure, or even that the researcher will be unable to find it. It is rather to assert that the structural framework operates by classifying each successive discourse event in the light of the immediately preceding one and, to state the matter in the broadest possible terms, irrelevance is always one of the speaker-options. A consequence of all this is that research in the area of spoken discourse will, for a long time, be data-based out of necessity: the difficulty of arguing by appeal to intuition is a fact that has to be lived with.

Conversational analysis

Currently, many of our insights into the structure of interaction come from the work of the Conversational Analysts, in particular Sacks, Schegloff and Jefferson. However, although many of their findings are fascinating and although Schenkein (1978:3) describes work by them and their colleagues as a 'promising movement towards an empirically based grammar of natural conversation', their descriptive methods create problems for others hoping to use their results, particularly for linguists accustomed to tightly defined categories.

Conversational Analysts were originally fugitives from a sociology they regarded as based on simplistic classification and they are well aware of Garfinkel's (1967) observation that you can never 'say in so many words' what you mean. Perhaps for these reasons they do not attempt to define their descriptive categories but instead use 'transparent' labels like *misapprehension sequence, clarification, complaint, continuation, pre-closing*. It will be instructive to look at some of their analyses to see the problems inherent in this type of description.

Sacks (n.d.) begins with the observation that a conversation is a string of at least two *turns*. Some turns are more closely related than others and he isolates a class of sequences of turns called *adjacency pairs* which have the following features: they are two utterances long; the utterances are produced successively by different speakers; the utterances are ordered – the first must belong to the class of *first pair parts*, the second to the class of *second pair parts*; the utterances are related and thus not any second part can follow any first part, but only an appropriate one; the first pair part often selects next speaker and always selects next action – it thus sets up a *transition relevance*, an expectation which the next speaker fulfils, in other words the first part of a pair predicts the occurrence of the second; 'Given a question, regularly enough an answer will follow'.

It is, however, no difficult matter to discover a question not followed by an answer and this raises a question about the status of the pair. Sacks argues that, whereas the absence of a particular item in conversation has initially no importance because there is any number of things that are similarly absent, in the case of an adjacency pair the first part provides specifically for the second and therefore the absence of the second is noticeable and noticed. Sometimes, either because he doesn't understand, or because he doesn't want to commit himself until he knows more or because he's simply stalling, a next speaker may produce not a second pair part but another first pair part. The suggestion is 'if you answer this one, I will answer yours'.

1	A: I don't know where the – wh – this address is	Q
	B: Well where do – which part of town do [you] live	Qi
	A: I live four ten East Lowden	Ai
	B: Well you don't live very far from me	A

Schegloff (1972) labels the embedded pair an *insertion sequence*, but one question which immediately arises is in what sense is the pair QiAi inserted into the pair QA; surely this is treating conversation as an accomplished product rather than a developing process, because A may never occur. In justification Schegloff argues that

> The Q utterance makes an A utterance conditionally relevant. The action the Q does (here, direction asking) makes some other action sequentially relevant (here, giving directions by answering the Q). Which is to say, after the Q, the next speaker has that action specifically chosen for him to do, and can show attention to, and grasp of, the preceding utterance by doing the chosen action then and there. If he does not, that will be a notable omission.

In other words, during the inserted sequence the original question retains its transition relevance, and if the second speaker does not then produce an answer it is noticeably absent in exactly the same way as it would be if there were no intervening sequence, and the questioner can complain about the lack of an answer in exactly the same way. Thus the argument is that adjacency pairs are normative structures, the second part ought to occur, and for this reason the other sequences can be regarded as being inserted between the first pair part that has occurred and the second pair part that is anticipated.

Jefferson (1972) proposes a second type of embedded sequence, the *side sequence*. She observes that the general drift of conversation is sometimes halted at an unpredictable point by a request for clarification and then the conversation picks up again where it left off. The following example is of children preparing for a game of 'tag':

2 Steven: One, two, three, (pause) four, five, six,
          (pause) eleven, eight, nine, ten
   Susan: Eleven? – eight, nine, ten
   Steven: Eleven, eight, nine, ten
   Nancy: Eleven?
   Steven: Seven, eight, nine, ten
   Susan: That's better

Whereupon the game resumes.

In Jefferson's analysis this side sequence, which she labels a *misapprehension sequence*, begins with a *questioning repeat* – an interrogative item which indicates that there is a problem in what has just been said, whose function is 'to generate further talk directed to remedying the problem'. Questioning repeats occur typically after the questioned utterance has been completed, because only then can one be sure that the speaker is not going to correct himself or explain the unclear item. An interrupting questioning repeat is liable to attract a *complaint* not a *clarification*, 'if you'd just let me finish'.

Jefferson suggests initially that the misapprehension sequence has a three-part structure, consisting of 'a statement of sorts, a misapprehension of sorts and a clarification of sorts'. The example above is in fact more complex, consisting of a statement followed by two misapprehension and clarification pairs. So far Jefferson's side sequence looks rather like Schegloff's insertion sequence. There are, however, two major differences: firstly, because the first item, the statement, is not a first pair part, the other items are in no sense inserted and thus there is no expectation of who should speak at the end of the sequence or of what type of utterance should follow; secondly, while the sequence misapprehension–clarification looks like a pair, there is actually a compulsory third element in the sequence, an indication by the misapprehender that he now understands and that the sequence is now terminated – 'That's better' in the example above, or 'yeah' in the example below.

3 Statement: If Percy goes with – Nixon I'd sure like that
   Misapprehension: Who
   Clarification: Percy. That young fella that wh – his daughter was
                     murdered (1.0)
   Termination: Oh yea:h Yeah

In addition, because the first item, the *statement*, is not a first pair part, the conversation cannot resume with the second pair part as happens after an insertion sequence, so there remains the problem of a *return*. Jefferson observes that:

It is not merely that there [occurs] a return to the on-going sequence, but that to return to the on-going sequence . . . is a task performed by participants.

She suggests that the return can be effected either as a *resumption* or as a *continuation* – a resumption is achieved by attention getters such as 'listen' or 'hey you know', which mark that there is a problem in accomplishing a return, while continuations, attempted by 'so' or 'and' are directed to 'covering-up' the problem, to proposing that there is no trouble. Thus the full structure is

4　　　　　　　　Statement:　　A:　And a goodlooking girl comes to you and [asks] you, y'know

	Misapprehension:	B:	Gi(hh)rl asks you to –
Side	Clarification:	C:	Wella its happened a lotta times
Sequence	Termination:	B:	Okay okay go ahead
	Continuation:	B:	So he says 'no' . . .

In trying to understand and use the descriptive categories outlined above the intending analyst has several problems. Firstly, *pair* is the only technical term which is defined, but pairs are also at times referred to as *sequences*; secondly, *sequence* is not defined but appears to be a structurally coherent collection of not necessarily successive utterances or utterance parts, up to four in number; thirdly, the exact status of *misapprehension sequence* is not clear but it is apparently a subclass of *side sequence*, although we have no idea what other types of side sequence there are.

From the way the authors describe and exemplify their categories it would appear that the real difference between Schegloff's insertion sequence and Jefferson's side sequence is that the former has a ready-made *return*, the second part of the question/answer pair, while for the latter it has to be 'worked at'. However, one could surely insert a misapprehension sequence inside Schegloff's Question/Answer pair – example (5) below looks unexceptional; would it, could it, then be classified as an insertion sequence?

5　A:　I don't know where the – wh – this address is　　Question
　　B:　Which one　　　　　　　　　　　　　　　　　　 Misapprehension
　　A:　The one you just gave me　　　　　　　　　　　 Clarification
　　B:　Oh yeah, yeah　　　　　　　　　　　　　　　　 Termination
　　B:　Well you don't live very far from me　　　　　　 Answer

Perhaps it was a mistake to assume that insertion and side sequences necessarily have different distributions; perhaps the main difference between them is the fact that they have different internal structures. As it is difficult to see how misapprehension and clarification differ in any fundamental way from question and answer respectively, one must assume that the structural difference lies in the *termination* element which completes the side sequence. However, there seems to be no reason why Schegloff's insertion sequence couldn't also have a termination.

1a A: I don't know where the – wh – this address is   Q
   B: Which part of the town do you live   Qi
   A: I live four ten East Lowden   Ai
   B: Ah yeah   Termination
    : Well you don't live very far from me   A

Thus one must conclude that in fact these two sequences only have different labels because they have been labelled from different perspectives – *insertion sequence* is a structural label, while *misapprehension sequence* is a semantic label which attempts to capture the relationship of the first item in the sequence to the preceding utterance.

There is a similar confusion in the labelling of the component units of the misapprehension sequence. Following an item labelled clarification one might expect an item which indicates that the addressee now understands (this is the apparent function of 'oh yeah, yeah' in example 3), and therefore labelled something like *acknowledgement*. In fact, the label given is *termination*, a structural not a semantic label and one which leads the reader to question why in that case the first item is not an *opener* or *initiator*.

In setting out to find misapprehension sequences in his own data the intending analyst faces a difficulty; to help him he has only Jefferson's observation that the sequences begin with a 'misapprehension of sorts' and the three analysed examples, (2), (3), (4) above. While it is easy to accept 'who' in example (3) as a misapprehension, the items in examples (2) and (4) look as if they would be more satisfactorily labelled as *challenge*, followed by a *correction* and a *justification* respectively.

As this brief discussion makes abundantly clear the descriptions of the Conversational Analysts with their transparent categories are deceptively attractive and apparently allow very delicate analyses. However, just as Katz and Fodor (1963) produced a sketch of an elegant way of describing the meaning of nouns in terms of distinctive features only to see Bolinger (1965) demonstrate that it was an illusion, so Conversational Analysts working with no overall descriptive framework run the risk of creating data-specific descriptive categories for each new piece of text to the last syllable of recorded conversation.

Linguistic description

In order to avoid the dangers inherent in a purely data-based description we have from the beginning attempted to locate our work within the theory of linguistic description presented in Halliday (1961), 'Categories of the theory of grammar'. Despite its title, and although based upon experience in describing phonological and grammatical structure, the paper is in fact an explicit, abstract discussion of the nature of linguistic description. Thus for anyone seeking, as we are, to describe a new kind of data following well-tried linguistic principles, it is a perfect starting-point.

The first questions one asks of a linguistic description are what are the descriptive units and how are they related to each other – as we have already seen these are not questions that are easy to answer for the units proposed by the Conversational Analysts. For any unit one must provide two kinds of information: what position or function it has in the structure of other larger units and what its own internal structure is.

Such information, about the interrelationships between units, can be presented very simply in terms of a rank scale, whose basic assumption is that a unit at a given *rank* – to take an example from grammar, *word* – is made up of one or more units at the rank below, in this case *morpheme*, and combines with other units at the same rank, that is other words, to make up one unit at the rank above, *group* or *phrase*.

Organizing descriptive units into a rank scale can be part of the heuristic process; as Labov observes (1972:121),

> formalisation is a fruitful procedure even when it is wrong:
> it sharpens our questions and promotes the search for answers.

It was their attempt to fit *utterance* into a rank scale which made Sinclair *et al.* (1972) realize that it was not in fact a structural unit and if we try to create a rank scale from the Conversational Analysts' descriptive units discussed above we get similarly enlightening results. One criterion for placing units at a particular point on a rank scale is relative size and thus we would expect the following:

sequence
pair
turn

However, in a rank scale, larger units are, by definition, related to smaller ones in a 'consists of' relationship, and we can in no way pretend that the Conversational Analysts' sequence consists of one or more pairs; rather both consist of two or more turns and thus we realize that structurally, sequence and pair are varieties or classes of the *same unit*, with pair being a label for one *subclass* of sequence just as transitive is a label for one kind of clause.

Distinguishing analytic units is only a first step; a description must then set out to isolate the different kinds or *classes* of unit at each rank, and these classes must be distinguished in terms of their *structure*, the way in which they are composed of particular units from the rank below in a particular sequence. For example at the rank of *clause* one can distinguish four major or primary classes *declarative*, *imperative*, *interrogative* and *moodless* according to the occurrence and relationship between two *elements of structure*, Subject and Predicator.

Declarative	S+P	He is writing
Interrogative	P‹S›	Is he writing/Where is he writing
Imperative	P	Write
Moodless	−P	Him

This is a very powerful description which can classify all free or main clauses into one of four classes. For the same reason it has disadvantages because there is an enormous number of relevant differences between clauses with which it does not cope: transitivity, polarity, voice, presence of adjuncts, and so on. However, all scientific description has the same problem, that of attempting to handle an infinite number of unique events by the simplest possible description. Halliday builds the solution into the theory; while remaining at the same *rank* one can take successive steps in *delicacy*, producing structures more and more finely distinguished, until every structural difference has been handled.

It will be evident from the example above that the structure of a unit is not, in fact, presented directly in terms of the units next below but rather in terms of *elements of structure* which are then related to the smaller units. Thus, clause structure is described in terms of the elements of structure S(ubject), P(redicator), O(bject), C(omplement), A(djunct) which are then in turn related to the classes of group, nominal, verbal, adverbial and prepositional, which realize them at the rank below. This apparently unnecessary double-labelling is in fact a crucial step, particularly when dealing with new data, as we shall soon see.

It is instructive to reconsider some of Schegloff and Jefferson's categories in these terms. From their articles discussed above we are led to assume, firstly, that there are at least two kinds of *sequence*, main and subordinate or major and minor; secondly, that at secondary delicacy there are at least two classes of subordinate sequence, insertion and side sequence, while at tertiary delicacy, it is implied, side sequences can be separated into misapprehension and other(s).

We noted that there are two ways in which side and insertion sequences are said to differ: they have a different structure and they occur in different environments. However, as we now realize, only the former is a statement about sequences, the latter is a statement about the structure of whatever is the unit above sequence. In other words, just as at clause rank in grammar the group realizing Subject may be embedded inside the group realizing Predicator, so in interaction, it is being suggested, there is a unit whose elements of structure are realized by sequences and which has at least the following possible realizations: AA, A‹B›, where B is recognized as an insertion sequence, and ABA where B is recognized as a side sequence. However, precisely because they do not have the technique of double labelling for units and elements of structure, Schegloff and Jefferson have conflated an observation about positional occurrence with one about internal structure. It is this confusion which allowed us to suggest earlier

(p. 55) that a misapprehension sequence could apparently occur in the same environment as an insertion sequence and to question what its status then was.

Initially, as we observed above, it looks as if there is no great problem in demonstrating that the two sequences are *structurally* distinct – one has a two-part structure, consisting of *question* and *answer*, the other a three-part structure consisting of *misapprehension*, *clarification* and *termination*. But misapprehension is a 'question of sorts' and clarification an 'answer of sorts' while, as we have seen, a termination is quite likely to follow a question/answer sequence. This time we see that we have a triple confusion between elements of structure, the units realizing them and degree of delicacy. Termination is a suitable label for an element of structure and would be most likely to combine with others like *initiation* and *response*. *Question* and *answer* are in fact classes of turn which are most likely to occur as realizations of the elements of structure initiation and response, while misapprehension along with *correction solicitor* and *appeal* (Jefferson and Schenkein 1978) are, if accepted as justifiable categories, almost certainly subdivisions of question at tertiary delicacy.

For Halliday 'shunting' backwards and forwards between and within ranks is an integral part of the heuristic process. What we have just attempted to do is redistribute the information presented in the labels and structural descriptions of side and insertion sequences in a way that will be both more enlightening and of more generality. We have ended up with the observation that at primary delicacy the two sequences are virtually identical – side sequence has the structure IRT, insertion sequence IR(T) – the other differences reported are now handled in the structure of the unit next above, whose existence has been deduced from theirs, and at tertiary delicacy in classes of the unit next below, *turn*. In so doing we have created the beginnings of a rigorous, generalizable description of discourse structure.

Ranks and levels

The lowest unit in a rank scale has, by definition, no structure, (otherwise it wouldn't be the lowest), but this doesn't mean that description necessarily stops there. Morpheme is the smallest unit of grammar and thus has no structure although, in a very real sense, morphemes do consist of phonemes or phonic substance. It is now one of the basic tenets of linguistics that there are two separate kinds of language patterning or *levels* – the phonological and the grammatical – each with its own rank scale, and the descriptive problem is to show how units at the level of grammar are *realized* by units at the level of phonology.

The unit at the highest rank in a particular level is one which has a structure that can be expressed in terms of smaller units, but which does not itself form part of the structure of any larger unit. Any attempt to describe structure assumes implicitly that there are certain combinations of units which either do not occur or, if they do occur, are unacceptable; such structures are classified as ungrammatical.

The corollary is that a potential unit upon whose structure one can discover no constraints in terms of combinations of the unit next below has no structure and is therefore not a unit in the rank scale. It is for this reason that sentence must be regarded as the highest unit of grammar, for, despite many attempts to describe paragraph structure and despite the obvious *cohesive* links between sentences, it is impossible to characterize paragraphs in terms of permissible and non-permissible combinations of classes of sentence. All combinations are possible and thus the actual sequence of sentence types within a paragraph depends upon topical and stylistic, but not grammatical considerations.

There are three possible outcomes to a search for linguistic patterning in spoken interaction: we may discover that all linguistic constraints end with the largest grammatical unit, the spoken sentence; we may discover that there is further grammatical patterning whose organizing principles have so far escaped discovery – this is not impossible because, although the tone group had generally been thought to be the largest unit of phonological patterning, we are now able to present evidence for the existence of one if not two larger units in the phonological rank scale (see Chapter 2). The third possibility, and the one we will attempt to justify, is that in order to describe further patterning in spoken discourse it is necessary to change *level*.

The reasons for postulating a new level, which we call *discourse*, are directly analogous to the ones given for separating phonology and grammar. Halliday (1961:243) argued that

> linguistic events should be accounted for at a number of different levels . . . because of the difference in kind of the processes of abstraction,

but he himself only considered the levels of form and substance. To these we add the level of discourse to handle language function.

In a complete analysis each level and its descriptive units handle part of the linguistic organization of a stretch of language, but there is no necessary correspondence between either the size or the boundaries of analytic units in different levels. As Halliday (ibid.:282–3) stressed, whereas

> [all] formal distinctions presuppose [some] distinction in substance . . . no relation whatsoever is presupposed between the *categories* required to state the distinction in form (grammar and lexis) and the *categories* required to state phonologically the distinction in substance which carries it.

A simple example of this fundamental principle is the plural morpheme, which, even in regular cases, is sometimes realized at the level of phonology by the unit *syllable*, horse/horse*s* and sometimes by the unit *phoneme*, cat/cats. There are, of course, much more complex cases and it is a similar lack of fit between units that provides strong support for postulating the existence of the new level, discourse.

Sinclair and Coulthard (1975) point out that not only can one of the smallest discourse units, the act *directive*, be realized by all the primary classes of the grammatical unit clause, but also that in many cases, as the following examples illustrate, the 'directiveness' appears to derive from the occurrence of the base form of the verb irrespective of whatever other grammatical items precede it. In other words the boundary of the discourse unit directive cuts right through the grammatical unit 'verbal group' assigning 'shut' to a different category from 'can', 'could' and 'to'.

6   (i)   shut the door
     (ii)   can you   shut the door
     (iii) I wonder if you could   shut the door
     (iv)   I want you to   shut the door
     (v)   please   shut the door
     (vi)   lets   shut the door

In discussing the separation of phonology and grammar as descriptive levels Halliday argues that conflation causes added complexity and also weakens the power of the description. It would now appear that grammatical description is suffering similar problems because grammarians are unwilling to acknowledge the existence of a further descriptive level. Sinclair and Coulthard (ibid.:121) suggest that

> a reasonable symptom of the need to establish a further level [is] the clustering of descriptive features in the larger structures of the uppermost level

and observe that the clause or sentence is currently being forced to cope with most of the newly discovered linguistic complexity:

> it now has to manage intricacies of intonation selection, information organization, semantic structuring, sociolinguistic sensitivity, illocution and presupposition, in addition to its traditional concerns.

All this suggests strongly that an artificial ceiling has been reached. However, it is one thing to perceive the problem, quite another to detail the solution, and so far we can do little more than offer interesting examples rather than fully worked out solutions of how the new level can help. One area of great importance in spoken interaction is the linguistic realization of interpersonal relationships. Intonational correlates of some aspects are discussed in detail in Brazil (1978a,b, 1985/1992) and thus we will concentrate here on grammatical ones.

In the example above it is fairly evident that relative 'status' and degree of 'politeness' (see Brown and Levinson 1978) affect the choice of clause type, but it may not be as obvious that the same factors can similarly affect the choice of tense, as in examples 7(iii) and (iv) below:

7 erm I'm organizing the departmental Christmas party this year

  (i) will you both be coming?
  (ii) could you tell me whether you and your wife will be coming?
  (iii) and I was wondering whether you and your wife will be coming?
  (iv) and I just wanted to know whether you and your wife would be coming?

There are massive problems facing any attempt to explain in grammatical terms both the inappropriateness of past time adverbs and the appropriateness and instanced occurrence of 'now' in examples like (iiia) and (iva):

  (iiia) and *now* I was wondering whether you and . . .
  (iva) and *now* I just wanted to know whether you and . . .

In coping with examples like this a description which sees tense selection as potentially a realization of a functional feature such as politeness, has considerable attraction.

From what has been said above it will be evident that we see the units of discourse as being realized by units of grammar in exactly the same way that grammatical units are realized by phonological ones, although at the moment we can do little more than discuss the nature of these discourse units; work on discovering the realization rules, or, looked at from the decoder's point of view, the interpretative rules, has hardly begun.

Meanwhile, we must show how, by adopting a three-level model, we are led to rethink the notion of *competence*. We have already suggested that the extension of a linguistic description to take in interactive discourse seems to make this rather radical step necessary.

Since 1957, competence has been related conceptually to the ability to discriminate between well-formed and deviant sentences. The application of the criterion of well-formedness has never been unproblematic, and developments in transformational/generative theory have tended to make its application more difficult rather than less so. If we consider it in relation to each of our postulated three levels in turn, we can throw some light on the problem.

Beginning with the phonological level, we note that any deviance can be recognized fairly easily, perhaps unequivocally. Initial /ŋ/, for instance, excludes any sequence of phonemes from the set of well-formed English words, as does final /h/, and sequences having certain specifiable combinations of phonemes medially are similarly excluded. Whatever the basis on which we classify the segments that enter into the phonological structures of a given dialect of English, the membership of those classes does not vary. We may, perhaps, relate this to the fact that there are physiological and physical aspects to the classification and thus the distinction between allowable and proscribed sequences is not entirely 'arbitrary' in the sense that it is observing distributional privileges.

When, however, we move to the formal level, the situation is not so simple. Admittedly, structure enables us to reject certain sequences as ungrammatical: 'cat the . . .' contravenes the rule that words of the word class [determiner] always precede the head of the nominal group. However, in the groups 'the cuddly black cat' and 'the black cuddly cat' the situation is somewhat different. 'Cuddly' is one of a large group of adjectives which belong to two separate subclasses of adjectives and it is the sequential position, before or after the colour adjective 'black' which determines the differential classification of 'cuddly' as a qualitative or classifying adjective. Here, it is his knowledge of nominal group structure that provides the hearer/reader with information about how to interpret a particular item. In fact the way in which the predictive power of the structural frame can be exploited to allocate words to classes quite different from those to which they are normally interpreted as belonging is a commonplace of literary commentary. A particularly vivid example is:

8   Thank me no thanking, nor proud me no prouds (*Romeo and Juliet*, III. v.)

but the phenomenon itself is very common. The point we are trying to make is that although the semantics of such a sentence may present difficulties, there is no real problem in providing a grammatical analysis. To recall the comparison with phonology, we may note that such exploitation is possible because items like 'cuddly', 'thank' and 'proud', as they are used conversationally, do not have a necessarily stable relationship with anything that can be objectively specified on an extra-linguistic basis. Exploitability would seem to be in inverse proportion to the stability of the relationship that is commonly assumed to hold for the word in question, a fact we can relate to the improbability of a closed-class item like 'the' being reclassified.

The intermediate position given to the formal level in our description accords with the observation that there structure sometimes separates the possible from the impossible (or perhaps more accurately, the probable from the highly improbable), but sometimes provides the basis for interpreting whatever elements actually do occur. Crossing the watershed between form and function we find a situation that complements the situation at the phonological level in an interesting way. In discourse we are concerned with an object created by the combined efforts of more than one speaker, and under these circumstances it is difficult to see how *anything* can be ruled out as 'not discourse'. To set out with the expectation that such a ruling will be possible, might, indeed, seem counter-intuitive. One speaker cannot place absolute constraints upon another speaker in any sense comparable with the way his apprehension of grammatical rules will block the production of certain sequences of elements within his own utterance. When 'mistakes' occur, and are remarked upon, they are usually of the type:

9 A: So the meeting is on Friday
   B: Thanks
   A: No, I'm asking you

where B wrongly classifies A's contribution, and rectification requires help of a metalinguistic kind from A. There is no way in which B can come to recognize the wrongness of his response by simply reflecting upon it in the way he might become aware of – and spontaneously correct – a grammatical mistake. The most promising theoretical assumption seems to be that a speaker can do anything he likes at any time, but that *what* he does will be classified as a contribution to the discourse in the light of whatever structural predictions the previous contribution, his own or another's, may have set up. To take an obvious and over-simplified example, an elicitation may get the response it predicts, or it may be followed by a totally irrelevant new initiation.

Reflection upon the latter possibility forces us to focus upon two important facts. The first is that, because of the predictive power of the structural frame, the first speaker would be likely to treat anything as a non-response only after he had failed to discern any possible relevance. Utterance pairs like

10 A: So the meeting is on Friday
    B: Tom will be back in town

where A hears B as meaning unambiguously either 'yes' or 'no' are common enough in most kinds of conversation. The absence of a deterministic relationship between form and function makes it possible for virtually any rejoinder to have coherence given the shared background of understanding of the participants. In our example, B's classification of A's utterance as an elicitation could itself have been made only on the basis of assumptions arrived at intersubjectively. It is partly because a quality of relevance, accessible only to participants, and valid only at the time and place of utterance, can attach to any utterance regardless of its form, that no generalized judgements about well-formedness in discourse can be made.

The problem of interpreting apparent non-sequiturs like (10) frequently confronts conversationalists and analysts alike. The satisfactory progress of interactive discourse depends upon participants seeing eye to eye about the classifying power of each contribution. In the case of (9) we can reasonably say that things went wrong because A's initiation is ambiguous, and because of this the misapprehension is easily rectified. Example (10) isn't so simple. B's contribution may, as we have said, fully meet the expectations of the initiation and so be seen from both participants' viewpoints as a response. There are other possibilities, however. B may have misunderstood the implications of A's initiation and so said something which, according to his own view of the state of convergence, could be a response but which A is unable to interpret as such because his view is different. Or

B may have interpreted A's comment in the way A intended but then responded on the basis of some assumed understanding which in fact was not accessible to A. Yet a further possibility is that B has exercised his option not to reply to the initiation. In a situation where both participants were fully aware of the structural implications of their own and each other's actions, B could simply have decided that, before pursuing the matter of Friday's meeting, there were other matters to consider. His re-initiation which ignores A's initiation might under some circumstances be considered rude, but his would depend on their relationship.

This brings us to the second point: if a speaker's behaviour *is* heard as deviant the deviance can be most satisfactorily characterized as deviance from a social norm. This is popularly recognized in the use of labels such as 'rude', 'evasive' and 'eccentric'. It is worth noting that, when speaker A fails to recover any coherent relationship between the two components of a pair like

11 A: Will you come for a drink?
    B: My brother's just left for the States

his analysis will reflect, among other things, his knowledge of B's manners, his drinking habits, even his state of mental health. As a linguistic event the latter's contribution simply represents one of the set of options open to him at this point in the discourse. What a competence/performance dichotomy might separate out as an 'error' must be regarded at the level of discourse as an event which has its own meaning, the latter being characterized not in terms of whatever judgements A may be induced to make of B but in terms of the prospective constraints that now apply to any rejoinder A might make.

Thus we are not arguing that interaction has no structure, but rather that the structural framework operates by classifying each successive discourse event in the light of the immediately preceding one.

FURTHER OBSERVATIONS ON EXCHANGE STRUCTURE

The definition of the exchange

Sinclair *et al.* (1972) defined the exchange as 'the basic unit of interaction' and we see no reason to disagree with this. It is basic because it consists minimally of contributions by two participants and because it combines to form the largest unit of interaction, the *transaction*. Sinclair *et al.* further suggested that there were three major classes of exchange, *eliciting*, *directing* and *informing*, whose initial moves function respectively to request a verbal response, to require a non-verbal response and to provide new information (in the most general sense of information).

This description obviously makes a very powerful claim about the nature of interaction, that there are only three basic types of exchange, a claim which may seem all the more surprising in the light of current work in speech act theory, pragmatics and ethnomethodology where large numbers of different exchange initiators have been isolated. However, to see these descriptions as necessarily in conflict is to misunderstand the nature of the original description which, as we discussed above, spreads out complexity along the scales of rank and delicacy.

For example the category *inform* includes what in many descriptions would be distinguished as *promise*, *prediction*, *statement*, to name but three. However, in order to demonstrate that these are structurally distinct units at secondary delicacy, and not merely different semantic labels for members of the same class, it would be necessary to demonstrate that, as well as sharing many possible realizations for next move as is evident in (12) below, there is also a set of possible next moves which follow them alone; it is this crucial criterion that no one has yet been able to meet.

12 I'll be there by eight   Great
    He'll be there by eight   } { Are you sure
    I know he'll be there by eight   Just in time to eat

Eliciting exchanges

Sinclair *et al.* observed that in the classroom the typical eliciting exchange was not *initiation–response*, IR, but rather *initiation–response–feedback*, IRF, where the third part functions to evaluate and/or comment upon the second. It is not difficult to explain the occurrence of this structure – most teacher questions are in some sense bizarre in that the questioner usually knows the answer already, while the answerer is himself often unsure and thus genuinely needs to be told whether the answer he has offered is the answer required. In many classrooms this structure is so powerful that if there is no evaluative third part it is 'noticeably absent', and its absence a clue that the answer is wrong:

13 T, I: Can you think why I changed 'mat' to 'rug'?
    P, R: Mat's got two vowels in it.
    T, F: Ø
    T, I: Which are they? What are they?
    P, R: 'a' and 't'.
    T, F: Ø
    T, I: Is 't' a vowel?
    P, R: No.
    T, F: No.

While such three part exchanges typify, more than anything else, classroom discourse, they do occur in other situations as well:

14 M: Have you brushed your teeth yet?
    C: Yes
    M: No you haven't

though, as here, they normally presuppose an asymmetrical status relationship. For this reason such exchanges in adult–adult interaction tend to be heard as aggressive:

15 A: What time did you come in last night?
    B: About midnight
    A: No, you didn't . . .

Other descriptions of interaction appear not to have recognized a similar three-part eliciting exchange, even though our discussion of misapprehension and insertion sequences above suggests that they certainly do occur. Nevertheless we want to argue that *all* eliciting exchanges have the potential of a three-part structure, while accepting that a two-part realization may, and in the case of polar responses often does, occur. As we can see in the following General Practitioner consultation, three-part exchanges are in fact by no means uncommon, though the third move is very different in kind from that in classroom discourse:

16 Doctor, I: And what's been the matter recently
    Patient, R: Well I've had pains around the heart
    Doctor, I: Pains – in your chest then
    Patient, R: Yes
    Doctor, I: Whereabouts in your chest
    Patient, R: On the – heart side, here
    Doctor, F: Yes
    Doctor, I: And how long have you had these for
    Patient, R: Well I had 'em a – week last Wednesday
    Doctor, F: A week last Wednesday

Follow-up

At this point we will start to draw on the description of intonation outlined in Coulthard (this volume, Chapter 2) and presented in detail in Brazil (1985/1992) in order to look in more detail at the options for the third part of the exchange.

    One of the teacher's major functions in responding to pupil replies is that of distinguishing right from wrong; so, and as we would expect, occurrences of high key 'yes' are frequent:

17 T: Would you say then that   P: Yes sir   T: //p YES //
    your pen was doing some work

18 T: Would you say then you're   P: energy sir   T: //p YES //
    using something

A teacher of course has more difficulty when responding to answers which are incorrect or only partially correct. Obviously he has the option of high key 'no' but seems only to use it at times of annoyance or exasperation:

19 T: What are three twos   P: eight sir   T: //p NO //

If at all possible he will use a mid key 'yes' which carries the meaning of agreement, and co-select referring tone to indicate incompleteness. Thus the move can be glossed as 'OK so far but . . .'.

20 T: can you tell me why do   P: to keep   T: //r YES //
      you eat all that food   you strong

21 T: and why would you want   P: to make   T: //r YES //
      to be strong   muscles

It is noticeable how rarely teachers use even mid key 'no' and it is instructive to look at the following occasion when it does occur.

22 T: Can you think what it means
    P: Does it mean there's been an accident further along the road
    T: //r NO //
    P: Does it mean double bend ahead
    T: //r NO //
    T: Look at the car
    P: Slippery roads
    T: //p YES //

Both teacher and pupils work hard to create a situation in which 'no' is a non-threatening, socially acceptable follow-up move. First the teacher implies that the question is a difficult one by changing from her earlier 'what is *x*' formulation to 'can you think what *x* means'; then the children respond with interrogatives which simultaneously mark the tentativeness of their answers and overtly request a 'yes/no' follow-up; finally the teacher does not select evaluative high key, but mid key and referring tone which together indicate that she is agreeing with their implied expectation that their answer is incorrect.

We have so far discussed 'yes' and 'no' co-occurring with high and mid key as options for the third move in an exchange; much more frequent, in fact, is a repetition or reformulation of the response. Teachers very often highlight part or the whole of a pupil's response by first repeating in high key, and thus marking it as important by contrast with whatever else might have been said, and then going on to produce a mid key, agreeing item:

23 T: How do you use your muscles
    P: By working
    T: //p by WOrking//p YES //

Reformulations in mid-key, where the key choice marks the item as additional information or as a suggested, contextually meaningful, paraphrase are quite common:

24 A: What time is it
    B: Ten o'clock
    A: // TIME to $_{GO}$ //

and we can see the teacher in the following example exploiting the option after a high key evaluative repetition:

25 T: Why do you put petrol in
    P: To keep it going
    T: //p ^{to} KEEP it $_{GOing}$ //p so that is will GO on the $_{ROAD}$ //

A common option in non-classroom discourse is low key which, when co-selected with 'yes' or a pure repetition, indicates that the move is doing little more than acknowledge receipt of information.

26 D: Whereabouts in your chest
    P: on the heart side
    D: //p $_{YES}$ //

27 A: What's the time
    B: ten o'clock
    A: //p ten o'$_{CLOCK}$ //

If the speaker reformulates in low key he is indicating that he doesn't feel he is adding any new information but simply verbalizing an agreement that the two versions are situationally equivalent in meaning:

28 A: What's the time
    B: ten o'clock
    A: //p $_{BED}$ time //

A REVISED DESCRIPTION OF EXCHANGE STRUCTURE

The theoretical discussion presented in the first section of this chapter and the new, intonation based, analytical insights presented on pages 66–8 above have prepared the ground for a critical re-evaluation of the account of exchange structure presented in Sinclair and Coulthard (1975) and a subsequent modification of the descriptive apparatus.

In identifying formal categories for the original analysis much reliance was necessarily placed on assumed contextual meanings which derived from apprehensions about what goes on in classrooms. In so far as the categories were labelled on a semantic basis it was hardly to be expected that they would always be appropriate for other types of discourse. Moreover, it was unlikely that discourse generated in the highly institutionalized setting of the classroom would exemplify the full range of options open to interactants in other situations.

However, perhaps the most important modifications we now propose arise from a more rigorous application of the principles underlying the formulation of rank-scale descriptions. In the original description the structure of exchanges was expressed in terms of three elements I(nitiation), R(esponse) and F(eedback) and the summary formula for all exchanges I(R)(F) indicated that all well-formed exchanges consisted minimally of two and maximally of three elements.

In addition, fully aware of Halliday's arguments in favour of 'double labelling', which we rehearsed above (p. 57), Sinclair and Coulthard set up three classes of move, *opening*, *answering* and *follow-up*, to label those units which realized the elements of structure IRF.

Sinclair and Coulthard proposed five major classes of exchange and labelled them, for ease of reference, according to the class of act realizing the head of the opening move and according to whether it was a teacher or a pupil who uttered it. We present below the structure and then an analysed example of each of five classes of exchange.

1 Teacher eliciting exchange: Structure

I with elicit as head
R with reply as head
F with evaluation as head

Example:
   I: What's the name of this cutter?
   R: Hacksaw
   F: The hacksaw

2 Teacher directing exchange: Structure

I with directive as head
R with react as head
(F) with evaluation as head

Example:
   I: I want you to take your pen and I want you to rub it as hard as you can on something woollen
   R: Activity
   F: None

3 Teacher informing exchange: Structure

I with inform as head
R with acknowledge as head

Example:
   I: Luckily, the French could read Greek
   R: Non-verbal Acknowledgement

4 Pupil eliciting exchange: Structure

I with elicit as head

R with reply as head

Example:
   I: Are the numbers for le – for the letters?
   R: Yes

5 *Pupil informing exchange:*   Structure

I   with inform as head.

F   with evaluation as head

Example:
    I: There's a letter missing from that up and down one
    F: Oh yes, you're right, it is

A number of features of this description caused misgivings even when it was first proposed, and they have continued to be sources of trouble in subsequent work. Firstly, there seemed to be too many classes of act at primary delicacy but no obvious way of reducing them. Secondly, it was disturbing to discover that each class of move was appropriate for only one place in structure, a phenomenon for which grammatical parallels are rare. Finally, the structure proposed for pupil informing exchanges, IF, was not satisfactory, while the alternative IR seemed no better. It could have been that all three features appeared to be problems only because the descriptive task was being viewed in the light of (possibly inappropriate) expectations carried over from the study of grammar. We can, however, derive some satisfaction from the fact that the alternative description presented below, which removes these problems, seems to be more satisfactory in other respects as well.

Elements of structure

In the original description initiation and response were conceived of as complementary elements of structure; a given realization of initiation was seen as prospectively constraining the next move, while a given realization of response was thought of as retrospective in focus and an attempt to be 'appropriate . . . [to the initiation] in the terms laid down' (Sinclair and Coulthard 1975: 45). The third element of structure, labelled *feedback*, was seen as an additional element in the exchange, not structurally required or predicted by the preceding response move, but nevertheless related to it.

The category label 'feedback' turns out, in retrospect, to have been an unfortunate choice. Not only did it imply that this element, unlike initiation and response, was defined semantically; it also led, at times, to conceptualization, and even definition, in highly specific semantic terms, as an item whose function it is 'to let the pupil know how well he has performed'.

We can now see that it was this very confusion that led to the problems with pupil informing exchanges. The pupil's informing move filling the initiation slot should, by definition, require a complementary move in the response slot. However, as the item which occurred in the slot tended to be one which in fact 'let the pupil know how well he/she had performed', it was categorized semantically, not structurally, and therefore labelled as feedback. In reality, the difference between teacher and pupil informing exchanges, which was handled in terms of exchange structure, IR as opposed to IF, should instead have been described as a difference in terms of the range of possible realizations in the response slot.

In reconsidering the three elements of exchange structure and their definitions we will now use the structural label *follow-up* for the third element. Two criteria will be used to define an element of exchange structure:

1 does the element generate constraints which amount to a prediction that a particular element will follow; and
2 has a preceding element predicted the occurrence of the element in question?

Using these criteria we can see that an initiation begins anew but sets up an expectation of a response, a response is predicted but itself sets up no expectations, while a follow-up is neither predicted nor predicting in this particular sense.

Predicting	*Predicted*	*Move type*
Yes	No	Initiation
No	Yes	Response
No	No	Follow-up
Yes	Yes	?

When we set out the definitional criteria in the form of a matrix like this, we discover a gap, and this prompts us to ask whether there is not also an element of exchange structure which is at the same time both predicted and predicting. Once we begin to search we discover that it is not in fact difficult to find pupil responses which appear to be actually looking for an evaluatory follow-up from the teacher:

T: Can anyone tell me what this means?
P: Does it mean 'danger men at work'
T: Yes

We have here, in the pupil's contribution, an element which partakes of the predictive characteristics of both response and initiation: to put it another way, we may say that it functions as a response with respect to the preceding element and as an initiation with respect to the following one. We can here make an interesting comparison with grammar, where phased predicators are frequently separated by an element of clause structure that 'faces both ways', standing as object to the first predicator and as subject to the second, for example: 'Let him go'. For much the same reason that Sinclair (1972) labels 'him' O/S, object/subject, we shall use the category R/I, response/initiation, to capture a similar double function.

It is probable that structures involving R/I are theoretically recursive, but examples seem to be rare, outside *Rosencrantz and Guildenstern are Dead*, and we can, by overlooking this complication, now propose an exchange structure consisting minimally of two structural elements, always I and R, and maximally of four:

I (R/I) R (F)

Move classes

After defining the elements of exchange structure we are now in a position to demonstrate that the second worry – that it was odd for there to be three major classes of move, opening, answering and follow-up, each appropriate to one and only one position in structure – was also well founded.

When we again look to grammar for comparison we notice that at the rank of group the class *nominal* can act at four of the five places in clause structure, S, O, C, A. We also notice, relevantly, that group classes are labelled according to their most important constituent unit, noun, verb, adjective, and not according to their position in the structure of the unit above, as was done for exchange structure. We therefore propose to abandon the labels *opening, answering, feedback*, and talk instead in terms of *eliciting, informing, acknowledging* moves. The labels are, of course, merely mnemonics and had the original analysis been correct this relabelling would have made no difference. The source of confusion we wish to avoid is that labelling classes of moves according to the elements of exchange structure they realize tends powerfully to reinforce the very expectation of a one-to-one relationship that the device of 'double labelling' was intended to avoid.

Part of the earlier difficulty in analysing classroom exchanges derived from the fact that pupil informs (opening moves with an informative as head) and pupil replies (answering moves with a reply as head) both tended to be followed by the same kind of item, a move with evaluation as head. However, when we look at other forms of interaction we discover that the situation is very similar – the set of items following informs is again very similar to that following replies – and the reason is not too difficult to discover: from a lexico-grammatical point of view the items realizing informs are very similar to those realizing replies.

It is this observation which leads us to argue that the majority of exchanges are basically concerned with the transmission of information and thus must contain one informing move, which can occur either in the Initiating or in the Responding slot. In some cases one participant offers a piece of information and then wants to know, minimally, that it has been understood and hopefully accepted and agreed with – in such cases, as the IR structure makes clear, the acknowledging move is socially required. In other cases the information is elicited and then the reason for its occurrence and its interpretation should not be problematic, so an acknowledging move is not essential though it often occurs – a fact captured by the observation that in such cases it occupies the Follow-up slot.

As soon as we conceptualize the exchange in these terms, with the initiating slot being used either to elicit or to provide information and the responding slot to provide an appropriate next contribution, an inform if the I was an elicit and an acknowledge if the I was an inform, we achieve the differential relationship between slots and fillers that we have been looking for:

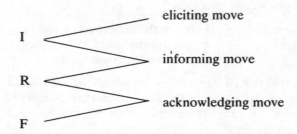

This simple representation also captures structurally the intuition that an initiating inform requires an acknowledgement whereas a responding inform does not.

It will be evident, even though this description has only been partially presented, that there will be more, though not many more, than the three move classes suggested in the original description, but this increase in complexity at move rank will be more than compensated for by a marked reduction in the number of primary classes of act.

Prospective classification

The powerful structural relationship between I and R means that any move occurring in the I slot will be heard as setting up a prediction that there will be an appropriate move in the R slot. The result is, as we briefly discussed on p. 63 above, that a speaker will make every effort to hear what follows his initiation as an appropriate response, and only in the last resort will he admit that it may be an unrelated new initiation. Thus, to take the simple case of an eliciting move in the I slot looking for information about polarity, it will classify *whatever* comes next as conveying polar (yes/no) information, if at all possible:

29 Can you come round tonight?
$$\begin{cases} \text{No} \\ \text{I've got an essay to finish} \\ \text{Thanks} \end{cases}$$

The joke in the following example from Labov (1972) derives from the fact that Linus either fails to interpret Violet's informing move as an adequate response, or deliberately rejects the underlying assumption that age is important.

30 Linus: Do you want to play with me Violet?
   Violet: You're younger than me. (Shuts door)
   Linus: She didn't answer my question.

The same interpretative strategy is used with wh-elicitations: all the items
in the response slot are interpreted as attempts to provide the required
information (although in selecting an interrogative version the speaker can
mark his information as potentially unreliable).

31 Where's the typewriter?
$\begin{cases} \text{It's in the cupboard} \\ \text{Try the cupboard} \\ \text{Isn't it in the cupboard} \end{cases}$

However, we must note that not all items following wh-elicits are informing moves. There will be occasions when the second speaker chooses to
produce an eliciting move, i.e. an R/I instead of an R, which simultaneously provides potentially unreliable information, and asks, through
the meaning carried by high termination, the original questioner to confirm
whether the offered information is in fact correct or not:

32 A: Where's the typewriter?
    B: //p ISN'T it in the ^{CUP}board //
    A: //p ^{NO} //

The limits of the exchange

In the earlier Sinclair and Coulthard version of exchange structure each move
class could only occur once and thus exchange boundaries were rarely
problematic. However, it has now been claimed that two eliciting moves can
occur in the same exchange and it will soon be suggested that two informing
moves can also co-occur. How then can one recognize an exchange boundary?

We argued earlier that the exchange is the unit concerned with negotiating the transmission of information and that it will contain an informing
move at I or R. We now want to argue that the exchange only carries one
(potentially complex) piece of information and its polarity, and that the
information and the polarity can only be questioned and asserted once. As
just presented it looks as if we are using semantic and not structural
criteria, but in fact we can support and exemplify our claims structurally,
for the power of the exchange is that as one progresses the available
options decrease rapidly.

Before we go any further we must subdivide both eliciting and informing
moves into two subclasses:

e_1 eliciting moves which seek major information
e_2 eliciting moves which see polarity information
i_1 informing moves which assert major information
i_2 informing moves which assert polarity information

We will now show that each of these moves can occur only once in a single exchange and also that they must occur in the sequence $e_1i_1e_2i_2$. We shall then have a very strong structural criterion which accounts for our intuition that when the same type of move occurs twice in succession we have an exchange boundary. Thus we recognize exchange boundaries between the following pairs of utterances even though the first exchange is structurally incomplete:

33 e_1 A: Where are you going?
    e_1 B: Why do you ask

34 i_1 A: Well, I've applied to fairly selective big, biggish civil engineering contractors
    i_1 B: Most of the people I'm applying to aren't pre-selective . . .

35 e_2 A: Would you like to come round for coffee tonight?
    e_2 B: Are you being serious

We must of course always be careful not to mis-analyse a particular linguistic realization; in (35a) below each of the alternatives offered for B could in other contexts be realizing respectively e_1, i_1, and e_2 moves, but here they are all interpretable as paraphrases of the basic i_2 realization 'yes'.

35a e_2 A: Would you like to come round for coffee tonight?
                ⎧ Who wouldn't
    i_2 B: ⎨ I'll be there by nine
                ⎩ Are you kidding

Although the most frequently occurring exchanges are the ones with the sequence e_1i_1 or e_2i_2 it is, as we mentioned above, possible to have the sequence $e_1e_2i_2$ as in example (32) above, and also i_1i_2 as in:

36 i_1 A: I think its raining
    i_2 B: //p YES//p it IS //

where, in a structure typical of classroom interaction, B proclaims the polarity of A's utterance without A suggesting it was ever in doubt. More typical, of course, following an informing move is a move indicating acceptance or understanding of the information:

36a i_1 A: I think its raining
    ack B: //p YES //p it IS //
    ack A: //p YES //

Whereas all the other moves can only occur once in a given exchange, acknowledge can, though it rarely does, occur twice, but in such cases it is almost invariably lexicalized, as in (36a) above, as a mid key 'yes' and is used by a speaker to 'pass' when it is his turn to speak and to allow the other speaker to select the next topic.

Residual problems

This new analysis of exchange structure while being intuitively more acceptable, obviously leaves several problems unresolved and creates others that apparently didn't exist before.

Informing moves

In what has gone before we have assumed and indeed implied that the distinction between class 1 informing moves and class 2 eliciting moves is unproblematic. However, there are times when it is unclear to which category an item belongs, because it is difficult to describe/delimit the boundary. For example, a high termination choice at the end of an informing move certainly constrains the other speaker to make a contribution, as in (37) and (38):

37 //r and so THEN // p i went to the MARket // $\left.\begin{matrix} \\ \\ \end{matrix}\right\}$ //p REally//
38 //p its ALready FREEzing //   //p GOSH //

and it is instructive to compare (37) and (38) with (37a) and (38a) which are unproblematically heard as elicitations.

37a //r and so THEN // p you went to the MARket // $\left.\begin{matrix} \\ \\ \end{matrix}\right\}$ //p YES //
38a //p you're ALready FREEzing //   //p SURE //

We are obviously on the borderline here – is it better to see utterances like (37) and (38), which appear to constrain the next speaker to verbalize his reaction to the information, as the most extreme type of inform, or the mildest of elicit? As the class of items which follow high termination items like (37) and (38) can also follow unproblematic informs and cannot follow class 2 elicits, it does appear more sensible to categorize (37) and (38) as informs, but there are still doubts.

Directing moves

We have so far not mentioned directing moves. Sinclair and Coulthard (1975) proposed a basic two-move structure for directing exchanges in the classroom, the initiating move realized minimally by a *directive*, the responding move minimally by a react defined as the performing of the required non-verbal action. The structure allowed for the occurrence, additionally, of an acknowledgement of the directive, like 'yes sir', though actual instances are rare and confined to exchanges between a teacher and a single pupil. Indeed the following hypothetical example could only occur in a class taunting its teacher:

39 Teacher: Open your books at page 39
    Class together: //p CERtainly, sir //

In other forms of interaction, between more equal participants, acknowledgement is much more common if not absolutely compulsory and one of the ways a child can, irreproachably, indicate his annoyance at being asked/told to do something, is by performing the action in silence with no acknowledgement. Indeed, the verbal acknowledgement is overtly requested in the most frequently occurring grammatical realizations of directives – the interrogative ones:

40 could you open the window
        open the window, will you

Here the interrogative simultaneously fulfils a double role: it provides for the verbal acknowledgement and also realizes 'politeness' by allowing the directive to masquerade as an elicitation – an exploitable masquerade as children know only too well:

41 Could you just $\left\{ \begin{array}{l} \text{Yes I could, but I'm a bit busy just now} \\ \text{No, I'm a bit busy just now} \end{array} \right.$

As philosophers have frequently pointed out the two major assumptions underlying directives are that the speaker has the right to ask the listener to do x and that the listener is, in the most general sense, agreeable or willing to do x. From what we know about termination, the key concord it predicts and the meanings of the choices in the key system, one would expect directives to end with a mid termination choice, looking for a mid key agreeing //p YES //, //p SURELy //, //p CERtainly //. It is thus quite fascinating to discover that most classroom directives, even those in a series and to the whole class, when no acknowledgement is possible or expected, also end with mid termination, symbolically predicting the absent agreement:

42 // FOLD your ARMS // LOOK at the WINdow // LOOK at the CEILing // LOOK at the FLOOR // LOOK at the DOOR //

Despite these interesting observations it is not clear whether it is better to regard directing moves as a separate primary class of move, or whether to regard them as a subclass of informing moves concerned with what the speaker wants B to do – certainly in terms of linguistic structure and realization the options following a directing move are remarkably similar to those following an informing move. Thus the final decision must depend on the significance attached to the non-verbal action.

Act classes

While we have argued that this new description will enable a marked reduction in the number of primary act classes, we have not yet fully worked out the new act classes, nor the way in which the primary classes will, or perhaps will not, make contact at secondary or tertiary delicacy with the apparently more delicate, though, as we have argued above, less rigorously defined, categories proposed by other analysts.

'Exchange structure' is a revised version of Coulthard and Brazil (1979) *Exchange Structure*. The first and third sections appear very much in their original form but the second section, 'Further observations on exchange structure', has been quite radically modified because it was concerned with introducing the Brazil description of intonation, which is now presented in detail in Chapter 2 above.

4 Priorities in discourse analysis

John Sinclair

From a linguistic perspective, the original discourse analysis work, revisited in Chapter 1, was motivated by a wish to make a description of spoken interaction, using the insights of the philosopher J.L. Austin (1962). Speech act theory offered a functional theory of meaning. It also gave a partial explanation of a class of descriptive problems in linguistics, namely those which expose an inconsistency between the meaning given by a straightforward description in terms of an established analytical framework, and a function in discourse that requires an unconventional description. Austin's notion of 'illocutionary force' was a powerful agent in reconceptualizing the way language relates to the world.

It seemed, indeed, that the conventional meaning of an utterance was but a stage in its interpretation; a preliminary statement of the organization of the components drawn from general knowledge about language of this kind to be found in grammars and dictionaries. When the utterance was viewed in context, another set of criteria applied, building on the analysis-for-meaning, and exhibiting the illocutionary force. So a statement like 'It's getting late' could acquire the status of a threat, a warning, a hint, a complaint, etc., depending on how it was said and in what context. Its conventional meaning was unaffected.

This argument suggested that there should be established a separate level of language description, which used the output from the grammar and the dictionary as input and which showed the relation between the utterances and their function when deployed in discourse. This level was called the level of discourse.

In suggesting a form of organization for the new level, the Hallidayan model of a taxonomic hierarchy was adopted (Halliday 1961) and the level of discourse was held to relate to the level of form as form did to the level of phonology. The building block: of discourse were the sentences and clauses of the grammar, but they took on new values. In the same way that the phoneme /s/ differs from the morpheme {s}, the sentence 'I see' differs from the move 'I see'.

The rank scale of act–move–exchange–(sequence)–transaction soon concentrated on the exchange, much as grammar was concentrating on the clause. Little was investigated above the exchange because it was recognized that the more extensive ranks in discourse were relevant not only to language, but had a status in social systems also. In any case the exchange proved fascinating enough.

The speech acts of the philosophers would be acts or moves in discourse; acts if there were other acts in the move. The linguistic model led naturally to a notion of structure which was absent from Austin. Instead of prescribing states of affairs in the world that enabled the speech acts to have their effect, there was a recognition of higher structures within which the acts had a predictable place. The exchange, and its characteristic three-part structure of initiation, response and follow-up, gave a linguistic context for the understanding of speech acts.

There is one major omission in the original account of formative influences on the study of discourse. That is C. C. Fries, whose introduction to his book *The Structure of English* is a forgotten landmark. The shaping influence of this book must have been subliminal because it was not consciously acknowledged or referred to; but Fries, struggling to vindicate received grammar using recorded telephone calls, made major advances in description. Sadly, he abandoned his insights when he came to the meat of his book, which is an unsuccessful attempt to provide objective criteria for a grammar.

At the end of the original study the research team was aware of a number of unresolved problems. A few of these are dealt with in the following sections of this chapter.

GENERALIZABILITY

The study focused on upper primary school classrooms, and it was not clear how much of the discourse patterning was ascribable to the genre and the situation, and how much was of more general validity. Subsequent work confirmed much of it, but showed that classroom discourse was not specially representative, and indeed had a number of unusual features. (A short review of classroom discourse may be found in Sinclair 1987.)

Despite the lack of general applicability, the model was widely used as a descriptive system for spoken interaction, and the following four years brought a large number of suggested improvements. Most of these consisted of additions to the list of acts – not surprising since the original list was specific to the classroom data. Very few were supported by data-oriented arguments.

A generalized and fairly comprehensive descriptive framework was prepared by Amy Tsui (1986) and it is to be hoped that a version of this research will shortly be published.

SITUATION

The description depended in part on features of the non-verbal situation. Perhaps it will never be possible to describe discourse without such recourse, but the work of scholars like Grice, Labov, and more recently Sperber and Wilson opens up conventions of description which are too sociologically dependent for the linguistic realities to be thoroughly observed and described.

It was conceded from the start that as the linguistic units increased in size, some of the description would have to be couched in non-linguistic terms, as in Ventola (1987) a move may be simultaneously a directive and a Sale Initiation (as the Italian 'dica', for example). This is not a double coding because the provenance of the two analyses is quite different. A directive is an Initiating move in the general structure of discourse, and a Sale Initiation is a category of sociolinguistic description which is not directly related to any linguistic unit or criteria.

Far from being a weakness, the lack of specificity of the higher units of the original model was seen as an element of flexibility, adaptable to the genre analysis of the future. Even the modest suggestion of transaction boundary markers turned out to be less than reliable in teacher talk, one major variable being the class size. Warren (forthcoming) points out that real life does not always measure up to the structural sequences that are expected of it. He also suggests that the study of spoken discourse may have been over-affected by the use of telephone calls and quiz programmes as data. They are much more predictably patterned than less specialized discourse; at the beginning and end of telephone calls there are set routines, no doubt stabilized because of a lack of shared environment.

One enduring problem is the rigorous description of the topic of conversations. To the observer it is an obvious feature of talk that it is about something; topics are proposed, supported, developed and concluded by the co-operative linguistic behaviour of participants. In current work, Hazadiah (1991) shows how Topic Frameworks form a rank between exchange and the transaction.

The relation between utterances and their discourse value was originally seen as being partly determined by aspects of the situation in which the language occurred. So it was said that if a teacher said 'Can you swim a length?' there is a potential ambiguity. If the teacher and pupil are poolside and the pupil suitably dressed, if swimming is not a proscribed activity at the time, and if other conditions favour it, the utterance may be taken as a command; otherwise a mere question.

This seems to rely far too much on the situation, and not enough on the context of the discourse. Commands to swim do not just appear in discourse out of the blue; they will be prepared for quite elaborately.

Subsequent work (Sinclair and Brazil 1982) built up a rule for interpreting initiations based on their grammatical structure. However, the relative importance of cotext and context has not been seriously explored. It is readily assumed by most commentators that since a listener has access to large quantities of knowledge of the world and its affairs, this knowledge will be deployed according to hints given in the text, using inferential processes. Thus is a text interpreted.

An alternative point of view, which I prefer, is to expect the text to supply everything necessary for its own interpretation; what we need is not an external knowledge base but a better understanding of text structure. If we do not rely on the text to indicate its own interpretation, then we invoke mysterious processes for which it is difficult to find evidence.

It is not, however, to be expected that texts will be fully explicit; the text will organize its meaning up to a point regarded as appropriate by the speaker; in interaction it is open to other participants to press for greater explicitness where they feel the need for it. Interpretations are always provisional during the course of a conversation, and a large number of points remain obscure because it is not regarded as important to clarify them.

STATUS OF MOVES

There were several problems associated with the number of moves in an exchange, and the status of the moves. A response to an elicitation is very often a statement. If this statement is not ellipted, then it looks suspiciously like an inform. But an inform is an initiation not a response.

The response to an inform is very often a simple acknowledgement, and in such cases there is often no follow-up element present. The realizations of responses and follow-ups overlap when they are minimal, such as *yes*, *mhm*.

Some responses take the form of questions, for example:

I   It's red
R   Dark red?
F   yes

(data from Francis and Hunston, this volume, Chapter 7)

These responses then have some of the character of elicitations, in that they strongly prospect an answer to their questions. But again, elicitations are initiations, that is they must come first in exchanges.

Various attempts were made to solve these problems, notably those of Coulthard and Brazil (this volume, Chapter 3), which are summarized and built into a revised model by Francis and Hunston (1987 and this volume, Chapter 7).

There were also further enhancements and elaborations of the model proposed from time to time, in particular Burton (1980) and Berry (1981). Burton emphasized the importance of moves which challenge presuppositions and contrasted them with all the others, which she called supporting moves. Berry concentrated on the transmission of information, and established a version of exchange structure which has been adopted by systemic linguists, and increases steadily in complication (O'Donnell, forthcoming).

I would like to put forward, in response to all this activity, a position which is not very far removed from the original one (Sinclair and Coulthard 1975), but which profits from the exposure which the discourse model has had over the years. In doing so I would like to deny any suggestion that there is a 'Birmingham School' of discourse, in the sense of a group of scholars working in a co-ordinated manner, increasing the dimensions of a shared position. The original work was mostly valuable as a known position, fairly clearly stated, which acted as a stimulus for further development. That development was varied and extensive, and no attempt has been made to meld it into a coherent whole. It should not, therefore, be assumed that I have accepted and incorporated any of the post-1975 work except as set out below and in other publications.

Discourse analysis prioritizes the interactive nature of language. In relation to the spoken language, this means that the co-operation of more than one individual is essential to its performance. But people are different in thought, word and deed.

From this I note three consequences:

(a) The social intentions of participants may well not coincide in an interaction. Therefore they strive to achieve their purposes by managing the future direction of the discourse. This is possible because each utterance provides a framework within which the next utterance is placed. Each speaker in turn thus has an opportunity to steer the discourse in the direction that best suits his or her purpose. This feature of discourse is called prospection.
(b) The vast complexity of human communicative behaviour must be reducible to a small number of simple activities. The simple management of prospection, particularly in real-time conversation, argues that people use a fairly simple model and elaborate it according to their needs and skills.
(c) No matter how co-operative people strive to be, it cannot be assumed that they correctly divine each others' intentions. The structure of conversations, as a consequence, provides a mechanism whereby they can check and compare their understanding of the discourse they are creating between them. In the exchange, this is realized by a move called *follow-up*.

Let us now examine these points in more detail.

PROSPECTION

The first point concerns prospection, as one of the structural foundations of the exchange. Each initiation prospects that the utterance following it will be interpreted under the same set of presuppositions as the initiation itself. If the putative response is not compatible with the prospections it will be interpreted as a challenge, and therefore the beginning of a new exchange.

The prospections specific to an exchange are derivable largely from the initiation. Hence the example above, 'It's red', sets up a prospection that a fully fitting response will confirm the accuracy of the statement; that any relevant response will concern the redness or otherwise of what *it* refers to. However, if the context suggests that the initiation is to be interpreted as a warning to stop a vehicle, a fully fitting response will couple an acknowledgement with some prompt verbal action.

In my judgement, the creation and maintenance of prospections should be the defining criterion of an exchange. The initiating move creates prospections which then determine the minimum extent of the exchange. Further moves in the exchange may make further prospections, but there is no need to classify them as initiations.

The control of prospection thus takes priority over the information model of the exchange, reducing its significance but not necessarily its relevance. It would not be appropriate here to assess the strengths and weaknesses of an information model; it is enough, I hope, to point out that the state of information transfer does not determine the structure of the exchange in the way that the state of the prospection does.

MULTIPLE CODING

The second point raises the vexed question of multiple coding. Levinson's critique of discourse analysis (1983:289ff), and Tsui's reply to it (1986) give strong accounts of the two positions. Since human behaviour is infinitely specific and infinitely subtle, it is ridiculous to assume that one designation, especially from a small set of choices, is sufficient to describe its total effect. But it is impossible to make an exhaustive description, and invidious to make a selective description. So the alternatives to a single coding are not really any better.

There are two strands of argument in favour of providing a single label for each discourse act and move. One is that people actually talk about discourse in terms of invitations, agreements, promises, etc., as if there was psychological reality to the labels, and the language contained a rich variety of labels. The other argument is that the language provides a full set of closed classes for secondary acts, such as responses, cues, reiterations and markers. The abundant use of these classes is only explainable by assuming that to each there corresponds a discourse function, and that speakers understand the discourse, at a primitive level at least, in terms of a small number of mutually exclusive alternatives. A well-known example of a closed class is the marker, which in classroom discourse is realized by one of *well*, *OK*, *now*, *good*, *alright*, *right*.

There will always be counter examples. For example fictional spies conduct exchanges which have two simultaneous meanings. All sorts of codes are used, for example by adults with children present. These are specialized and marginal types of discourse, perhaps of a similar status as ironies – in fact the literary figure of dramatic irony is one such example.

But just as the existence of irony does not disturb the normal way of interpreting language, the existence of complex conversations does not disturb the normal way of interpreting normal conversations.

I find it preferable, given this evidence, to make a general assumption that each act and move realizes a single choice from a finite set. There is no doubt that it makes for a simple analysis, but it requires sensitive interpretation in doubtful cases, and of course it has to be set aside on the very rare occasions when the general assumption is not valid.

THE THIRD MOVE

Is conversational discourse made up essentially of two-move structures or three-move structures? The conversation analysts (Sacks MS; Schegloff 1973) talk in terms of adjacency pairs, such as question and answer. Much observed talk is of this kind, and certain types of conversational routine have routinely two moves in their exchanges.

On the other hand, classroom discourse, which was our original reference point, is noticeably three-move. So are quiz games, interrogations, many service encounters and a lot of everyday talk. The problem is not going to be resolved by a majority vote – by counting up whether the greater quantity of talk is two-part or three-part in its exchange structure. We must seek an explanation of the variability of the exchange.

Where there is a clear third move, it has a function which is different from that of Initiation and Response. It offers an opportunity for participants to check that they are agreed on the function of the previous pair, to comment on the exchange as it stands, to react to the response in the context of the initiation.

> I Why? Did you wake up late today?
> R Yeah, pretty late.
> F Oh dear.
>
> (data from Francis and Hunston)

Presumably not all exchanges require this kind of support. Where participants are well known to each other, in familiar situations and without specific business to transact, it may be possible to have long stretches of two-move conversation without the need for follow-up. Special routines like form-filling or running through a series of checks are so obvious in their goals that there may be no need to check all the time that both participants understand the state of the discourse.

There is always the option, however, and in many types of discourse the third move is virtually obligatory. In any kind of didactic or supervisory discourse, it gives feedback to the person under supervision which is essential to the efficient conduct of affairs.

I   Put the chopsticks away Ann-Marie
R   A'right (puts them down)
F   Good girl

(data from Francis and Hunston)

The third move in this example is quite distinctive, and restricted to areas of discourse where one participant has the right to evaluate the behaviour of another. In general discourse F moves can range from mumbles transcribed as *Hah*, *Yeah*, *Mm*, to reactions like *Whatever*, *Oh dear*, and on to substantial structures like *That's what I would have thought too*, and *Yeah, my feet hurt* (data from Francis and Hunston).

ENCAPSULATION

The mechanism of the F move is that it contains a reference to the IR pair. The reference may be explicit, as in *That* in the example above, or implicit, as in *Yeah*, *Mm*, etc. In the latter examples the reference has to be retrieved by considering exactly what is being assented to. Although little more than a low-intonation mumble, these all have the effect of indicating that, for the speaker, the discourse is proceeding coherently; the other participants then have an opportunity to say otherwise, but it is expected that they will agree and be reassured by the F move.

A reaction like *Oh dear* is a reaction to a proposition which is split between the I and R moves; in the example above the proposition is something like 'the person I am speaking to woke up pretty late today'. In order to understand the F move, we must retrieve I and R.

This mechanism is called encapsulation (Sinclair, forthcoming) and is one of the two principal mechanisms of coherence in discourse structure. It is essentially retrospective in nature but is quite different from ordinary cohesion because it encapsulates complete IR pairs. The other one is prospection, already featured in this chapter.

AN OUTLINE MODEL OF DISCOURSE STRUCTURE

Each Initiation move in spoken discourse prospects a Response, unless it is a simple articulation of a proposition. The Response, being prospected, concludes an adjacency pair and opens the possibility of encapsulation by an F move. Another participant may make a Challenge move after I or R, and thus begin a new exchange.

An Initiation which does not prospect a Response may still get one; otherwise an F move may directly follow the Initiation. Additional F moves are optional.

The F move is only obligatory in certain specialized varieties of discourse: its likelihood depends on a number of variables. But it is a permanent option in the structure of the exchange, following an I-without-R or an IR pair. The prospection of F is not the same as the prospection of

R by I. Whereas to prospect R, an I must set up specific presuppositions, to prospect F, an I or an IR pair must simply occur.

Basic structures:

I-prospects-R	=	I
Challenge	=	C
I-without-R	=	I*

$$I \; R \; (F)$$
$$I* \; (F)$$
$$I \; C = I \ldots$$
$$I* \; C = I \ldots$$
$$I \; R \; C = I \ldots$$

PLANES OF DISCOURSE

The F move, by encapsulating, and the I move, by prospecting, are overtly contributing to the discourse management. They are operating on an *interactive plane* of discourse (Sinclair 1981). The R move, in that it fits the presuppositions of the I to some extent, is also operating on the interactive plane.

The other plane of discourse is the *autonomous plane*. This is where the meaning of the discourse is managed; where each new move, once its interactive contribution has been taken account of, is related to the preceding meaning as the text has organized it. As Hazadiah (1991) says, the autonomous plane shows the product of discourse, the shared meaning; the interactive plane shows the process, the means whereby the meaning is made available for sharing. Every utterance has a value on both planes.

A challenge breaks the presuppositions and precipitates a new exchange. It therefore cancels the interactive value of the previous move, leaving only its contribution to the autonomous plane. The challenge, like the Follow-up, contains an encapsulation; but whereas the F move is usually terminal in the exchange, the challenge is initial. In exchanges whose Initiation is a Challenge, the subject matter becomes the discourse itself.

> I was supposed to get up at about seven o'clock
> I (Challenge): What do you mean you were supposed to
> (data from Francis and Hunston)

In the above example, the main clause 'What do you mean' is clearly a query about language, and not directly about getting up.

CONCLUSION

Figure 1 shows a few developments of the original model, notably the challenge. It is not obligatory for an exchange to contain an F move, but it is an available option in every exchange. When R is specifically prospective, F is obligatory.

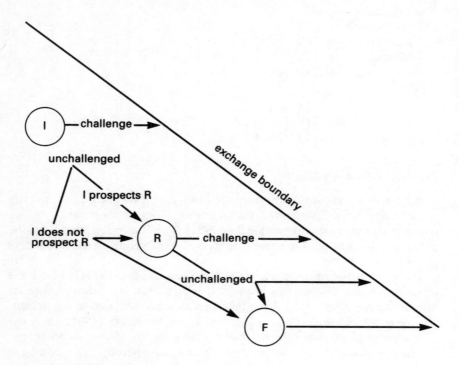

Figure 1: Exchange structure

If an Initiation is a simple informing move, and the next utterance encapsulates it, then IF is a valid structure. R is only necessary when prospected.

There is no need, in this model, for double codings because they are not felt to be characteristic of the vast bulk of discourse. There is no reference to primary and secondary knower, or indeed to any states of awareness of participants. This is because models based on the exchange as a device for information transfer do not lead us to the interactive structure, but to some analysis suitable, perhaps, for the autonomous plane.

The model presented here is intended to cover general conversations. Some specialized genres have special conventions, and would lead to elaborations or simplifications of the model. However, I feel that it is important to make full and detailed statements about the general nature of discourse, describing the way these structures are deployed in particular types of conversation. The need for a level of discourse, where the higher patterns of language can be described without reference to any particular social use, is fairly obvious.

5 A functional description of questions

Amy Tsui

INTRODUCTION

The term 'question' has been used in the linguistic and speech act literature as though it is generally understood what a 'question' is. Unfortunately, an examination of the studies on 'questions' shows that the term has never been clearly defined. It has been used as a semantic category (see Quirk *et al.* 1972, 1985), as an illocutionary act (see for example Lyons 1977, 1981; Huddleston 1984), and as a kind of 'request' or 'directive' (see for example Katz 1977; Katz and Postal 1964; Gordon and Lakoff 1975; Labov and Fanshel 1977; Burton 1980). Sometimes an utterance is identified as a 'question' because it is interrogative in form and sometimes because it expects an answer or some verbal performance from the addressee. In other words, the term 'question' is sometimes taken as a syntactic category and sometimes a discourse category; as a result, the term remains vague and ill-defined. In what follows, I shall examine some of the studies of 'questions'.

QUIRK *et al.*'s STUDY OF 'QUESTIONS'

Let us start with the study of 'questions' by Quirk *et al.* (1972, 1985).[1] Quirk *et al.* define 'questions' as a semantic class which is primarily used to seek information on a specific point (1985:804). They propose that there are three major classes of 'question' according to the answer they expect (1985:806):

1 Those that expect affirmation or negation, as in 'Have you finished the book?' YES/NO questions.
2 Those that typically expect a reply from an open range of replies, as in 'What is your name?' or 'How old are you?' WH-questions.
3 Those that expect as the reply one of two or more options presented in the question, as in 'Would you like to go for a WÁLK or stay at HÕME?' ALTERNATIVE questions.

Let us examine these three classes one by one.

Yes/no questions

According to Quirk *et al.*, yes/no questions are usually formed by placing the operator before the subject and using 'question intonation', that is a rise or fall–rise. Another typical characteristic of yes/no questions is the use of non-assertive forms 'any', 'ever', etc., which denote neutral polarity that leaves open whether the answer is 'yes' or 'no'. However, Quirk *et al.* point out that a yes/no question can be biased towards a positive or a negative answer. For example, assertive forms such as 'someone' may be used, in which case the question has a 'positive orientation', e.g. 'Did SOMEONE call last night?', 'Has the boat left ALREADY?' These questions are biased towards a positive answer. They indicate that the speaker has reason to believe that the answer is 'yes'; he is asking for confirmation of his assumption (1972:389). This means that the expected answer is 'yes' and thus a 'no' answer would be contrary to that expectation. As for questions like 'Isn't your car working?', Quirk *et al.* suggest that they have negative orientation. This negative orientation, however, is complicated by an element of surprise or disbelief. The implication is that the speaker had originally hoped for a positive response, but new evidence suggests that the response will be negative. There is therefore a combination of old expectation (positive) and new expectation (negative) (1985:808). The expected answer is 'no', and 'yes' would be contrary to his expectation. Quirk *et al.* further remark that because the old expectation tends to be identified with the speaker's hopes and wishes, negatively orientated questions often express disappointment or annoyance. The examples they give are 'Can't you drive straight?' and 'Aren't you ashamed of yourself?'

From Quirk *et al.*'s analysis of yes/no questions so far, we can detect three problems. Firstly, if the classification of questions is made on the basis of the answer they expect, then there should be three classes of questions: one class expecting a 'yes' answer, a second expecting a 'no' answer and a third with no expectations. However, it should be noted that there are three classes of questions only in terms of the predicted form of the answer. In terms of the *communicative choice* realized by the answer, there are only two classes of questions because a 'yes' answer to a positively biased question realizes the same communicative choice of confirming the speaker's assumption or expectation as a 'no' answer to a negatively biased question. This can be supported by the fact that sometimes negatively biased questions can get a 'yes' or a 'no' answer, both realizing a confirmation. For example, the question 'You mean he didn't recognize you?', which is negatively biased, can be responded to by 'Yes', meaning 'you are right, he didn't recognize me', or 'no', also meaning 'you are right, he didn't recognize me'. Both answers confirm the speaker's assumption. Hence, both negatively and positively biased questions belong to the same functional class: questions whose discourse function is to elicit confirmation.

Secondly, if we are looking at the function or the communicative choice realized by the expected answer and not its form, then a 'yes' answer to the question 'Have you been to Paris?' and a 'yes' answer to the question 'Has the boat left ALREADY?' have different functions. The first 'yes' is an elliptical form of 'Yes, I have been to Paris' which supplies the information whereas the second 'yes' is an elliptical form of 'Yes, your assumption is correct' which confirms the speaker's assumption. In other words, the difference between these two questions is not so much that one has neutral polarity and the other has biased polarity, but rather that one seeks information and the other seeks confirmation. The former is therefore similar to wh-questions which seek information, such as 'What country have you been to?' except that the information it seeks is more specific (cf. Churchill 1978). It is only because English has a yes/no answering system that we are misled into believing that the function of questions like 'Have you been to Paris?' is to elicit a 'yes' answer (hence a confirmation) or a 'no' answer (hence a disconfirmation) and therefore they have a different function from wh-questions (see the discussion on Alternative Questions, pp. 96–8 below, and examples 25 and 26).

That the so-called neutral polarity yes/no questions are in fact information seeking questions can be further supported by the fact that they do not necessarily expect either a 'yes' or 'no' answer. The utterance 'Are you still here?' spoken with high termination (Brazil *et al.* 1980) by the speaker to his colleague working in the office at 7 o'clock in the evening does not expect either a 'yes' or 'no' answer. It functions as an information question tantamount to 'Why are you still here?'. A mere 'yes' or 'no' response from the addressee would be odd or interpreted as unwillingness to interact with the speaker.

Thirdly, those 'questions' which express disappointment and annoyance seem to expect neither a 'yes' nor a 'no' answer. Either a 'yes' or a 'no' answer to 'Can't you drive straight?' would be considered a cheeky remark or a retort. Silent acquiescence is likely to be the expected response. Hence it is doubtful whether such utterances should be considered to belong to the category of 'questions' as defined by Quirk *et al.* at all.

Similar problems can be found in their handling of tag questions. Tag questions are considered a further type of yes/no question which conveys negative or positive orientation. Quirk *et al.* propose four types of tag questions:

Type 1   He likes his JŌB, DOÉSn't he?   (Rising tone)

Type 2   He doesn't like his JŌB, DOÉS he?   (Rising tone)

Type 3   He likes his JŌB, DŌESn't he?   (Falling tone)

Type 4   He doesn't like his JŌB, DŌES he?   (Falling tone)

Each of these four types asserts the speaker's assumption and invites a response. Each, they say, has different assumptions and expectations:

Type 1   Positive assumption + neutral expectation
Type 2   Negative assumption + neutral expectation
Type 3   Positive assumption + positive expectation
Type 4   Negative assumption + negative expectation

(Quirk *et al.* 1985:811)

Quirk *et al.*'s analysis of tag questions is problematic. According to their analysis of the expected answers, there are three and not four different expected answers to tag questions. Both Types 1 and 2 expect either 'yes' or 'no'. But again it should be noted that this is a classification in terms of form; in terms of communicative choice, there are only two types because the 'yes' answer in Type 3 and the 'no' answer in Type 4 both realize the same communicative choice of agreeing with the speaker's assumption.

Further, one can question whether a tag question can have neutral expectation. The very construction of a tag question suggests that the speaker has certain assumptions and is biased towards a certain answer. As Hudson (1975) points out, tags are always conducive; they cannot be neutral (p. 24). For a tag question with a rising tone, the discourse context or the context of environment has led the speaker to cast doubt on his assumption and he invites the addressee to confirm it (see also Brazil 1984a:43).

In other words, a tag with a rising tone (i.e. Types 1 and 2) is biased towards an expected answer rather than neutral. It invites the addressee to confirm the speaker's assumption. This can be supported by the fact that a confirmation will be spoken in mid key, indicating that the answer fulfils the expectation, whereas a denial is likely to be spoken in high key, indicating that the answer is contrary to the expectation (see also Brazil *et al.* 1980). For example:

1   (C:4:14)[2]
    S: //p i THINK you did that THIS year //r+ DIDn't you //
    G: //p oh YEAH //

G's response is spoken in mid key. If the answer was 'no', it would have been spoken in high key. For example,

2   (BCET:A:20)
    B: //p it's not TOO late to apPLY now //r+ IS it //
    C: //p YEAH //p i THINK so //r+ they're ALL full up //

C's response, 'yeah', which disconfirms the speaker's assumption, is spoken in high key, indicating that it is contrary to B's expectation. As for a tag spoken with falling tone, the speaker has no doubt about his assumption and the addressee is invited to agree with him. For example,

3 (C:4:3)
   G: //p Fox is his FIRST-name //p ISn't it //
   S: //p RIGHT //
4 (ibid.:26)
   G: //p sounds like a soCIety of MOLEs //p DOESn't it //
   S: ((laughs))

In (4), S responds to G's tag question by laughing, which is commonly used as a minimal indication of agreement. This kind of response would be unacceptable for a tag with a rising tone because it would require a more explicit response of a confirmation or disconfirmation.

Thus, although both types of tag question expect a 'yes' (or 'no') answer from the addressee, the function that they realize is different. While a 'yes' (or 'no') answer to a rising tag realizes a confirmation, a 'yes' (or 'no') answer to a falling tag realizes an agreement. The difference can be best seen by comparing (1) with (5) below.

5 (On a sunny day)
   A: //p it's a LOVEly day //p ISn't it //
   B: //p YES //

While S's question in (1) seeks confirmation from G, A's question in (5) cannot possibly seek confirmation from B that it is a lovely day because the truth of the asserted proposition is self-evident. It functions to get B to agree with him that it evidently is a lovely day (see Brazil 1984a:36).

Thus we can see that in terms of the function or communicative choice realized by the expected answers, there are only two types of tag question, not four: one which expects *agreement* and one which expects *confirmation* from the addressee.

The third type of question which falls under yes/no questions, according to Quirk *et al.*, is declarative questions which are items that are identical lexico-grammatically to declaratives but function as questions because they are spoken with rising intonation. For example, 'You've got the exPLŌsives?' Declarative questions are said to invite the hearer's verification, that is, either a 'yes' or a 'no' answer (see 1985:814).

This analysis of declarative questions is questionable. Firstly, the very fact that the question should be presented in declarative form suggests that the speaker has certain assumptions and the utterance is biased towards an expected response. Brazil (1985) suggests that in the utterance //r+ you preFER THAT one //, the speaker is heard as 'proffering a tentative assessment of common ground' and the response expected is a 'confirmation of a proclaimed endorsement, yes' (pp. 155–6). A response which denies the tentative assessment of the speaker can of course occur, but it will be contrary to the expectation and is likely to be spoken in contrastive high key. Secondly, Quirk *et al.* have overlooked the fact that 'declarative questions' can also be realized by a declarative sentence spoken with a falling intonation. For example, the arrowed utterance in (6):

6 (B:C:A:1:2)
   H: I I don't know, see, he has a son at, was in the school last
      year ah does he have to re-apply?
   X: Ah yes, I think so.
→ H: So we'll have to fill out one of those forms again.
   X: Yes.

H is not telling X that he has to fill out a form but asking for confirmation.
As Brazil (1985) points out, in saying 'you prefer that one' with a proclaiming (i.e. falling) tone and mid-termination, the speaker is not likely to be
telling the hearer about his preference but rather asking him to respond to
the tentative assertion. Similarly, the utterance 'John prefers that one',
spoken with a falling tone in a situation where the addressee is privy to
John's preference functions as a 'question'. Labov and Fanshel have made
similar observations. They state that if the speaker makes a statement
about a B-event with a falling intonation (which they call declarative
intonation) then it is heard as a request for confirmation. This is supported
by their findings in a series of interviews: negative responses to the
declarative question 'And you never called the police' were in the form of a
simple 'No' whereas positive responses required some indication of surprise as well, such as 'Oh yes, I called them' (1977:101). The requirement
of an indication of surprise for positive responses shows that they are
contrary to the expectation of the declarative question.
     Thirdly, declarative questions can also function as information questions
in certain contexts and the answer expected is a supply of information.
Consider the following example given by Brazil:

7 (Brazil 1985:159)
   Doctor: //p where do you GET this pain //
   Patient: //p in my HEAD //
→Doctor: //p you GET it in your HEAD //

As is evident from the discourse context, in the arrowed utterance, the
doctor is not so much asking the patient to confirm but rather, as Brazil
points out, is 'asking for greater precision – a recycling of the question, so
to speak, by behaving as though the patient had not yet selected a response, and leading perhaps to "Yes. Behind my eyes" ' (1985: 159).

Wh-questions

The second class of questions is wh-questions, which are information-
seeking and seem to be the least problematic category. They are realized
by wh-words, usually spoken with falling intonation and the answer
expected is the missing piece of information denoted by the wh-word. They
are considered to constitute a category distinctly different from questions
seeking neutral polarity and questions seeking confirmation. However,
things are not quite so simple; consider the following wh-questions:

8 What did you say?

9 What do you mean?

We can say that they expect the answer to be the supplying of information. But they are different from questions like 'What did you do yesterday?' in that they invite the addressee to repeat and/or to clarify whatever was said previously. In other words, these questions take the discourse backwards: they are about the discourse itself. Coulthard distinguishes them from information-seeking questions realized by wh-interrogatives by calling those which seek clarification of the preceding utterance 'Return' and those which seek repetition 'Loop' (see 1981:21ff).

Consider also the following questions:

10 What time shall we meet?

11 Where shall I meet you?

These questions invite the addressee not only to supply the missing information signalled by 'what time' and 'where' but also to commit himself to a specific time and place of meeting. Take the following piece of data for example.

12 (B:B:A:3:3)
    A: What time?
    B: Let's say about seven.
    A: Seven o'clock huh, okay.

Once the 'information' supplied by B is endorsed by A, both A and B have committed themselves to doing something at the specified time. That wh-questions like the above are not simply information-seeking can be seen firstly by comparing (13) with (14) and (15).

13 A: What's the time?
    B: Seven.
    A: Thanks.

14 A: What time shall we meet?
    B: Five o'clock.
→?A: Thanks.

15 A: Where shall we meet?
    B: At the Peninsula Hotel.
→?A: Thanks.

Example (13) is a perfectly acceptable exchange whereas (14) and (15) are not. In (13), speaker A asks for a piece of information, and when B supplies the information, a thanking from A is in order. By contrast, in (14) and (15), A's thanking B is odd because B is not supplying a piece of missing information.

Secondly, comparing (12) and (13) we can see that the 'information' supplied in B's utterance in exchange (12) is negotiable whereas that in exchange (13) is not. In the former, A may not accept the time specified by B, in which case further exchanges will be produced until a time acceptable to both is settled upon, as we can see in the following piece of data:

16 (B:B:B:6:2)
    X: When are we going to get together?
    H: Anytime. How about tonight?
    X: Well, I, I, (pause) I can't get together until um maybe
        Sunday.
    H: Alright, Sunday.

H's suggestion of 'tonight' as a time for meeting is not accepted. A further exchange results in which H and X agree to meet up on Sunday.

The above discussion suggests that wh-questions can realize various functions and that it is therefore doubtful whether wh-questions constitute a single class.

Alternative questions

The third class of questions proposed by Quirk *et al.* is alternative questions. According to them, there are two types of alternative question: the first type resembles a yes/no question and the second a wh-question. For example:

17 Would you like CHŎcolate, vaNÍLla or STRÀWberry?

18 Which ice cream would you LÌKE, CHŎcolate, vaNÍLla or
    STRÃWberry?

The first type is said to differ from a yes/no question *only* in intonation (my emphasis). Instead of the final rising tone, it contains a separate nucleus for each alternative, that is, there is a rise on each item except for the last one where a fall occurs, indicating that the list is complete (1985:823). The second type is a compound question: a wh-question followed by an elliptical alternative question. Its 'full' form is something like the following:

19 Which ice cream would you LÌKE? Would you like CHŎcolate,
    vaNÍLla or STRÃWberry?

There are two points that I wish to raise here: firstly, it is true that alternative questions have at least two different syntactic forms, but do they realize two different categories of questions in terms of the expected answer? Secondly, is it justified to establish alternative questions as a third category? In other words, do they constitute a class of question distinctly different from yes/no and wh-questions?

To address the first point, let us look at the answer expected to (17) and (18). For both, the expected answer is one of the three stated choices. In other words, classified in terms of prospected answer, they belong to the same type of question although they have different syntactic structures. They both invite the addressee to inform the speaker of his choice. To address the second point, let us compare alternative questions and wh-questions. Look at the following exchanges initiated by an alternative question and a wh-question.

20 A: How are we going to get there?
    B: By BŪS.

21 A: Will we get there by BŪS or TRĀIN?
    B: By BŪS.

In both exchanges, A's utterance invites B to supply a piece of information. The only difference is that in exchange (21), the information that B supplies is one of the alternatives offered by A. In other words, both are *information-seeking* questions.

Let us now compare alternative questions with yes/no questions. Quirk *et al.* differentiate them as follows:

22 Alternative:
    A: Shall we go by BŪS or TRĀIN?
    B: By BŪS.

23 Yes/no:
    A: Shall we go by bus or TRĀIN?
    B: No, let's take the CĀR.

Example (23) is considered to be a different category of question from (22) because (23) can be responded to by 'yes' or 'no' whereas (22) cannot. The answer to (22) must be lexicalized. However, what Quirk *et al.* have overlooked is that the 'yes' or 'no' answer to (23) is only a preface to the stating of a choice which must also be lexicalized. This is supported by the fact that a response consisting of only 'yes' or 'no' without the stated choice is self-evidently incomplete. Consider:

24 A: Shall we go by bus or TRĀIN?
  ?B: No.

Hence, like (22), the expected answer to (23) is the stating of a choice. The only difference between the two is that in the former, the choice is selected from a restricted set whereas in the latter, it is selected from a potentially unrestricted set. In this sense, alternative questions and yes/no questions are similar (see also Jespersen 1933). In fact, in some languages, for example Portuguese and Mandarin Chinese, which do not have a 'yes/no' answering system, the answer to a yes/no question is always lexicalized as in alternative questions. For example:

25 (Portuguese)
    A: Queres café? (Do you want coffee?)
    B: Quero (I want)

26 (Mandarin Chinese)
   A: nā diěn yǐng hǎu kàn má? (Is that film good?)
   B: (a) hǎu kàn (good)
       (b) bù hǎu kàn (not good)

Indeed, in Mandarin Chinese, yes/no questions are often presented in alternative form. It is linguo-centric and even misleading to call these questions 'yes/no questions'. (26), for example, would often occur as 'nā diěn yǐng hǎu bù hǎu kàn?' (Is that film good or not good?) The expected answers to both forms are the same: 'hǎu kàn' (good) or 'bù hǎu kàn' (not good).

We may conclude by saying that in terms of expected answer, alternative questions do not constitute a separate category but rather belong to the category of information-seeking questions.

Exclamatory questions

Finally, I wish to discuss briefly what Quirk *et al.* call 'exclamatory questions' which are considered a minor type of question. Exclamatory questions are considered to function like exclamations although they have the form of a question. They can take the form of a negative polar question with a final falling instead of rising tone, such as 'Hasn't she GRŌWN!' and 'Wasn't it a marvellous CŌNcert!' or they can take the form of a positive polar question, also with a falling intonation, such as 'Am I HŪNgry!', 'Did he look anNŌYed!' Quirk *et al.* point out that the first form invites the addressee's agreement. This suggests that the answer expected would be the same as questions which seek agreement with the speaker's assumption or belief, for example, 'She has grown, HĀSn't she?'. Hence the former belongs to the same category as the latter. As for the second form of exclamatory question, the expected answer is more often an acknowledgement than an agreement. This is true for exclamatory questions such as 'Am I HŪNgry!' where the experience is entirely personal and therefore can only be acknowledged; but it is also true for questions like 'Did he look anNŌYed!' which are often responded to by an acknowledgement such as 'oh DĪD he'. Here we can see that exclamatory questions which elicit agreement in fact belong to the same category as tag questions which elicit agreement, and those which elicit an acknowledgement belong to an entirely different category of utterance.

Form versus communicative choice

From the above discussion, it can be seen that the characterization and classification of 'questions' proposed by Quirk *et al.* is very unsatisfactory. Although they claim that their classification is made according to the response expected, the above discussion reveals that very often precedence is given to syntactic form rather than expected response. The three major classes of questions that they propose are in fact based on surface form. Even when they do look at the expected response, it is often the form of the response that is being attended to rather than the function or the communicative choice realized by the response.

'QUESTION' AS 'ILLOCUTIONARY ACT'

Let us now look at the characterization of 'questions' as illocutionary acts. Lyons (1977) characterizes 'question' as an utterance with a particular illocutionary force. He asserts that the difference between a question and a statement is that the former contains a feature of doubt and that one of its felicity conditions is that the speaker should not know the answer to his question. He asserts that although questions are normally associated with the expectation of an answer from the addressee, this association is conventional and is independent of the illocutionary force of the question. He argues that this analysis of questions enables us to subsume various kinds of rhetorical questions instead of having to treat them as abnormal or parasitic upon information-seeking questions (see p. 755). The inconsistency of this characterization of 'question' can be seen from two objections that I shall raise below.

Firstly, if the expectation of an answer is independent of the illocutionary force of a 'question', then there is no need to differentiate the following two sentences:

27 Is the door open?

28 The door is open, isn't it?

In both sentences, the speaker expresses doubt as to whether the door is open. Yet, Lyons distinguishes between the two by pointing out that a sentence like (28) 'puts to the addressee the positive proposition p (which the speaker is inclined to believe to be true and assumes the addressee will accept), but at the same time explicitly admits in the tag the possibility of its rejection' (p. 765) and that the function of the checking tag is 'expressly to solicit the addressee's acceptance or rejection of the proposition that is presented to him' (ibid.). A sentence like (27), however, is

> neutral with respect to any indication of the speaker's beliefs as to the truth value of p and when they are asked of an addressee, unless they are given a particular prosodic or paralinguistic modulation, they convey no information to the addressee that the speaker expects him to accept or reject p.

> (ibid.)

This means that one of the crucial differences between (27) and (28) lies in the different answers expected of the addressee. By differentiating the two, Lyons is taking the expected answer into consideration.

Secondly, according to Lyons's characterization of 'questions', it is difficult to see how rhetorical questions can be considered a kind of 'question'. Consider the following example,

29 (B:H:B:5:5)
    H and M are talking to a colleague who just joined the department.
    H: But I think he might be threat – a threat to the very insecure Chinese folk around here.
→   M: Who cares?
    H: And ah that that sh-

M's utterance 'Who cares?' is commonly referred to as a rhetorical question. But it does not express doubt, nor does it imply that M does not know the answer to the question. It is a remark on H's opinion that the new colleague will be a threat to his Chinese colleagues. This is supported by the fact that after M's remark, H does not supply an answer but rather continues to express his opinion.

What Lyons, as well as Quirk *et al.*, seems to be doing is trying to offer a description which takes into account both syntactic form and discourse function. Therefore, different and inconsistent criteria are used in the identification and classification of 'questions'. The result is that the category of 'question' becomes a half-way house between a syntactic category and a discourse category. As Anthony points out:

A definition which attempts to cover utterances as syntactically and functionally disparate as those which we intuitively label questions necessarily reduces itself to near-vacuity.

(1974:6, quoted in Stenström 1984)

'QUESTION' AS 'REQUEST'

Let us now turn to a characterization of 'questions' which moves completely away from syntactic form to function – the characterization of 'questions' as 'requests' and 'directives'. 'Questions' have been characterized by some as 'requests' which have the purpose of eliciting information (see, for example, Katz 1972, 1977, Katz and Postal 1964, Gordon and Lakoff 1975, Labov and Fanshel 1977). It has been suggested by Postal, G. Lakoff, Ross and others that the logical form of 'questions' should be REQUEST (a, b, TELL (b, a, S)) and not ASK (a, b, S); 'a' being the speaker and 'b' the addressee. In other words, it should be 'I request that you tell me' instead of 'I ask you'. 'Questions' have also been characterized by others as a kind of 'directive' on the ground that a 'directive' is an instruction to perform something and 'questions' are instructions to make a verbal performance. For example, according to Burton (1980) 'Tell me your name' is a 'directive' to make a verbal performance, and according to J. Willis (1981), a 'question' in which a student is instructed to say something is characterized as 'Direct:verbal'. While this kind of characterization is superior to that of Lyons and Quirk *et al.* in that it does not confuse form and function, it is not without problems.

Sadock (1974) points out that it is wrong to say that all 'questions' are to be represented as 'requests', specifically 'requests for information'. He provides the following evidence to support his argument: requests can take sentence adverbial 'please' but there are many types of questions that can be used as indirect requests with which 'please' cannot occur. For example, * 'Don't you think you should please take out the garbage?'; true questions allow the pre-tag 'tell me' but requests do not, for example, 'Tell me, take out the garbage, will you?'; and so on (p. 90). Lyons (1977) points out that questions are not a kind of request because 'No' in response to yes/no questions such as 'Is the door open?' is an answer to the question whereas 'No' to 'Open the door please' is refusing to do what is requested.

To Sadock's and Lyons's arguments, I wish to add that there is a crucial difference between the two, which is that utterances referred to as 'questions' elicit or prospect a very different response from requests. A question elicits an obligatory verbal response and the interaction between the speaker and the addressee is completed entirely at the verbal level. Even when the response is non-verbal, it is merely a surrogate of the verbal response. For example:

30 A: Are you going home?
   B: (shakes head)

B's non-verbal response here is a surrogate of the verbal response 'no'. A request, however, elicits an obligatory non-verbal response with perhaps an accompanying verbal response and the interaction is completed at the non-verbal level. In other words, 'questions' have a different discourse function or consequence from 'requests' and therefore they should not be subsumed under the latter (see also Stubbs 1983:75).

Since the category 'question' is vague and ill-defined and cannot be subsumed under either 'requests' or 'directives', I propose to call those utterances which elicit solely a verbal response 'Elicitations'.

ELICITATIONS

The term 'Elicitation' is first introduced by Sinclair and Coulthard (1975) to describe utterances in the classroom which elicit a verbal response. They write,

> An elicitation is an act the function of which is to request a linguistic response – linguistic, although the response may be a non-verbal surrogate such as a nod or raised hand.

(1975:28)

The term 'Elicitation' is used here as a discourse category to describe any utterance, both inside and and outside the classroom, which functions to elicit an *obligatory* verbal response or its non-verbal surrogate.

I shall now attempt to make a classification of 'Elicitations' according to the different responses prospected.

SUBCATEGORIES OF ELICITATION

Elicit:inform[3]

Let us start with the kind of Elicitation which invites the addressee to supply a piece of information. Consider the following pieces of data.

31 (B:A:A:2:1)
→   H: What time will you be finished?
     X: Lecture finishes at about quarter past twelve.

32 (B:E:A:4:3)
→   X: Are you a literature section / or a language studies.
     H: No no I'm I'm not I'm language side, but
        I would like to see the two sides bridged myself.

33 (B:B:A:3)
→   B: Do you do you have wheels?
     A: Yes, I drive, it's Donald's car.

34 (Schegloff 1972:107)
→   A: I don't know just where the – uh – this address / is.
     B: Well, where do – which part of the town do you live.
     A: I live at four ten east Lowden.
     B: Well, you don't live very far from me.

35 (B:C:B:1:9)
     E: D'you have an O.U.P. here, or you haven't got it?
     F: No, ah I asked them, they haven't got it, so I got it from New York.
→   E: You have to get it from New York huh?
     F: Yeah just write, just write them a letter, they'll probably send it by
        air mail too, for free.

For (31), it will be generally agreed that H's utterance asks for a piece of missing information. X's utterance in (32) is similar to H's utterance in (31) in that it also invites the addressee to supply a piece of information, except that the answer prospected here is one of the alternatives supplied. B's utterance in (33) is what Quirk *et al.* refer to as a 'neutral polarity yes/no question' in which the speaker does not have any assumptions as to whether the answer is 'yes' or 'no'. As mentioned before, although the prospected answers to this kind of utterance are usually in the form of 'yes' or 'no', they do not and cannot possibly realize a confirmation or disconfirmation because there is no speaker assumption to confirm or disconfirm. They are in fact the missing information that the speaker seeks. A's utterance in (34) is declarative in form. However, we can see that A is not giving B a piece of information but rather seeking information. It is equivalent to 'Where is this address?'. Finally, E's utterance in (35) is a declarative plus a questioning particle. This kind of surface form commonly realizes a confirmation-seeking Elicitation. But in this particular context, its function is obviously not to seek confirmation since what it appears to seek confirmation of has already been given in the preceding utterance and there does not appear to be any hitch in communication between E and F. E's utterance is therefore seeking further information about obtaining the book from New York. Hence we can say that the arrowed utterances in (31)–(35) all realize the same discourse function. Let us call them 'Elicit:inform'.

There is a kind of Elicit:inform which needs discussion here: that in which the addressee is invited to supply a piece of information which the speaker already possesses. It is the kind of Elicitation performed in the classroom where the teacher checks to see if the pupils know the answer. The function of this type of Elicit:inform is very different from that in social discourse. A comparison of the following three exchanges will highlight the difference:

36 T: What is the time?
　　P: It's ten o'clock.
　　T: Well done.

37 A: What's the time?
　　B: Ten o'clock.
　?A: That's right.

38 (Coulthard and Brazil 1981:90)
　　A: What time did you come in last night?
　　B: About midnight.
　　A: No, you didn't.

(36) is a typical classroom exchange: the evaluative third part indicates to the pupil whether his answer is right or wrong. Its absence would be considered odd or a clue that the answer is wrong (see Coulthard and Brazil this volume, Chapter 3). (37) is considered odd because of the presence of the evaluative third part since it is part of the pragmatic presupposition that the speaker does not know the answer (see also Searle's felicity conditions for 'questions' in Searle 1979).

As for (38), A's evaluative utterance is often heard as aggressive. This is because part of the pragmatic presupposition of B's response is that the information provided by B is true and/or is believed by B to be true. By saying 'No, you didn't' A is challenging this presupposition. When the context of situation makes it clear that A is not only challenging the presupposition that the information provided is true, but also the presupposition that B believes it to be true, then A is in fact challenging B's sincerity. A's evaluative utterance is therefore very face-threatening.

Despite the difference between these two types of Elicit:inform, I do not want to set up a separate subcategory to account for the classroom type, for two reasons. Firstly, the response prospected by both types is the same. Secondly, whether the speaker wants to know the answer or to know if the addressee knows the answer or not is not signalled in the Elicitation itself. Even in the classroom, it is sometimes difficult to decide which is the case. Any experienced teacher will agree that very often the former is taken to be the latter by students. This kind of knowledge-checking Elicit:inform is not identifiable by the analyst or even the addressee. Very often, it is not until the speaker produces a third move that the addressee or the analyst knows whether the speaker already has the answer to the Elicitation. In other words, it is only in retrospect that we are able to say which type of Elicitation has been performed. As we are dealing with the prospective classification of utterances, the difference discussed above does not justify the setting up of a separate subcategory.

Elicit:confirm

The second subcategory is Elicitations which invite the addressee to confirm the speaker's assumption. It can be realized by tag interrogatives (both reversed polarity tags and copy tags), declaratives, positive and negative polar interrogatives. The following arrowed utterances are all instances of Elicit:confirm.

39 (C:4:14)
→ S: // p i THINK you did that THIS year // r + DIDn't you //
   G: Oh yeah.

40 (B:B:A:1:2)
→ F: // p JOHN would know // r+ WOULD he //
   H: Yeah, John would know.

41 (B:E:A:4:3)
→ X: // p these ARE students in the ENGlish department //
   H: That's right, they're all English majors.

42 (B:D:A:1:2)
→ C: // p the WHITE building // r+ where they have the psyCHOlogy
    department and everything //
   D: Psycho, law, you name it, oh they're all in there.

43 (B:F:A:1:3)
→ E: // p DIDn't ah // r YEVtuSHENko // r+ write a POem about that //
   F: Yeah, that's right.

44 (B:B:A:2:1)
→ X: // p is that YOU HENry //
   Y: Yes, that's right, yeah.

In all of the above arrowed utterances, the declarative, or the declarative associated with the interrogative, expresses what the speaker assumes to be true and the speaker is inviting the addressee to confirm that his assumption is true.

In (39) and (40) the rising tag invites the addressee to confirm the speaker's assumption. The arrowed utterances in (41) and (42) are declarative in form, with the former spoken with a falling tone (p) and the latter in rising tone (r+). In both cases, the addressee has better knowledge of the subject matter than the speaker. Hence they realize the function of seeking confirmation from the addressee. If it were vice versa, (41) would realize the function of giving information and (42) would realize the function of seeking confirmation that the addressee knows which building the speaker is referring to. The following is an example of the latter.

45 (B:A:A:1)
   H: //p HEY //p i i forGOT something //p i HAVE to go to
      LUNCH today //p with ALice // ((laughs)) //o to SEE the //p YOU
      know //o THE //
   X: ((laughs))
   H: //p the ah VIDeotape //r+ of that SHOW //r+ we DID at the
      hoTEL //
   X: Yup, yup.

Here, H seeks confirmation from X that he knows which videotape he is referring to.

Hence, the discourse function of an utterance depends not only on the intonation, but also on the situation and who knows what (see Brazil 1985). However, it should be noted that the context of situation does not always help to disambiguate the discourse function. For example,

46 (Coulthard and Brazil 1981:84)
   A: So the meeting's on Friday.
   B: Thanks.
   A: No I'm asking you.

In cases like this, the discourse function of the utterance will only be disambiguated as the discourse unfolds.

E's utterance in (43) is a negative polar interrogative. According to Quirk *et al.*, 'negative questions' have a negative orientation: they are biased towards a negative answer. However, E's utterance is not negatively conducive. Quite the contrary, it prospects a positive response confirming the speaker's assumption that Yevtushenko did write a poem. Whether a negative polar interrogative is positively or negatively conducive depends on the context. For example, if A, upon seeing B still in bed at eleven in the morning, says 'Don't you have lectures today?' then the expected answer to the utterance is obviously negative. A positive answer would be contrary to the expectation.

Finally, in (44), X assumes that the person on the other end of the line is Henry and he invites the addressee to confirm his assumption. X's utterance is what Quirk *et al.* would describe as a positively biased 'yes/no question'. However, as we can see, there are no assertive forms like 'someone' or 'already' in the utterance. The positive orientation is achieved by making 'you' prominent. Even when an assertive form like 'someone' is used, the utterance is not necessarily positively orientated. For example, the utterance 'Did someone CALL last night?' with the prominence on 'call' is not positively orientated. It is equivalent to 'Did anyone CALL last night?'. Both of them mean 'Was there a caller?'. Unless 'someone' is prominent the utterance is not positively orientated and 'someone' is not contrastive to 'anyone'. (I'm grateful to David Brazil for pointing this out to me.) In other words, prosodic features like prominence are important factors in determining what kind of Elicitation an utterance realizes.

In all of the above utterances the prospected response is confirmation. The addressee can of course respond by a disconfirmation, but the response will be contrary to the expectation and is likely to be spoken in contrastive high key. It should be noted, however, that sometimes we do find a confirmation in response to an Elicit:confirm spoken in high key.

47 (C:4:28)

    G: //p i MEAN they //r+ ISn't the LION rock TUNnel //

    //r+ a tunnel through a ^{MOUNtain} //

→ S: //p ^{YEAH} // that's probably the closest survival tunnel for us.

In (47), 'yeah' confirms the speaker's assumption and yet it is spoken in high key. This is because although intonationally a mid key is used to indicate that the response accords with the speaker's expectation, the addressee may choose to use a high key for emphatic purpose or in a particular context to indicate surprise, delight or annoyance (see Coulthard and Brazil, this volume, Chapter 3). In this case, S's use of a high key conveys an additional meaning which is paraphrasable as 'yes, that's right, I hadn't thought of that before'.

Similarly, a disconfirmation can be spoken in mid key which is normally used to indicate confirmation or agreement. The following piece of data is an example.

48 (BCET:A:4)

    C: //p was THIS caroline ^{SPENce} //

→ A: //p NO //p this is a FRIEND of caroline spence //

In (48), 'no' disconfirms C's assumption that A was talking about Caroline Spence. Yet, it is spoken in mid key. This can be explained by social considerations. By choosing mid key, the speaker is presenting his response as though it is not contrastive to the speaker's expectation, hence making the response less face-threatening and socially more acceptable.

Elicit:agree

The third subcategory is those which invite the addressee to agree with the speaker's assumption that the expressed proposition is self-evidently true. It initiates what Brazil (1984a:36) refers to as a 'world-matching' exchange, or in Labov and Fanshel's terms an exchange about an 'AB-event' (1977:80). It is most commonly realized by tag interrogatives and negative polar interrogatives, both spoken with a falling tone. The following arrowed utterances are instances of Elicit:agree.

49 (BCET:A:34)
→ B: //r i supPOSE he's a bit SENile now //p ISn't he //
    C: He looks it.

50 (C:4:53)
    (G and S are talking about a kind of bread made by the Hopi.)
    S: It's just, oh, the taste is, it's the most delicious thing that I've ever had, light blue, translucent.
→ G: // doesn't that SOUND like a NICE name for bread //
    //p HOpi BLUE bread //
    S: ((laughs))
    G: It's like something you get from a health foodstore, Hopi blue bread ((laughs))

In the arrowed utterances, the speaker assumes that the expressed proposition is self-evidently true. All he is doing is inviting the addressee to agree with him, hence establishing the existing common ground between himself and the addressee. The nature of this kind of Elicitation is best seen in exchanges like the following.

51 (On a sunny day)
    A: Lovely day, isn't it?
    B: Yes, beautiful.

As I have pointed out above, A's proposition is self-evidently true. Hence A is not asking B to confirm that his proposition is true, but rather to agree with him that it self-evidently is (see Brazil 1984a:36). Elicit:agrees like the above are often used to start a conversation, particularly between strangers. Other examples are the use of Elicit:agrees like 'Are you John Matthews?' or 'You must be John Matthews' to start a conversation in an encounter at a party or at the beginning of an interview when names are already known. Since what the addressee is invited to agree with is self-evidently true, the speaker is bound to be successful in eliciting the expected response. This establishes the common ground between the speaker and the addressee and serves to 'promote social mutuality' and paves the way for further interaction (see Brazil 1984a:34).

'Elicit:commit'

There is yet another subcategory of Elicitation which differs from the above three subcategories in that it elicits more than just a verbal response from the addressee. It also elicits commitment of some kind. Let us identify it as 'Elicit:commit' for want of a better label. Consider the following example:

52 (C:1:A:4:1)
→ J: Can I talk to you?
　　S: Sure. Come in. Let's close the door. Have a seat.

The purpose of J's Elicitation is not just to elicit a 'yes' answer from S, but also to get S to commit herself to a talking session. As Goffman (1981) points out, the intent of the question 'Have you got a minute?' is to open up a channel of communication which stays open beyond the hoped-for reply that satisfies the opening. In other words, in (52), the interaction is not completed at the production of a response from S, but rather at the production of a series of exchanges. The following example is, therefore, odd:

53 A: Can I ask you a question?
　　B: Sure.
　　?A: Ø

Hence this kind of Elicitation not only invites an obligatory response but also invites commitment on the part of the addressee to further interaction.

Another kind of Elicitation which can be considered an Elicit:commit is that realized by the type of wh-interrogative discussed above (see examples 10 and 11) which invites the addressee to enter into a contract with the speaker. The following is another example:

54 (B:C:A:5:1–2)
→ X: Where shall I meet you?
　　H: Well, ah I'll be finished with class at five. It is right in Tsimshatsui, so maybe we'll meet you at the Peninsula, between say five-fifteen and five-thirty?
　　X: OK wonderful.

As I have already pointed out above, utterances like X's Elicitation above initiate an exchange in which the speaker endorses the 'information' elicited in the third part. Once the endorsement is given both the speaker and the addressee have committed themselves to a future action.

This subcategory of Elicitation bears strong similarity to 'requests' in the sense that if responded to positively, it will involve commitment to a further action or a further exchange. There is nevertheless an important difference: a verbal response is obligatory in the former whereas it is not in the latter.

Elicit:repeat and Elicit:clarify

Finally, there are two subcategories of Elicitation which are meta-discoursal: they refer to the discourse itself. One prospects a repetition of the utterance preceding the Elicitation and the other prospects a clarification of a preceding utterance or preceding utterances. We may label the former Elicit:repeat and the latter Elicit:clarify. The former is realized by wh-interrogatives such as 'Who/When/Where/What did you say?', 'Say that again?' or words such as 'Sorry?', 'Pardon?' or 'Huh?'. It should be noted, however, that the utterance 'What did you say?' realizes an Elicit:repeat only when 'what' is prominent and is usually spoken with a rising tone (r+). If 'you" is prominent then it realizes an Elicit:inform. The following is a possible contextualization of the latter.

55 A: He asked me if he could borrow my car.
→ B: and what did YOU say?

Here B is not asking A for a repetition, but rather to report what he said. It is therefore an Elicit:inform and is usually spoken with a falling tone.

Elicit:clarify has a greater variety of realizations. It can be realized by wh-interrogatives such as ' What do you mean?', ' Which room?', 'Where?' or a high key repetition of a word or phrase in the preceding utterance. For example,

56 (BCET:A:1)
    C: Do you get the bus?
    B: Yeah.
→ C: The bus?
    B: And the tube.

C's utterance, spoken with high key, elicits clarification of B's preceding response.

To summarize we may say that there are six subcategories of Elicitation: Elicit:inform, Elicit:confirm, Elicit:agree, Elicit:commit, Elicit:repeat, Elicit:clarify.

CONCLUDING REMARKS

In the above examination of conversational data, I have characterized any utterance which prospects an obligatory verbal response as an 'Elicitation' irrespective of its syntactic form. This characterization avoids the inconsistency of using syntactic criteria for some utterances and discourse criteria for others; it avoids confusing labels such as 'exclamatory questions' and 'declarative questions' where in the former, the term 'question' refers to the interrogative form whereas in the latter, the term 'question' refers to the discourse function; it also avoids the lumping together of utterances which have different discourse consequences such as the characterization of 'questions' as 'requests'.

NOTES

1 The analysis of questions in Quirk *et al.* (1985) is basically the same as that in Quirk *et al.* (1972).

2 The conversational data used here consist of face-to-face and telephone conversations between native speakers of English. B stands for telephone conversations and C stands for face-to-face conversations. (BCET) stands for Birmingham Collection of English Texts. I would like to thank the English Department, University of Birmingham, for allowing me to use their data.

   The following transcription notations are used: // marks a tone unit boundary; / marks overlapping utterances; CAPITALS mark PROminent SYLLables.

3 In Tsui (1987), I labelled this subcategory 'Elicit:supply'. I have changed it to Elicit:inform to bring it into line with the other 5 subcategories in which the label signifies the kind of response prospected by the Elicitation.

'A functional description of questions' is a substantially modified version of 'On elicitations', first published in Coulthard (1987a) *Discussing Discourse*, 80–106.

6   Caught in the act: using the rank scale to address problems of delicacy

Dave Willis

SOME PROBLEMS IN DISCOURSE ANALYSIS

When is a statement a question, and when is a question not a question? Or, to be more precise:

> How . . . does a hearer know when a declarative structure has the function of a question, and how does he know that a clause does or does not ask a question depending on where it occurs in a sequence of clauses?
>
> (Sinclair and Coulthard 1975)

The question I want to examine here is very close to this. Sinclair and Coulthard identify three major problems in the analysis of the apparently loosely structured discourse of desultory or casual conversation. The third of these they describe as 'the ambiguity inherent in language'. This ambiguity, they say,

> . . . means that people occasionally misunderstand each other; more often for a variety of reasons, people exploit the ambiguity and pretend to have misunderstood:
>
> Dad: Is that your coat on the floor again?
> Son: Yes. (goes on reading)

> The father is using the resources of the language to avoid giving a direct command to his son; he uses a formulation which betrays irritation but is as far as he can go towards the polite 'Could you pick up your coat please?' However, because he uses an interrogative formulation, his son is able to ignore the intended command and reply as if it were a question.
>
> (ibid.)

Because of problems like this Sinclair and Coulthard decided to begin their quest for a structural description of discourse in the classroom situation, in which the teacher was in front of the class teaching, and therefore likely to be exerting the maximum control over the discourse.

Since 1975 the description has been developed and diversified. These developments are well exemplified and documented in Coulthard and Montgomery (1981) and in this volume. The work of Brazil (1975, 1978a, 1978b) and Coulthard and Brazil (1979) looks closely at the function of intonation in structuring discourse and in doing so extends and enhances the description; Burton (1980) focuses on casual conversation and introduces the valuable notion of *challenging moves*; Francis and Hunston (this volume, Chapter 7) offer a development of the system to handle telephone conversations; while Ventola (1987) extends the system to provide an ethnographic analysis of service encounters. These are all attempts to describe data in which the discourse is not predictably controlled as by a teacher in a classroom.

The advantages of working within a structural description of discourse are clear. The distinctive feature of a structural description is that the elements in the description and their possible combinations must be rigorously defined. This means that descriptions which are based on the same structural criteria are directly comparable. It is possible to reveal similarities and differences between different discourses and different genres of discourse once these have been subjected to the same structural analysis.

The original Sinclair–Coulthard system of analysis is based on Halliday's (1961) rank scale description of grammar. The ranks in the model are lesson; transaction; exchange; move and act, and these are related to one another in a 'consists of' relationship. A *lesson* is made up of a series of *transactions*, which in turn is made up of a number of *exchanges*. *Exchanges* are made up of *moves*, which in turn are made up of acts. I would like to look first at the ranks of exchange and move.

There are two types of exchange: *Boundary exchanges* and *Teaching exchanges*. I want to look at teaching exchanges. A teaching exchange has three elements of structure: Initiation (I), Response (R) and Feedback (F). The structure of the exchange is specified as I(R)(F). This I(R)(F) exchange structure dictates that all exchanges consist of at least an Initiation and that this Initiation may be followed by either a Response or a Feedback. If there is a Response this may in turn be followed by a Feedback.

This I(R)(F) exchange structure defines the potential for an Opening move followed by an Answering move followed in turn by a Follow-up move. All the possible realizations of this exchange structure are to be found in the data. An exchange may consist simply of an Opening move:

T: A group of people used symbols to do their writing. They used pictures instead of, as we write, in words.

In this case the move is realized by a single act, an *inform*. An Opening move of this kind requires no Answering move on the part of the pupils. A directive exchange, on the other hand, typically has an IR structure, consisting of a teacher Direct:

T: Now you can do them in any order you like. Let's see if you can sort out which is which.
P: NV.

which elicits a non-verbal response from the pupils as they set about complying with the directive.

The most typical classroom exchange, however, uses the full IRF structure. This is when the teacher asks a question (I), a pupil responds (R) and the teacher evaluates that response (F):

T: What is it?
P: Pair of scissors.
T: Pair of scissors. Yes pair of scissors.

The prevalence of exchanges of this kind is one of the most striking features of the Sinclair and Coulthard data. But exchanges of precisely this kind in which the move at F serves to evaluate the move at R are rare outside the classroom. Consider the following exchange taking place between a husband and wife in their sitting room:

A: What's that you've got?
B: A pair of scissors.
A: A pair of scissors. Yes, a pair of scissors.

There is certainly something distinctly odd about this. We do not typically evaluate responses in this way unless we are in something like the teacher–pupil relationship. It is for this reason that Burton (1980) rejects the F move and replaces it with a *challenge*.

A LOOK AT INFORMING AND ELICITING EXCHANGES

Berry (1981), however, points out that it is not the three-part structure in itself which is odd outside the classroom. It is the evaluative function of the Follow-up move which is very much a part of the teacher role and therefore typical of the classroom situation and unusual outside the classroom. There is nothing remarkable about the three-part structure in itself. Consider, for example:

A: What's that you've got?
B: A pair of scissors.
A: Oh.

Here the 'Oh' simply serves to acknowledge the response, not to evaluate it. Berry goes on to elaborate the Sinclair and Coulthard model in order to account for the difference between the evaluative follow-up in the classroom and the kind of acknowledgement which is so common in everyday discourse. She argues that the acceptability, and indeed prevalence, of evaluative follow-up in the classroom is a feature of the teacher's role, a role which she describes as that of *primary knower* or K1. She points out that in other situations which involve a K1 there is nothing remarkable about evaluative follow-up. In support of this she cites an exchange between a quizmaster and a contestant:

Quizmaster: Which cathedral has the tallest spire?
Contestant: Salisbury.
Quizmaster: Yes.

In such an exchange, she says, the initial question is not a 'real' question in the sense that it is a request for information on the part of the speaker. It is a 'pseudo-question'. The quizmaster knows the answer very well and simply puts the question in order to ascertain whether or not the contestant knows the answer, just as teachers ask questions to see if pupils know the answer.

Within Berry's description a true question, one which seeks to elicit information, will be asked not by a *primary knower*, K1, but by a *secondary knower*, K2. The exchange given above, incorporating a 'real' question is analysed as:

(I) K2: What's that you've got?
(R) K1: A pair of scissors.
(F) K2f: Oh.

Where K2f is a Follow-up move acknowledging the response to a question. In an exchange like the quizmaster/contestant example, K1, the quizmaster, is not seeking but *witholding* information which he is prepared to divulge only after he has ascertained whether or not K2, the contestant, is able to supply it unaided. For this reason Berry offers the following analysis:

(I) DK1: Which cathedral has the tallest spire?
(R) K2: Salisbury.
(F) K1: Yes.

DK1 is a move in which the questioner defines the knowledge to which he as K1 has access, the name of the cathedral with the highest spire, but delays providing that information by defining it in the form of a question rather than revealing it in the form of a statement. It announces the *delay* of a K1 move. The K2 move offers information, but at the same time waits for confirmation of that information. K1 provides that confirmation.

This is an elegant analysis which has a number of obvious attractions. We have seen that the two exchanges are essentially different. Berry's analysis reveals that difference. It does so by identifying the roles fulfilled by the questioners – K1 in the case of the teachers and quizmasters and K2 in most other cases. It also underlines the similarity in function of:

(I) K2: What's that you've got?

and

(R) K2:   Salisbury.

Both of them request information – in the case of (I) K2, an answer to a question, and in the case of (R) K2, confirmation of an answer. This explains why an F move is obligatory in the classroom, but not as a general rule. The witholding of acknowledgement after a 'real' question would not be in any way unusual:

(I) K2:   What's that you've got?
(R) K1:   A pair of scissors.
(I) K2:   My kitchen scissors?
(R) K1:   Yes.
(F) K2f: Oh.

In an exchange with (I) DK1, however, an (F) K1f is obligatory. If it is missing something must be done to repair the omission. In the classroom pupils usually make the repair by interpreting the lack of (F) K1f as a negative evaluation.

Berry's analysis is, then, a revealing one. But it rests on the initial identification of the questioner as K1 or K2. How would the analysis work with the following exchange:

Father: What time did you get in last night?
Son: Eleven o'clock.
Father: Yes.

There is nothing in the father's question to reveal his K1 status. At this stage he has simply asked a question. From the analyst's point of view there is no reason to identify that question as (I) DK1. It is the third move in the exchange, the father's 'Yes', which reveals the true status of the opening move.

Berry's K1/K2 distinction was designed to elaborate the Sinclair/Coulthard analysis to account for different types of initiation. But if we look back to the original Sinclair/Coulthard classroom analysis we find that there already is an element in the analysis which can be invoked to account for this difference. We looked above at the way the exchange structure is realized through moves, but we did not look at the next rank in the scale, the rank of *act*.

The typical teaching exchange has been exemplified as:

T: What is it?
P: Pair of scissors.
T: Pair of scissors. Yes, pair of scissors.

In this example each move consists of a single act. The Opening move is realized by an *elicitation*. This requires a verbal response, which is provided in the Answering move which is realized by a *reply*. This is followed by a Follow-up move realized by an *evaluate*. Sometimes moves are more elaborate than this. Here:

T: I've got some things here too.	(starter)
Hands up.	(cue)
What's that, what is it.	(elicit)

is made up of three acts – a *starter*, which prepares students for what is to come; a *cue*, which encourages students to offer their answers; and an *elicit*, a question which carries the basic function of the move. So a move can be made up of a series of acts. This is one reason why we need to go to the rank of act for a full description. There is another reason too. We saw earlier that I, R and F were places in structure which were filled or realized by moves taken from specified classes. In the same way moves serve as places in structure which are filled in turn by acts.

If we look at:

T: What is it?
P: Pair of scissors.
T: Pair of scissors. Yes, pair of scissors.

at the rank of move we have an Opening move, an Answering move and a Follow-up move. And if we look at:

A: What's that you've got?
B: A pair of scissors.
A: Oh.

also at the rank of move, we have exactly the same analysis. But if we move to the rank of act we have quite a different picture. In the first exchange we have a Follow-up move realized by an evaluate:

> Realized by statements and tag questions, including words and phrases such as 'good', 'interesting', 'team point', commenting on the quality of the reply, react or initiation, also by 'yes', 'no', 'good', 'fine', with a high–fall intonation.
>
> (Sinclair and Coulthard, this volume, p. 21)

In the second exchange, however, the Follow-up move is not realized by an evaluate. Strictly according to the system described in Sinclair/Coulthard an *evaluate* must be present in a Follow-up move in the classroom since only an evaluate can function as the head, that is to say the *obligatory* element in the Follow-up move. There are, however, places in their analysis where the Follow-up move is realized not by an evaluate but by an *accept*. On one occasion a pupil takes the initiative and tells the teacher something about a recent television programme. This is followed by an eliciting exchange:

T: When was this?
P: On Monday I think.
T: Good gracious me, that's fairly recently.

Here the teacher's Follow-up move is described as being realized by an *accept*. There are problems with the analysis. An *accept* is described as:

Realized by a closed class of items – 'yes', 'no', 'good', 'fine', and repetition of pupil's reply, all with neutral low fall intonation. Its function is to indicate that the teacher has heard or seen that the informative, reply or react was appropriate.

(ibid.:20)

This does not cover the teacher's follow-up in the example given. In addition to this, *accept* in the model is described as a *pre-head* and not a head act. This means that it cannot stand on its own. It must be followed by a *head*, in the case of an eliciting exchange by an *evaluate*.

There is, however, another candidate which might function as the head of a Follow-up move in an eliciting exchange. In an informing exchange the head of the Follow-up move may be an *acknowledge*:

realized by 'yes', 'OK', 'cor', 'mm', 'wow' and certain non-verbal gestures and expressions. Its function is simply to show that the initiation has been understood, and, if the head was a directive, that the pupil intends to react.

(ibid.:20)

If we extend the scope of this act and allow it to stand as the head of a Follow-up move in an eliciting exchange we can offer an alternative analysis. The phrase 'Good gracious me' can be analysed as an *acknowledge* standing as the head of the Follow-up move. The supporting ' . . . that's fairly recently' can be analysed as a *comment*:

realized by statement and tag question. It is subordinate to the head of the move and its function is to exemplify, expand, justify, provide additional information.

(ibid.:20)

We now have an IRF exchange. The I is realized by a pupil elicit which is in turn realized by a single act – *elicit*. The R place in the exchange structure is filled by an Answering move which is realized at the rank of act by a reply. The F is now filled by a Follow-up move made up of an *acknowledge* as head and a *comment* as post-head.

By allowing for an *acknowledge* as head of a Follow-up move we have an analysis which allows us to distinguish between exchanges which, in Berry's terms are initiated by a DK1 and those which are initiated by a K2. If at the rank of act we have an *evaluate* as head then the exchange has a DK1 initiation, as in:

Father: What time did you get in last night?
Son: Eleven o'clock.
Father: Yes.

Here the father reveals his opening move as DK1 by evaluating the son's reply. He is in effect saying 'I knew all the time that you came in at eleven. I was just checking to see if you would give me an honest answer.'

If, on the other hand, we have an *acknowledge* as head then we have a K2 initiation, as in:

A: What's that you've got?
B: A pair of scissors.
A: Oh.

There is, then, no need to distinguish initially between K2 and DK1. The nature of the exchange is revealed later by the head of the Follow-up move. The roles of teachers and quizmasters will be marked by the fact that they regularly evaluate responses. Eliciting exchanges outside the classroom and the quiz show, which are typically initiated by Berry's K2, will normally have an *acknowledge* as head of the Follow-up move. But if they are DK1 exchanges they will have an *evaluate*. This marks the initiation retrospectively as DK1. The DK1 and K2 tags have become redundant. The information they carried is now carried in the analysis at the head of the Follow-up move.

It may be argued, however, that the analysis is still incomplete. There is a difference between the son's 'Eleven o'clock' and the quiz contestant's 'Salisbury'. The difference is that the son is operating in the K1 and not the K2 role. But this is a difference which is concealed by the Berry analysis too. There is another point to make here. In the classroom or the quiz show situation respondents may regard themselves as K1 without challenging the status of the teacher or the quizmaster. There is no reason why we should not have a pupil or contestant with confidence in their ability to provide the information requested. They may show this confidence by replying with falling intonation so that their response has the status of an inform. If, however, they have no such confidence they may reveal this by using rising intonation:

A: Which cathedral has the tallest spire?
B: Salisbury?
A: Yes.

Alternatively they may reveal it by answering a question with an overt interrogative:

A: Which cathedral has the tallest spire?
B: Is it Salisbury?
A: Yes.

If we introduce another act as a possible head and classify 'Salisbury' or 'Is it Salisbury' as an *offer* we have taken the analysis a stage further. We can now distinguish between an exchange in which the respondent accepts the role of K2 and one in which he lays claim to the authority of a K1.

I am, therefore, proposing two amendments to the original Sinclair/Coulthard model:

1 *acknowledge* should be acceptable as the head of a Follow-up move in an eliciting exchange.

2 we should introduce *offer* as another possible head act in the Answering move. This will enable us to distinguish between a tentative response which requests confirmation and a response which claims authority which will be realized as a *reply*.

This in turn enables us to make a further distinction. After an Answering move with *offer* as head, a Follow-up move is obligatory. After an Answering move with a *reply* as head a Follow-up is optional. Some situations, the classroom is certainly one, will be characterized by the fact that this option is regularly taken up.

THE ANALYSIS APPLIED TO DIRECTIVE EXCHANGES

Berry (1981) goes on to transfer the notion of K1/K2 roles in informing and eliciting exchanges to deal with directive exchanges. Instead of a primary knower (K1) and a secondary knower (K2), directive exchanges involve a primary doer (A1) and a secondary doer (A2). Just as K2 requests information so A2 requests action. And just as K1 can either withhold and at the same time define knowledge (DK1) or supply knowledge, so A1 can either define and withhold action (DA1) or carry out an action. This gives exchanges as follows:

A: Let me open the door for you.	(DA1)
B: Thank you.	(A2)
A: (opens door)	(A1)
B: Thanks.	(A2f)
A: Will you open the door please?	(A2)
B: (opens door)	(A1)
A: Thanks.	(A2f)

This analysis also allows for the most typical directive exchanges – those in which an undertaking is given to carry out an act at some future date, but which have, for the time being, no A1 element:

A: Will you come tomorrow please?	(A2)
B: Yes, of course.	(DA1)

In place of the A1 element there is an agreement on the part of one of the participants to carry out some action in the future. Such an agreement is equivalent to a commissive. Searle would say it 'counts as' a commissive. The exchange here is incomplete, however. Just as a K1 move is obligatory after a DK1 so A1 is obligatory after DA1. J.D. Willis (1987) suggests that for this reason an exchange with DA1 but no A1 should be regarded as a bound exchange. The full exchange would be A2; DA1 . . . A1, with the A1 supplied when B does in fact come tomorrow.

After re-examining Berry's proposals for informing and eliciting exchanges and after having found a mechanism at the rank of act which makes the K1/K2 distinction redundant, we can perhaps do the same with directive exchanges. We can propose an act to be called a *commissive*, one in which a participant undertakes an obligation to fulfil some specified action at some time in the future. We would then have:

A: Will you come tomorrow please?   (elicit)
B: Yes, of course.   (commissive)

In this case, just as an *evaluate* at the head of the Follow-up move in an eliciting exchange marks the initiation as a K2 in Berry's terms, so a *commissive* as head of an Answering move in a given exchange shows that the Opening move in that exchange has been interpreted as a *direct*.

J.D. Willis (1987) looks at a number of problematic exchanges in which an initiation which has the form of an *inform* or an *elicit* is interpreted as a *direct*:

1 A: Is that your coat on the floor again?
   B: Yes. (picks up coat)

2 A: Is that the salt over there?
   B: Sorry. (passes salt)

3 A: The room's a bit dusty.
   B: Sorry. I'll do it as soon as I can.

4 A: Why don't you send a telegram?
   B: Yes. OK.

But if we include the possibility of a *commissive* these exchanges cease to be problematic. Examples (1) and (2) create relatively little difficulty anyway. The non-verbal action in each case provides a *react* which shows that the initiation has been treated as a *direct*. In these cases the *react* is the head of the move with an accompanying verbal act as pre- or post-head. In the case of (3) and (4), the words 'I'll do it as soon as I can' and 'OK' are commissives. In uttering them the speaker undertakes an obligation to carry out an action in the future. The utterance of a commissive as the head of an Answering move has the effect of saying 'I understand your initiation as a *direct*', and therefore has a reclassifying force. If we accept this analysis the next stage is to look at data and see how such commissives are realized.

J.D. Willis (1987) goes on to consider the difference between:

5 A: It's hot in here.
   B: Yes, isn't it?

6 A: It's hot in here.
   B: The window's jammed.
   A: Oh, I see.

and

7 A: It's hot in here.
   B: I'm sorry. I'll open the window.

It was proposed that the initiation in each of these cases be regarded as an *inform*, but that in (7) this *inform* be reclassified as a *direct*. The reclassifying mechanism is marked by 'I'm sorry' which is seen as accepting the need for some action. In the light of our introduction of a *commissive* a different interpretation is possible. Example (7) is exactly parallel to (3) and (4) above. It is the commissive, 'I'll open the window' which has the effect of showing that the initiation is interpreted as a *direct* and which is the head of the Follow-up move. The words 'I'm sorry' make up a pre-head act, let us call it a *pre-commissive*, which introduces the commissive.

Given this analysis the initiating moves are seen as having illocutionary *potential* rather than illocutionary force. In (5), (6) and (7) the initiation has the interactive force of an *inform*. It may or may not be the case that any or all of these initiations were intended as directives. But in an analytical model we have no way of retrieving A's intentions. We can only describe the discourse as it unfolds. We cannot claim privileged insight into the participants' knowledge and intentions. In (5), therefore, we have an IF exchange. A produces an *inform* and B responds with an *acknowledge*. In (6) we have three moves:

A: It's hot in here.   (I/opening/inform)
B: The window's jammed.   (I/opening/inform)
A: Oh, I see.   (F/follow-up/acknowledge)

In (7), however, we have a two-move exchange:

A: It's hot in here.   (I/opening/inform)
B: I'm sorry. I'll open the window.   (F/follow-up/Pre-commissive
                                               + commissive)

Because of the commissive at the head of the Follow-up it is the directive potential of the Opening move that is actualized in the discourse. This may or may not have been A's intention, but that is the stage the discourse has now reached. A is seen as having issued a *direct* to which B has responded with a *commissive*.

A POSSIBLE ANSWER TO THE PROBLEMS

In answer to our original question:

> How . . . does a hearer know when a declarative structure has the function of a question, and how does he know that a clause does or does not ask a question depending on where it occurs in a sequence of clauses?
>
>   (Sinclair and Coulthard 1975:2)

I would say he doesn't *know* but he is free to exploit the illocutionary

potential of an utterance by putting on it whatever reasonable interpretation he wishes. Once he has signalled that interpretation then the potential is established. This, of course

> means that people occasionally misunderstand each other; more often
> for a variety of reasons, people exploit the ambiguity and pretend to
> have misunderstood.

(ibid.:5)

If this is to be realized in an analysis of the discourse we must have some
means of showing what potential has been realized. I have suggested that
we can do this at the rank of act.

An analysis of this kind faithfully reflects what is happening in the
discourse. A given utterance may be treated as a K1 or a K2 elicit. How it
operates in the discourse depends not simply on the structure of the
initiation but also on how the participants choose to regard it. An *evaluate*
tags the opening elicit as K1 and, if this is a common feature of the
discourse, tells us a good deal about the relationship between the participants. An *acknowledge*, on the other hand, tags the opening elicit as K2,
which is likely to be the norm outside settings like the classroom and the
quiz show.

The recognition of a *commissive* act enables us to distinguish between an
elicit and a *direct* in the same way. Whenever the Answering move has a
commissive as head this tells us that the Opening move has been treated as
a directive. It makes no difference what the intentions of the original
speaker were. The discourse has reached the stage where we have in play a
commissive which realizes the illocutionary potential of the preceding act
as directive. In analyses of this kind it is the patterning at the rank of act
which allows us to identify illocutionary potential.

'Caught in the act: using the rank scale to address problems of delicacy' is a
substantially modified version of 'An analysis of directive exchanges', first
published in Coulthard (1987a) *Discussing Discourse*, 20–43.

7 Analysing everyday conversation

Gill Francis and Susan Hunston

INTRODUCTION

The system of analysis presented in this chapter was developed for an undergraduate course in Discourse Analysis taught by the authors at the National University of Singapore. Students on the course were required to analyse a five-minute stretch of recorded talk, using a system outlined for them in lectures and further discussed in tutorial sessions.

From a pedagogical point of view, our aim was to define precisely the analytical categories so that the students could apply them with confidence, but at the same time present a system which would be flexible and adaptable enough to cope with a wide variety of discourse situations: casual conversations between friends and family members, child–adult talk, commercial transactions, professional interviews, radio phone-ins, and even air-traffic controllers' talk. From a theoretical point of view, we sought to interpret, integrate and systematize the various adaptations and refinements of the original Sinclair–Coulthard model (1975) which have emerged from Birmingham over the past ten years. The sheer quantity and range of our data (over a hundred transcripts) provided us with an opportunity to formulate a substantially revised version of the model which, we feel, reflects accurately the nature of different types of talk while remaining true to the spirit of the original model and its fundamental underlying principles.

In the ensuing discussion, it is assumed that the reader is familiar with Sinclair and Coulthard (1975); Sinclair and Brazil (1982); and Coulthard and Montgomery (1981), especially the chapters by Coulthard and Brazil (ch. 4), Stubbs (ch. 5), Berry (ch. 6), and Brazil (ch. 7). The first of these (Sinclair and Coulthard 1975) provides the theoretical background to our own approach and presents with great clarity the system as it was conceived at that stage.

It is in Coulthard and Montgomery (1981) that problems which arose when the system was applied to other data are discussed, and certain alterations proposed. Some of these adaptations have far-reaching implications for the system as a whole, yet nowhere is the revised system set out with the precision of the original 1975 version. This chapter seeks to repair this omission.

In particular, two radical changes to the notion of 'exchange' are proposed (1981:ch. 4). Firstly, the one-to-one correspondence between move and element of exchange structure is abandoned. The position in Sinclair and Coulthard (1975) may be summarized thus:

Element of structure	*Move*
Initiation ———————	opening
Response ———————	answering
Follow-up ———————	follow-up

In Coulthard and Montgomery (1981) this is reformulated as:

Element of structure	*Move*
Initiation	eliciting
Response	informing
Follow-up	acknowledging

Secondly, there is discussion about the limits of the exchange: how long it may be and what it may contain. The decision as to whether to place an utterance in the same exchange as a preceding utterance, or whether to interpret it as initiating a new exchange, may be made on the grounds of intonation, or according to the type of information being sought or given (notably whether such information is a decision between 'yes' and 'no' or whether it is the kind of information expected in response to a wh-question). It is apparent from these discussions that the exchange is now potentially longer than the three moves originally envisaged. An additional element of structure – R/I – has been incorporated, and typical exchanges range from, for example, the IR structure to I R/I R F F. The various possibilities can now be expressed as:

$$I \ (R/I) \ R \ (F^n)$$

(see Coulthard and Montgomery 1981:112)

Data

The data presented and discussed in this chapter is a complete telephone conversation between two native speakers of English (pp. 157–61 below). The two participants are close friends and call each other frequently. This type of discourse was chosen for two reasons: firstly because the lack of paralinguistic features such as gestures and eye-gaze allows us to pre-empt the possible criticism – a valid one in the case of face-to-face interaction – that only video recording can capture all the features of conversation.

Secondly, it was an easy way to obtain a short interaction complete with all the rituals of greeting and leave-taking.

The data collected by our students, to which reference is also made, consists largely of two-party conversations. Singaporeans make up the vast majority of participants, and the data contains many examples of features of Singapore English.

THE SYSTEM OF ANALYSIS

In the following pages we will first present a summary of the rank scale, basing the diagrammatic representations of structure on those set out in Sinclair and Coulthard (1975). For each rank other than the Interaction we will provide three-column lists representing the structure of each class or unit at that rank, proceeding downwards from Transaction to Act. The first column gives the elements of structure of the class or unit, and the second column shows the possible combinations of these elements of structure. In the third column, the elements of structure are associated with the classes or units at the rank next below, showing which among these may realize each element. This section is followed by a more detailed explanation of the system of analysis, with detailed descriptions of each unit and further explanations where necessary.

It must be noted that the system we present applies particularly to everyday conversation – we have omitted the categories more typical of 'formal' situations. For example, we have not included the element of move structure 'select' and the acts which realize it (*cue*, *bid* and *nomination*) on the grounds that it is a feature whose use is restricted to the classroom, formal discussions where speaking rights are controlled by a chairperson, and certain types of quiz game. It does not occur in two-party everyday conversation.

Summary of the system of analysis

RANK I: INTERACTION
No structural representation possible at this stage.

RANK II: TRANSACTION

Elements of structure	*Structures*	*Classes of exchange*	
Preliminary (P)	(P) M (M^2 ... M^n) (T)	P.T:	Organizational
Medial (M)		M:	Conversational
Terminal (T)			

RANK III: EXCHANGE
(1a) Organizational Boundary

Elements of structure	*Structures*	*Moves*	
Frame (Fr)	Fr	Fr:	framing

(1b) Organizational: Structuring, Greet, Summon

Elements of structure	Structures	Moves	
Initiation (I)	IR	I:	opening
Response (R)		R:	answering

(2) Conversational

Elements of structure	Structures	Moves	
Inititiation (I)	I (R/I) R (Fⁿ)	I:	eliciting
			informing
			directing
Response/ (R/I)		R/I	eliciting
Initiation			informing
Response (R)		R:	informing
			acknowledging
			behaving
Follow-up (F)		F:	acknowledging

RANK IV: MOVE

(1) Framing

Elements of structure	Structures	Acts	
signal (s)		s:	marker
head (h)	(s) h	h:	framer

(2) Opening

Elements of structure	Structures	Acts	
signal (s)	(s) (pre-h) h (post-h)	s:	marker
pre-head (pre-h)		pre-h:	framer
			starter
head (h)		h:	metastatement
			conclusion
			greeting
			summons
post-head (post-h)		post-h:	comment

(3) Answering

Elements of structure	Structures	Acts	
signal (s)	(s) (pre-h) h (post-h)	s:	marker
pre-head (pre-h)		pre-h:	starter
head (h)		h:	acquiesce
			reply-greeting
			reply-summons
			reject
post-head (post-h)		post-h:	comment
			qualify

(4) Eliciting

Elements of structure	Structures	Acts	
signal (s)	(s) (pre-h) h (post-h)	s:	marker
pre-head (pre-h)		pre-h:	starter
head (h)		h:	inquire
			neutral proposal
			marked proposal
			return
			loop
			prompt
post-head (post-h)		post-h:	comment
			prompt

(5) Informing

Elements of structure	*Structures*	*Acts*	
signal (s)	(s) (pre-h) h (post-h)	s:	marker
pre-head (pre-h)		pre-h:	starter
head (h)			receive
		h:	informative
			observation
			concur
			confirm
			qualify
			reject
post-head (post-h)		post-h:	concur
			comment
			qualify

(6) Acknowledging

Elements of structure	*Structures*	*Acts*	
signal (s)	(s) (pre-h) h (post-h)	s:	marker
pre-head (pre-h)		pre-h:	receive
head (h)		h:	terminate
			receive
			react
			reformulate
			endorse
			protest
post-head (post-h)		post-h:	comment
			terminate

(7) Directing

Elements of structure	*Structures*	*Acts*	
signal (s)	(s) (pre-h) h (post-h)	s:	marker
pre-head (pre-h)		pre-h:	starter
head (h)		h:	directive
post-head (post-h)		post-h:	comment
			prompt

(8) Behaving

Elements of structure	*Structures*	*Acts*	
signal (s)	(s) (pre-h) h (post-h)	s:	marker
pre-head (pre-h)		pre-h:	starter
			receive
			reject
head (h)		h:	behave
post-head (post-h)		post-h:	comment
			qualify

Expanation of the system of analysis

The previous section presented a downward view, showing how the elements of structure of each rank are realized by classes or units at the rank next below. The explanation given in this section will begin from the rank of Act and proceed upwards, again in accordance with the layout of Sinclair and Coulthard (1975).

Acts

Acts are the units at the lowest rank of the *discourse level* of language patterning, and are realized at the level of grammar and lexis. (For a discussion of linguistic levels and approaches towards accounting for the lack of fit between discourse function and grammatical form, see Sinclair and Coulthard (1975:ch. 3).) The following list of acts includes all those which occur in the sample analysis at the end of this chapter. The list includes some which do not occur there but which are included for two reasons:

1 They are necessary to an intonational paradigm. For example, *terminate*, *receive* and *react* are realized respectively by low, mid and high key repetitions and 'yes' items, so we include *react* although it does not occur in our data sample.
2 They are essential to a description of the basic functions of language, one of which is asking others to do things. We have no example of a *directive* in our data, but we nevertheless include it and the other act uniquely associated with this function, *behave*.

Our students' data provided innumerable examples of the whole range of acts listed.

The acts of everyday conversation

Label	Symbol	Realization and function
framer	fr	Realized by a closed class of items: (i) 'OK', '(all) right', 'anyway' and their variants, where the item precedes an exchange-initial move head ('anyway' may also be embedded in a move head); (ii) 'well', 'now', 'good' and their variants, where the item precedes an exchange-initial move head and is said with high key falling intonation followed by silent stress. When it precedes an *ms* or *con* it realizes the pre-head of an opening move in a Structuring exchange; when it precedes any other exchange-initial move head it realizes the head of a framing move in a Boundary exchange. Its function is to mark boundaries in the conversation, where such an interpretation is consistent with considerations of topic.
marker	m	Realized by the same closed class of items as *fr*: (i) 'OK' etc. where the item precedes a non-exchange-initial move head; (ii) 'well' etc. (also 'oh', 'er(m)' and 'look') where not said with high key falling intonation. Realizes the signal element of all moves. Its function is to mark the onset of a move.

starter	s	Realized by statement, question, command or moodless item. Realizes the pre-head of an opening, answering, eliciting, informing, directing or behaving move. Its function is to provide information about or direct attention towards the act realizing the move head.
meta-statement	ms	Realized by statement, question or command. Realizes the head of an opening move in a Structuring exchange. Its function is to structure the conversation prospectively in some way, and to obtain a warrant for doing so.
conclusion	con	Realized by a statement or question often with anaphoric reference. Realizes the head of an opening move in a Structuring exchange. Its function is to 'tie up' a particular topic, and to obtain a warrant for doing so.
acquiesce	acq	Realized by 'yes' and other items indicating assent, both verbal and non-verbal. May also be realized by silence, interpreted as a default mechanism whereby failure to protest (*rej*) is an indication of acquiescence. Realizes the head of an answering move in a Structuring exchange. Its function is to provide a warrant for a suggestion as to prospective (*ms*) or retrospective (*con*) structuring made by the other participant in a two-party conversation.
greeting	gr	Realized by a closed class of items which form the first-pair parts of the adjacency pairs used in the rituals of greeting and leave-taking: 'hello', 'hi' 'good morning', '(good)bye(-bye)', 'have a nice/ good day', 'be seeing you' and their variants. Realizes the head of an opening move in a Greet exchange. Its function is self-explanatory.
reply-greeting	re-gr	Realized by a closed class of items which form the second-pair parts of the adjacency pairs used in the rituals of greeting and leave-taking: 'hello', 'hi', 'good morning', '(good)bye(-bye)', 'fine thanks (and you?)', 'thank you', 'same to you', 'yeah see you', and their variants. Realizes the head of an answering move in a Greet exchange. Its function is self-explanatory.
summons	sum	Realized by the ringing of the telephone, a knock at the door, etc., or the calling of somebody's name.

Realizes the head of an opening move in a Summon exchange.

Its function is to engage another participant in a conversation or to attract his/her attention.

| reply-summons | re-sum | Realized by the items used to answer a telephone ('hello', the giving of one's number, etc.) or the door (opening it, calling 'come in', etc.) or by 'yes', 'what?' and other indications of attention (both verbal and non-verbal) given upon hearing one's name called.

Realizes the head of an answering move in a Summon exchange.

Its function is to indicate willingness to participate in a conversation, or that one is giving one's attention. |

inquire   inq   Realized by questions which seek information as opposed to a 'yes' or 'no' answer, i.e. wh-questions and ellipted forms of these.

Realizes the head of an eliciting move (except at I^b in Clarify and Repeat exchanges).

Its function is to elicit information.

neutral   n.pr   Realized by questions which seek a 'yes' or 'no'
proposal   answer, i.e. questions beginning 'Do you', 'Are you', etc, and ellipted forms of these.

Realizes the head of an eliciting move (except at I^b in Clarify and Repeat exchanges).

Its function is to elicit a decision between 'yes' and 'no'.

marked   m.pr   Realized by questions which seek a 'yes' or 'no'
proposal   answer, where the form of the question indicates the polarity of the expected answer, i.e. questions beginning 'Don't you', 'Aren't you', etc. It is also realized by declaratives said with 'questioning' intonation and declaratives followed by tag questions.

Realizes the head of an eliciting move (except at I^b in Clarify and Repeat exchanges).

Its function is to elicit agreement.

return   ret   Re .lized by question, often ellipted.

Realizes the head of an eliciting move at I^b in a Clarify exchange.

Its function is to seek clarification of a preceding utterance.

loop   l   Realized by a closed class of items: 'pardon', 'what', 'eh', 'again', and their variants, said with rising intonation.

Realizes the head of an eliciting move at I^b in a Repeat exchange.

Its function is to elicit the repetition of a preceding utterance which was not clearly heard.

prompt	p	Realized by a closed class of items: 'hah' (with rising intonation), 'come on', 'go on give me an answer', 'guess' and their variants. Realizes the head of an eliciting move at I^b in a Re-initiation exchange, or the post-head of any other eliciting move, or the post-head of a directing move. Its function is to reinforce the point of a preceding utterance, whether this was to elicit an *i*, a *conc* (etc.) or a *be*. When it realizes a move-head, it follows a silence on the part of 'B'.
observation	obs	Realized by statement. Realizes the head of an informing move at I (Inform exchange). Its function is to offer 'information' which is already part of the shared knowledge of the participants in the conversation. In other words it has a predominantly phatic function.
informative	i	Realized by statement or by 'yes' and 'no' items and their variants, both verbal (e.g. 'I (don't) think so') and non-verbal (e.g. nods and shakes of the head). Realizes the head of an informing move at I (Inform exchange); or at R/I or R (Elicit exchange) where the head of the eliciting move at I or R/I is realized by either *inq* or *n.pr*. Its function is to supply information or to give a decision between 'yes' and 'no'.
concur	conc	Realized by low or mid key 'yes' and 'no' items and their variants, both verbal and non-verbal; or by repetition or paraphrase. Realizes the head or post-head of an informing move at R/I or R (Elicit exchange) where the head of the eliciting move at I or R/I is realized by *m.pr*. Its function is to give agreement.
confirm	conf	Realized by high key 'yes' and 'no' items and their variants, both verbal and non-verbal; or by repetition or paraphrase. Realizes the head of an informing move at R/I or R (Elicit exchange) where the head of the eliciting move at I or R/I is realized by *m.pr*. Its function is to give or assert agreement.
qualify	qu	Realized by 'qualified' statement or by tentative 'yes' and 'no' items (where tentativeness is intonationally signalled) and their variants, both verbal ('to some extent yes', 'no not really', 'well I suppose so (not)', etc.) and non-verbal (e.g. shrugging the shoulders).

Realizes the head of an informing move at R/I or R (Elicit exchange) where the head of the eliciting move at I or R/I is realized by *n.pr* or *m.pr*; or the post-head of an answering, informing or behaving move.

Its function is to qualify a decision or an agreement by indicating that its polarity is not unconditional, or to detail conditions and exceptions.

reject	rej

Realized by statement or by 'yes' and 'no' items and their variants, both verbal and non-verbal. May also be realized by silence, interpreted as a default mechanism whereby failure to supply a *re-gr*, *re-sum*, *i*, *conc*, *conf*, *qu* or appropriate *be* is an indication of rejection.

Realizes the head of an answering move in a Structuring, Greet or Summon exchange: or the head of an informing move at R/I or R (Elicit exchange): or the pre-head of a behaving move in a Direct exchange.

Its function is to refuse to acquiesce to a suggestion as to the structuring of the conversation; or to refuse to give an appropriate answer to a *gr* or a *sum*, or to reject the underlying presuppositions of an *inq*, *n.pr* or *m.pr*; or to indicate unwillingness to comply with a *d*.

terminate	ter

Realized by low key 'yes' and 'no' items, and their variants, both verbal and non-verbal; or by low key repetition.

Realizes the head and/or post-head of an acknowledging move at R and/or F.

Its function is to acknowledge a preceding utterance and to terminate an exchange (although it may be followed by further acknowledging moves).

receive	rec

Realized by mid key 'yes' and 'no' items and their variants, both verbal and non-verbal; or by mid key repetition.

Realizes the head or pre-head of an acknowledging move at R and/or F; or the pre-head of an informing move at R (Elicit exchange); or the pre-head of a behaving move.

Its function is to acknowledge a preceding utterance or (as pre-head) to indicate that the appropriate *i*, *be*, etc. is forthcoming.

react	rea

Realized by high key 'yes' and 'no' items and their variants, both verbal and non-verbal; or by high key repetition.

Realizes the head of an acknowledging move at R and/or F.

Its function is to indicate positive endorsement of a preceding utterance.

reformulate	ref	Realized by statement which paraphrases a preceding utterance. Realizes the head of an acknowledging move at R and/or F. Its function is to acknowledge a preceding utterance or offer a revised version of it.
endorse	end	Realized by statement or moodless item. Realizes the head of an acknowledging move at R and/or F. Its function is to offer positive endorsement of, sympathy with, etc., a preceding utterance ('good idea', 'you poor thing', 'well I never', 'very interesting', etc.).
protest	prot	Realized by statement or by 'yes' and 'no' items and their variants. Realizes the head of an acknowledging move at R and/or F. Its function is to raise an objection to a preceding utterance; it acknowledges the utterance while disputing its correctness, relevance, appropriateness, the participant's right to have uttered it, or anything else.
directive	d	Realized by command. Realizes the head of a directing move. Its function is to request a non-verbal response, i.e. an action.
behave	be	Realized by action. Realizes the head of a behaving move. Its function is to provide a non-verbal response to a preceding *d*, whether this involves compliance, non-compliance, or defiance.
comment	com	Realized by statement. Realizes the post-head of all moves except framing. Its function is to exemplify, expand, explain, justify, provide additional information, or evaluate one's own utterance.
engage	eng	Realized by 'mm', 'yeah' and low or mid key 'echoes'. Does not realize any element of move structure (hence it always appears in parentheses in the 'act' column of an analysis). Its function is to provide minimal feedback while not interrupting the flow of the other participant's utterance.

Notes on the acts

1 An act must always begin with a new tone unit: for example 'well' is not identified as a *marker* unless there is a tone unit boundary between it and

whatever follows it (compare exchange (13) with exchange (27) of the sample analysis).

2 For a discussion of the way in which the terms 'statement', 'question' and 'command' are used above, see the section on 'situational categories' in Sinclair and Coulthard (1975:29ff). It is important to appreciate that a question, for example, is not always realized by an interrogative.

3 Where an Elicit exchange is referred to above, the term must be taken to include the three bound-Elicit exchanges: Clarify, Repeat and Re-initiation.

4 We make no claim that the above definitions cover all the possibilities as to what acts may be realized by or realize, or what functions they fulfil. Nor do we claim that the list is complete. Indeed we believe that it is neither feasible nor desirable to present a complete inventory of all the acts necessary to analyse every conceivable conversation. Each new set of data will inevitably require adaptations and additions at act level.

Moves

Acts combine to form moves: each act realizes one element of move structure. As the table on pp. 125–7 shows, there are eight moves: *framing*, *opening*, *answering*, *eliciting*, *informing*, *acknowledging*, *directing* and *behaving*; the first three realize elements of structure of Organizational exchanges, and the other five of Conversational exchanges.

The structure and function of moves

The structure of each move is given in the table on pp. 125–7. It will be noted that the framing move has an optional *signal* and an obligatory *head*, while all the other moves have an optional *signal*, *pre-head* and *post-head*, and an obligatory *head*. The function of each move is most easily seen in terms of the acts which realize its head, so these are given after each move heading.

1 Framing: *framer*
Its function is to mark boundaries in the conversation.

2 Opening: *metastatement, conclusion, greeting, summons*
Its function is to initiate a conversation (or perhaps close it, if the head is realized by a *greeting* or a *conclusion*), or to impose structure on it in some way, and to obtain a warrant for doing so. (We also recognize that a *greeting* and *reply-greeting* pair may constitute a minimal interaction.)

3 Answering: *acquiesce, reply-greeting, reply-summons, reject*
Its function is to indicate willingness to participate in a conversation, or to provide a warrant for suggestions as to structuring made by the other participant (or not to do any of these things, if a *reject* is used).

It will be noted that the acts which realize the heads of opening and answering moves are related to the exchange in which these moves occur. When the head of an opening move is realized by *metastatement* or *conclusion*, and of an answering move by *acquiesce*, the exchange is Structuring. When the same structural elements are realized by *greeting* and *reply-greeting*, or by *summons* and *reply-summons*, the exchanges are Greet and Summon respectively. It would have been possible to remove this sort of act–exchange link only by creating three 'pairs' of moves instead of one; we preferred not to complicate matters in this way.

It is further evident that the heads of opening and answering moves form complementary pairs, such that the realization of one predicts that of the other: a *summons* is followed by *reply-summons* and so on. Only *reject* is common to all three exchanges.

4 Eliciting: *inquire, neutral proposal, marked proposal, return, loop, prompt*
Its function is to elicit information, a decision between 'yes' and 'no', agreement, clarification or repetition, depending on which act realizes its head. A further link between act and exchange exists here. The head of an eliciting move in an Elicit or Re-initiation exchange may be realized by *inquire, neutral proposal* or *marked proposal*; in the case of a Re-initiation exchange only, it may also be realized by *prompt*. In a Clarify exchange the head is realized by *return* only, and in a Repeat exchange by *loop* only. (We note that this sort of act–exchange link is present in the 1975 description also.)

5 Informing: *observation, informative, concur, confirm, qualify, reject*
Its function is to offer information, or to supply an answer appropriate to a preceding eliciting move (or inappropriate, if a *reject* is used). The head of an informing move at I (Inform exchange) may be realized by *observation* or *informative*. The head of an informing move at R/I or R (Elicit exchange) may be realized by *informative, concur, confirm, qualify* or *reject*; in other words the last four are always answers. This link between act and exchange, which in this particular case can be expressed in terms of elements of exchange structure, is an inevitable consequence of abandoning the one-to-one correspondence between move and element of structure (see p. 124).

6 Acknowledging: *terminate, receive, react, endorse, protest*
Its function is to provide positive or negative follow-up, its nature and polarity depending on which act realizes the head.

7 Directing: *directive*
Its function is to request an immediate or future action.

8 Behaving: *behave*
Its function is to supply an action, either in accordance with a preceding *directive* (in which case if it has a pre-head this will be realized by *starter* or *receive*) or in defiance of it (in which case the optional pre-head will be realized by *reject*).

Directing and behaving form a complementary pair of moves: A asks B to do something and B does it (or does not do it, or does something else). We suggest however that directing and acknowledging may *also* form a complementary pair: A asks B to do something, not now but later; B acknowledges the request with a *receive* or an *endorse*, say, or perhaps with a *protest*.

Exchanges

Moves combine to form exchanges: each move realizes one element of exchange structure. There are two major classes of exchange: Organizational and Conversational. As the table on pp. 125–7 shows, there are two subclasses of Organizational exchange, distinguished structurally as well as functionally. The first subclass consists of the Boundary exchange, which has only one element of structure, Fr. The second consists of three exchanges: Structuring, Greet and Summon, which have two obligatory elements of structure, I and R.[1] The class of Conversational exchange consists of the following units: Elicit, Inform, Direct, and the three bound-Elicit exchanges Clarify, Repeat and Re-initiation. Bound-Elicit exchanges are so named because they are bound to preceding exchanges and they all have eliciting moves at I^b. All Conversational exchanges, with the exception of Direct (see below) have the structure I (R/I) R (F^n), where I and R are obligatory. R/I is optional, but it shares with R the property of being predicted, in that I predicts either R/I (which in its turn predicts R) or just R. F is always optional and unpredicted. Direct is the only exchange which does not have the optional element R/I, a statement which we must ask the reader to take on trust, since to give the reasons for this would occupy too much space.

The structure, function and realization of each unit will now be given, with examples from either our own data or our students'. The reader will note that the realization of R/I is not given for each exchange type: R/I is always realized by an eliciting move (in which case R is realized by an informing move) or by an informing move (in which case R is realized by an acknowledging move). This is explained in full on pp. 145–9 below.

In the examples, acts are also included for the sake of completeness. 'e.s' stands for element of structure. Where the example is taken from our data sample, the exchange number is given on the left.

---

1 Organizational

(a) Boundary
Structure: Fr, realized by a framing move.
Function: to mark boundaries in the conversation.

Example 1	*act*	*e.s*	*move*	*e.s*
A: Well	m	s	framing	Fr
anyway	fr	h		

(b) Structuring, Greet, Summon
Structure: I R, where I is realized by an opening move and R by an answering move.

(i) Structuring
Function: to structure the conversation, prospectively or retrospectively. In the following example, *acquiesce* is realized by silence, hence the parentheses.

Example 2	act	e.s	move	e.s
42 A: OK	fr	pre-h	opening	I
Danny I must go	ms	h		
B: ∅	(aqu)	h	(answering)	R

(ii) Greet
Function: to greet or take leave, observing conventional procedures.

Example 3	act	e.s	move	e.s
49 B: Well have a nice day	gr	h	opening	I
A: Thank you	re-gr	h	answering	R

(iii) Summon
Function: to engage another participant in conversation, or to gain his/her attention.

Example 4	act	e.s	move	e.s
16 A: Hey Danny	sum	h	opening	I
B: Yeah	re-sum	h	answering	R

2 Conversational
(i) Elicit
Structure: I (R/I) R (F^n), where I is realized by an eliciting move, R by an informing move, and F by an acknowledging move.
Function: to elicit information, decision, or agreement.

Example 5	act	e.s	move	e.s
8 B: Why (#)	s	pre-h	eliciting	I
did you wake up late today?	n.pr	h		
A: Yeah pretty late	qu	h	informing	R
B: Oh dear	end	h	acknowledging	F

(ii) Inform
Structure: I (R/I) R (F^n), where I is realized by an informing move, and R and F by acknowledging moves.
Function: to offer information.

Example 6	act	e.s	move	e.s
33 B: It's a bit *strange* you know	obs	h	informing	I
A: Yeah interesting	ref	h	acknowledging	R

(iii) Direct

Structure: I R (F^n), where I is realized by a directing move, R by a behaving or acknowledging move (see pp. 135–6 above) and F by an acknowledging move.

Function: to request immediate or future action.

Example 7	*act*	*e.s*	*move*	*e.s*
A: Put the chopsticks down Ann-Marie	d	h	directing	I
B: Alright	rec	pre-h	behaving	R
(puts them down)	be	h		
A: Good girl	end	h	acknowledging	F

(iv) Clarify (bound-Elicit)

Structure: I^b (R/I) R (F^n), where I^b is realized by an eliciting move, R by an informing move, and F by an acknowledging move.

Function: to elicit clarification of a preceding utterance.

Note: In this and other examples of bound-Elicit exchanges given below, the preceding exchange is also supplied and the boundary between the two marked by a broken line, as in the sample analysis below.

Example 8	*act*	*e.s*	*move*	*e.s*
13 A: You got home all right? (#)	s	pre-h	eliciting	I
you weren't too tired?	m.pr	h		
B: Well er (2)	m	s	informing	R
I got up pretty late myself	i	h		
I mean I – I was supposed to get up at about seven o'clock	com	post-h		
14 A: What d'you mean you were supposed to	ret	h	eliciting	I^b
B: Well I had the alarm clock on for seven	i	h	informing	R
A: Hah (low key)	ter	h	acknowledging	F

(v) Repeat (bound-Elicit)

Structure: I (R/I) R (F^n), where I^b is realized by an eliciting move, R by an informing move, and F by an acknowledging move. In the following example, R/I is realized by another eliciting move, and R (as usual) by an informing move.

Function: to elicit repetition of a preceding utterance.

Example 9	*act*	*e.s*	*move*	*e.s*
27 A: Well what *was* it then?	inq	h	eliciting	I

B: Sorry?	l	h	eliciting	I^b
A: What was it then?	inq	h	eliciting	R/I
B: I don't know you know I mean I'm just trying to work out and see	s	pre-h	informing	R
I mean it could be *anything* wh – helium doesn't get converted	i	h		

(vi) Re-initiation (bound-Elicit)

Structure: I^b (R/I) R (F^n), where I^b is realized by an eliciting move, R by an informing move, and F by an acknowledging move.

Function: to indicate that an informing move is still required: it follows a silence on the part of B. In the following example, it follows another bound-Elicit exchange (a Clarify – see sample analysis below).

Example 10	*act*	*e.s*	*move*	*e.s*
44 A: Is that OK? (#)	ret	h	eliciting	I^b

---

45 Hah?	p	h	eliciting	I^b

Transactions

Exchanges combine to form transactions: each exchange realizes one element of transaction structure. As the table on pp. 125–7 shows, the transaction has only one obligatory element of structure – M – which is realized by one exchange. As the notation (M^2 . . . M^n) indicates, each subsequent exchange realizes M^2, M^3, M^4, etc. – there is no upper limit. Most transactions consist of several exchanges realizing Ms.

The other two elements of structure – P and T – are optional. When P or T occurs, it is realized by one or more of the units comprising the Organizational class of exchange – Boundary, Structuring, Greet and Summon. M is realized by one of the units comprising the Conversational class of exchange – Elicit, Inform, Direct, and the three bound-Elicit exchanges.

In the absence of an exchange (or exchanges) realizing P, there is a further way in which the beginning of a new transaction may be recognized, and that is by intonation. When a participant selects *high key* and *proclaiming tone* for the first tone unit of an utterance, the utterance is seen as transaction-initial. An example of this occurs in exchange (124) of our data sample (see p. 159), where A says: 'Did you enjoy last night'. The information supplied by intonation is reinforced by the obvious 'topic-change' occurring at this point.

In all cases, in fact, the identification of a transaction boundary should be consistent with considerations of topic, since the transaction is basically a *topic-unit*. We do not propose here to go into the thorny question of 'topic', which must remain a pre-theoretical and intuitive notion. It must be stressed, however, that the linguistic signal (*framer* or intonation contour) is necessary but not entirely sufficient evidence for a transaction boundary.

The transaction differs from units lower down the rank scale in that while we can identify its boundaries, we can say little about its internal structure. We do not know how the various Conversational exchanges realizing the Ms combine, or even whether the structure of a transaction can be described in terms of linguistic patterning. Moreover, since we can suggest no *impossible combination* of exchanges, one of Sinclair and Coulthard's four criteria for a linguistic system (1975:16–17) cannot be met.

The transaction, then, is a less satisfactory unit altogether than those lower down the rank scale.

Interactions

Transactions combine to form the highest unit on the rank scale, the interaction. Again, however, little can be said about the internal structure of an interaction.

One problem which has been raised concerns the defining of its limits. Coulthard suggests (1981:14) that perhaps greetings and leave-takings should not be seen as part of the structure of a particular interaction, but rather as markers of the beginning and end of situations during which interactions occur. In the course of a project which involved asking doctors to record their interviews with patients, it was noted that 'one doctor . . . decided that the greetings were not part of the interview and only turned on the tape-recorder after these preliminaries, while another turned off the tape-recorder before he dismissed the patient.' Secondly, Coulthard argues, primary-school pupils usually begin and end their day by greeting and taking leave of their teacher, while in the course of the day a number of interactions – or lessons – take place which are not marked in this way.

We would not, however, wish to place greetings and leave-takings outside the limits of the interaction on the grounds that, if they are seen simply as marking the beginning and end of situations, they can no longer be subjected to internal analysis. In our data sample, there is one transaction (the last one) which is made up entirely of three Greet exchanges and one Structuring. To see a closing transaction like this (and it clearly qualifies as a transaction)[2] as part of a situation but not as part of an interaction would be to 'jump' a rank, which is inconsistent with the fundamental principles of rank-scale analysis.

Our data sample happens to be a complete interaction; it contains 'opening' and 'closing' transactions which define the interaction boundaries. We do not wish, however, to elevate this observation into a generalization about 'boundary transactions', since we do not have enough data. The majority of our students' transcripts, on the basis of which this description was formulated, did *not* consist of complete interactions, but were randomly selected stretches of discourse within them. A much larger body of complete interactions needs to be investigated before any structural statements as to their boundaries can be made.

Secondly, there is the question of whether interactions exhibit any further evidence of internal structure. Here the problem is that where interactions do appear to be structured, this is usually the result of situational factors. For example, the structure of a doctor–patient interview is affected by such factors as institutional setting and the goals of the participants. The fact that examination will precede diagnosis, and diagnosis will be followed by prescription has little to do with *linguistic* structure. And for everyday conversation, we have no evidence even of this sort of structuring.

Following Sinclair and Coulthard, then, we describe the interaction as 'an unordered series of transactions', bearing in mind that this does not mean that they do not display order but that this 'order' has not as yet been, and perhaps cannot be, characterized in linguistic terms.[3]

Having set out the framework of the analytical system, we will now go on to look at some of the key areas and problematic issues, particularly those concerning exchange structure.

RESTRICTIONS ON MOVES

On pp. 136–9 we set out the elements of structure of different exchanges and the moves which may realize these elements. The following diagram summarizes the restrictions upon where in an exchange a move may occur:

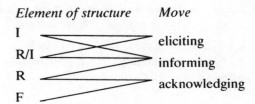

Element of structure   Move

This shows, for example, that an eliciting move may realize I or R/I but not R. This is, of course, consistent with the predictive nature of the eliciting move (see pp. 145–9 below): it must realize a predictive element of structure.

The informing move is of particular importance in the Sinclair–Coulthard system because of the assertion that 'exchanges are basically concerned with the transmission of information' (Coulthard and Montgomery, 1981:99). Exceptions to this are the Organizational exchanges, which are concerned with the organization of a conversation rather than its content, and certain Direct exchanges.[4]

The other exchanges, however (Elicit, the three bound-Elicits, and Inform), are seen as 'information units' and must contain an obligatory informing move at the appropriate 'slot': I R/I or R. It follows that the structure

| eliciting | I |
| acknowledging | R |

is impermissible, even though it may appear to be a theoretical possibility. How, then, are we to interpret the following exchange, where an eliciting move is acknowledged but no information is given?

Example 11	*move*	*e.s*
Interviewer: How do you intend to achieve this?	eliciting	I
Politician: That's a very interesting question	acknow-ledging	R

Intuition here seems to accord with theory in classing this exchange as deviant, and so we reject the analysis given above. Rather, the second utterance is in fact the pre-head of an informing move. If no *informative* occurs as head of the move, both the move and the exchange are incomplete. The analysis would look like this:

	act	*e.s*	*move*	*e.s*	*exch*
Interviewer: How do you intend to achieve this?	inq	h	eliciting	I	Elicit (incomp)
Politician: That's a very interesting question	s	pre-h	(informing)	R	

Whilst it is essential for an exchange to contain an informing move, that move cannot occur at F. Consider the following exchange from our data:

Example 12	*act*	*e.s*	*move*	*e.s*	*exch*
15 A: Well	m	s	eliciting	I	Elicit
your alarm clock doesn't seem to work	m.pr	h			
B: No it did	rej	h	informing	R	
I think I turned it off	com	post-h			
A: Mm	ter	h	acknow-ledging	F	
It's you that doesn't work	com	post-h			

As the utterance 'It's you that doesn't work' is not heard as the start of a new exchange (on the grounds of intonation) it cannot be classed as informing, and this would remain the case even if there were no preceding move head as there is here.

To turn to acknowledging moves, these can occur at R or F, but they cannot initiate an exchange or occur at R/I. This is consistent with the concept of the exchange as a unit in which information is transmitted: the acknowledging move is seen as a response or a reaction to the information. There is, then, no 'Acknowledge' exchange to parallel Elicit and Inform.

Given the acknowledging move's special status in this respect, we also see that it is the only move which may occur at two places in the I R F exchange, that is at *both* R and F of the same exchange. This is unique because neither the eliciting move nor the informing move can occur at both I and R unless an R/I element is also present (see the diagram on p. 141). It should be noted that when an I R F exchange consists of the three moves

informing	I
acknowledging	R
acknowledging	F

only the first acknowledging move is predicted (see p. 136). The third move is unpredicted, or entirely optional, and is therefore coded as F. An example from our data is:

Example 13	*act*	*e.s*	*move*	*e.s*	*exch*
41 B: Especially when the Chinese opera turned out to be (#) er a group of Chinese madrigal singers or something	obs	h	informing	I	Inform
A: If it was	ref	h	acknow-ledging	R	
B: (laugh) Wh-whatever	end	h	acknow-ledging	F	

Returning now to eliciting and informing moves, we note that although it is not permissible for the same move to realize two elements of structure in an I R F exchange, once the element R/I is introduced further possibilities come into play. Indeed, as there are only three moves (leaving aside the Direct exchange) it is clear that one move will have to be repeated, since acknowledging cannot occur at R/I. The following are examples from our data of exchanges with two informing or two eliciting moves.

Informing moves at I and R:

Example 14

		act	e.s	move	e.s	exch
21	A: I mean you know it's not (laugh) important it's just er a peculiar physical fact that helium yesterday was lighter than air and today it's heavier	i	h	informing	I	Inform
	B: Really?	m.pr	h	eliciting	R/I	
	A: Yeah (high key)	conf	h	informing	R	
	isn't that weird	com	post-h			

Eliciting moves at I and R/I:

Example 15

	act	e.s	move	e.s	exch
46 B: Sorry what was that?	l	h	eliciting	I^b	Repeat
A: Can I – I'll talk to you when I get there	m.pr	h	eliciting	R/I	
B: Yeah (mid key)	conc	h	informing	R	

If the exchange is to have definable limits, however, there must be restrictions on how these moves may be realized. We find Coulthard and Brazil's rules based on a distinction between e_1, i_1 (seeking or asserting major information) and e_2, i_2 (seeking or asserting polarity) (Coulthard and Montgomery 1981:101) unhelpful here, and we prefer to formulate the restrictions in terms of acts. Basically we state that if there are two eliciting or two informing moves in one exchange, their heads must be realized by different acts. (The only exception is discussed below and exemplified in Example (18).) An Inform exchange, for example, may begin with an *informative* and then have a *concur, confirm, qualify* or *reject* realizing a later informing move head. Example (14) above contains both an *informative* and a *confirm*. Similarly an Elicit exchange beginning with, say, an *inquire* may also contain a *neutral* or *marked proposal*. The following invented example illustrates the phenomenon:

Example 16

	act	e.s	move	e.s	exch
A: (doing crossword puzzle) What's an anagram of 'clay paste'?	inq	h	eliciting	I	Elicit
B: Could it be 'catalepsy'?	n.pr	h	eliciting	R/I	
A: Yes that seems to fit	conf	h	informing	R	

Finally, a bound-Elicit exchange may have a *return, loop* or *prompt* realizing the head of an eliciting move at I^b; a further eliciting move will be allowed within the same exchange because its head will be realized by an *inquire* or a *neutral* or *marked proposal*.

Example (15) above contains both a *loop* and a *marked proposal*. Examples (14) and (15) above illustrate the most common occurrences of the structural element R/I, i.e. it tends to occur in Inform and bound-Elicit exchanges. (It is also common in primary knower initiated Elicit exchanges, which are discussed in the next section.)

There is, however, a further possibility: an exchange in which the act *informative* does occur twice, but where the occurrences can be distinguished from each other in terms of the lexical items which realize them. According to our definitions, an *informative* may be realized in two ways:

(a) an assertion of major information, such as would be elicited by a wh-question. It may occur at I or at R.
(b) an assertion of polarity in answer to a *neutral proposal*. It occurs at R. Polarity answers to *marked proposals* are coded *concur*, *confirm*, *qualify* or *reject*, depending on whether and how far they confirm the underlying presuppositions of the proposal. A *neutral proposal*, which expects no particular answer, contains no such presuppositions, or at least not overtly. We therefore take *informative* to be the more appropriate coding. An example of this sort of informative is:

Example 17	*act*
B: Are you still in NS	n.pr
A: No	i

We propose that an exchange may contain one of each type of *informative*, for example:

Example 18	*act*	*e.s*	*move*	*e.s*
A: It's red	i	h	informing	I
B: Dark red?	n.pr	h	eliciting	R/I
A: Yes	i	h	informing	R

In exchange and move terms, therefore, this is coded in the same way as:

Example 19	*act*	*e.s*	*move*	*e.s*
A: It's red	i	h	informing	I
B: Dark red I suppose	m.pr	h	eliciting	R/I
A: Yes (mid key)	conc	h	informing	R

PREDICTABILITY AND THE EXCHANGE

The elements of structure of the exchange, I, R/I, R and F, are defined by Coulthard and Brazil in terms of predictablity. The definitions may be summarized as follows:

	Predictive	Predicted
I	+	−
R/I	+	+
R	−	+
F	−	−

In subsequent discussions, however, the notion of predictability has been associated with the closely related concept of obligatory/optional. Making the same association, we state the rules as follows:

(a) I is always obligatory and predictive;
(b) As I is predictive it must be followed by R/I or R;
(c) If R/I occurs it must be followed by R;
(d) F is always optional.

The above rules raise two problems for analysts. Firstly, the following typical classroom exchange can no longer be coded in the 'traditional' manner:

Example 20	*move*	*e.s*
T: What's this?	eliciting	I
P: A saw	informing	R
T: Yes, it's a saw	acknowledging	F

The third utterance in this exchange cannot be F, as F is by definition always optional/unpredicted yet the acknowledging move of a teacher-initiated Elicit exchange is obligatory/predicted in that pupils expect to be told whether their answers are 'right' or not (Sinclair and Coulthard 1975:51).

We approach this problem through the following reasoning. Any Elicit exchange which is initiated by a primary knower must consist of at least three parts. This is consistent with Berry and with the Sinclair and Coulthard (1975) notion of a Teacher-Elicit exchange. As the third part is obligatory it must be predicted by the second part. The structure of the Elicit exchange of Example (20) is therefore I R/I R, with the moves remaining the same as in the Example. This correspondence between moves and elements of exchange structure is indicated in the diagram on p. 141 above.

The second problem is that if R is predicted it cannot be optional. In other words, the structure I (R) is a contradiction in terms. Unfortunately, this suggests that Berry's example, reproduced below, is an incomplete exchange:

Example 21
Guide (conducting party round cathedral): Salisbury is the English cathedral with the tallest spire
(Coulthard and Montgomery 1981:126)

Such one-part exchanges are frequently found, yet if I is predicting, the exchange must be two-part. Neither is it possible to propose that I is not predicting where it is realized by an informing move. Apart from the theoretical difficulties this would raise (F and I would become indistinguishable), it is counter-intuitive in examples such as the following (from our data) where the exchange is heard as incomplete:

Example 22

	move	e.s
A: I mean nothing could have	informing	I
happened to it (high termination)		

We propose that under normal circumstances the minimum number of moves in an exchange (other than a Boundary exchange – see above, p. 136) is two. In other words, R is obligatory whatever the exchange type. This is because both participants are obliged to give evidence of taking part in the conversation (assuming of course that it is a dialogue as opposed to a multi-party conversation), and, specifically, of listening or 'paying attention' to each other. This may be argued informally as follows. If speaker A volunteers information 'out of the blue', she needs confirmation that B has heard her, and has absorbed the information. The information must therefore be acknowledged. If, on the other hand, speaker B as secondary knower elicits a piece of information from speaker A, it is obvious that B is listening for an answer and therefore the information need not actually be acknowledged for the exchange to be well-formed. In other words, an informing move at I must be followed by an acknowledging move at R, whereas an identical informing move at R, following an eliciting move at I, does not predict an acknowledging move at F. This explains why the utterance

Example 23

A: Geoff rang	I

is incomplete, needing the acknowledgement

B: Oh thanks	R

whereas

B: Any messages	I
A: Geoff rang	R

is complete. An additional

B: Oh (thanks)	F

is polite but optional.

There are, however, two circumstances under which the predicted R may not occur, yet the exchange remains complete. The first is where one of the participants (or group of people) has curtailed speaking rights and, moreover, is assumed to be listening and absorbing information simply by being present. The obligation to provide acknowledgement has been suspended by an unspoken agreement under the terms of which one participant in the conversation is the speaker and the other is the listener. This listener's role is institutionalized for school pupils, for example, who are not expected continually to acknowledge the teacher's informing moves. In the case of tourists being given information by a guide (as in Example (21) above) the state is a temporary and optional one.

The second circumstance in which an exchange is complete even though the predicted R is not realized is when the R part is implied by what precedes it and what follows. This is discussed in full on pp. 152–6 below, but we include an example here by way of illustration:

Example 24
A: Oh hold on I've got to get the extension hold on

This realizes the opening move of a Structuring exchange (see p. 137 above), which in theory requires an answering move at R. As the utterance is a *metastatement*, however, and as the silence or 'holding on' which follows is taken as an accepting sort of silence, an *acquiesce* occurring at R is coded even though it is unrealized by an utterance. It is for this reason that we extended the definition of *acquiesce* to include silence (see p. 129 above).

There remains one fundamental difficulty which analysts face and which is inherent in the definitions of elements of structure in terms of predictability. As the table on p. 146 shows, both F and I are unpredicted. If there is a secondary knower eliciting move at I we can predict that what will follow will be an informing move at R (leaving aside for the moment the possibility of R/I). It is this, of course, which predisposes us to hear the utterance following a question as an answer, if at all possible. After that, however, we can make no predictions and cannot tentatively code in advance as we can with R. What follows may be an acknowledging move at F or a new initiation. This 'third' contribution may be an eliciting move, identified either by its form as in exchange (14) of our data, or because it is heard thus by the other participant as in exchange (11). In this case there is no problem, as the move must be coded as I. (It should be noted, however, that where the coding depends upon how an utterance is interpreted by the other participant (as in exchange 11), it is carried out retrospectively.) If the 'third' contribution is not an eliciting move, however, the coding decision is based entirely on the content and/or intonation of the utterance. It often happens in casual conversation that the utterance following the answer to a question is a 'comment' or an 'observation' which is indeterminate between an acknowledging move at F and an informing move initiating a new exchange. An example from our data is:

Example 25

36	A:	(laugh) What do you mean good exercise it	I[b]
	B:	(laugh) I mean walking round looking for the fair was exercise	R
	A:	Yeah my feet hurt	F? I?

(Actually we decided to code it as F)

As the 'third' utterance is one tone unit, which means there can be no exchange boundary within it, the problem of indeterminacy remains unsolved and a decision must be taken by the analyst. Similar problems are discussed in the next section.

DOUBLE LABELLING

One criticism often levelled at the Sinclair–Coulthard system is that it assumes that each utterance or part of an utterance has one and only one function (e.g. Open University 1981:23). So each act must be either, say, a *qualify* or an *informative*, a move must be either eliciting or acknowledging, and so on. Yet, the critics claim, in practice a single act or move can perform two functions at once.

The system as amended in Coulthard and Brazil (1981) does allow for an element of structure which is both predicted and predicting: R/I. In a sense this represents a dual function. At the ranks of move and act, however, such double labelling is not used. The utterance is coded according to its 'dominant' function. In the following made-up examples, we may code the third utterance as R/I but must decide between eliciting and informing at the rank of move.

Example 26	*move*	*e.s*
A: What's the time?	eliciting	I
B: What?	eliciting	I[b]
A: What's the time?	eliciting	R/I
B: Four o'clock	informing	R

If the third utterance is not structurally or intonationally an interrogative, the moves are re-coded as follows (although 'yes' is both a statement and a question):

Example 27	*move*	*e.s*
A: What's the time?	eliciting	I
B: The time?	eliciting	I[b]
A: Yes	informing	R/I
B: Four o'clock	informing	R

(Note that the various eliciting and informing moves in these exchanges are realized by different acts. The exchanges therefore satisfy the criteria laid down on p. 144.)

The above problem is relatively simple as it involves labelling within the exchange. A more severe difficulty arises when an utterance which appears to have a dual function occurs at the boundary between one exchange and another. This frequently happens in casual conversation where participants may produce a string of utterances, each one simultaneously responding to what has gone before and initiating something new. Wells *et al.* (1981) suggest that such exchanges can be seen as overlapping, with the linking utterances realizing simultaneously the second element of one exchange and the first element of the next. Below are some examples from our data and that of our students, analysed using chained exchanges after the Wells model. (Other Wells innovations are not used. Wells would label the moves Solicit, Give and Acknowledge and does not use the notation R/I.)

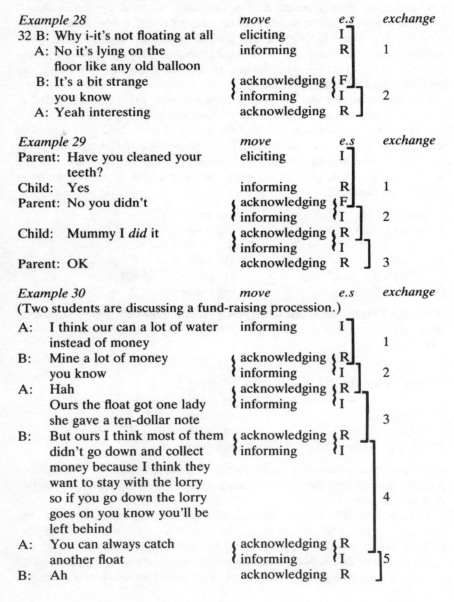

Example 28	move	e.s	exchange
32 B: Why i-it's not floating at all	eliciting	I	
A: No it's lying on the floor like any old balloon	informing	R	1
B: It's a bit strange you know	acknowledging / informing	F / I	2
A: Yeah interesting	acknowledging	R	

Example 29	move	e.s	exchange
Parent: Have you cleaned your teeth?	eliciting	I	
Child: Yes	informing	R	1
Parent: No you didn't	acknowledging / informing	F / I	2
Child: Mummy I *did* it	acknowledging / informing	R / I	
Parent: OK	acknowledging	R	3

Example 30   move   e.s   exchange
(Two students are discussing a fund-raising procession.)

		move	e.s	exchange
A:	I think our can a lot of water instead of money	informing	I	1
B:	Mine a lot of money you know	acknowledging / informing	R / I	2
A:	Hah Ours the float got one lady she gave a ten-dollar note	acknowledging / informing	R / I	3
B:	But ours I think most of them didn't go down and collect money because I think they want to stay with the lorry so if you go down the lorry goes on you know you'll be left behind	acknowledging / informing	R / I	4
A:	You can always catch another float	acknowledging / informing	R / I	5
B:	Ah	acknowledging	R	

Analyses of this type satisfy the intuition that exchanges are linked together in a way that rigidly-defining horizontal lines between them tend to mask. Such a solution, however, wreaks havoc with a hierarchical system of analysis. For the exchange to be a unit which will combine with other exchanges to form larger units, or transactions, it must have clearly defined boundaries and there must be limits on what it can contain. Otherwise it is impossible to apply the notion of rank scale to ordinary spoken discourse. Although our data includes sequences which can be analysed like Examples (28)–(30), these are relatively rare, and the analysis which is more in accord with the Sinclair–Coulthard system is at least equally satisfactory.

Another motivation that may lead the analyst to see a need for double labelling is that an utterance may have a significance for the conversation as a whole which is not captured by the restricted nomenclature of act, move and exchange. An example from our data is:

Example 31
A: Oh (#) no we were just leaving actually
B: Oh

The long-term function of this exchange is to limit the overall length of the conversation: A warns B that the time available is short and that any important matter should be raised at once.

The Sinclair–Coulthard system of analysis, however, approaches discourse on a moment-by-moment basis. Each utterance is classified in terms of its effect on the immediately following utterances. As the exchange of Example (31) has no immediate effect upon the limits of the conversation it can be classified only as 'Inform'. Its larger-scale significance remains uncoded.

Similarly, the Sinclair–Coulthard system codes utterances in terms of their effect on the discourse only, not upon the participants in that discourse. Observers of interaction know that, for example, the answer to a question may have a significance far in excess of its role as the realization of an informing move at R. In the following utterances, B's responses may be classified as a joke, a mild insult, and an expression of affection respectively.

Example 32
(A proselytizer (A) at a bus-stop attempting to convert a bystander (B))
A: Where will you stand on Judgement Day?
B: Still here I expect, waiting for the number 11 bus

Example 33
A: Do you have the time?
B: There's a clock right in front of your eyes – says ten to four doesn't it

Example 34
A: Will you hold my bag?
B: For you my love I'd hold an elephant

Such classifications reflect a concern with the relationship between the participants in the conversation rather than with the structure of the conversation itself. It is worth noting, however, that conversations have many dimensions, all of which are important. Only one of these dimensions is captured in a description of the structure of discourse.

INCOMPLETE EXCHANGES AND IMPLIED ELEMENTS

Where a predicted element of an exchange is missing, the exchange must be classified as incomplete. Example (35) is a list of the incomplete exchanges which occur in various places in our data:

		e.s	exchange
Example 35			
(i) 3 B: Hello		I	Greet (incomplete)
(ii) 6 A: Hello		I	Greet (incomplete)
(iii) 9 A: So I've got to get him off to school		I	Inform (incomplete)
(iv) 18 A: Why doesn't it float any more		I	Elicit (incomplete)
(v) 20 B: What do you mean it doesn't		I^b	Clarify (incomplete)
(vi) 22 B: What do you mean it doesn't float any more		I^b	Re-initiation (incomplete)
(vii) 23 A: I mean nothing could have happened to it		I	Inform (incomplete)
(viii) 24 A: But I			(incomplete)
(ix) 40 A: Still Ben had a nice time.		I	Inform (incomplete)
(x) 48 A: Bye-bye		I	Greet (incomplete)

Two types of apparent omission from this list need to be explained. Firstly exchanges which appear incomplete but which are followed by bound exchanges, such as exchange (27), are not coded as incomplete. The second apparent omission is the following:

Example 36	act	e.s	move	e.s	exchange
34 A: Anyway look	fr	pre-h	informing	I	Inform
I have to be off OK	i	h			

Here, the R part of the exchange would seem to be 'missing', but we do not consider this to be the case. Our line of reasoning runs in this way. If the exchange were taken in isolation, it would be classified as a Structuring exchange:

Example 37	act	e.s	move	e.s	exchange
34 A: Anyway look	fr	pre-h	opening	I	Structuring
I have to be off OK	ms	h			
B: ∅	(acq)	h	(answering)	R	

In isolation this Structuring exchange would begin the pre-closing sequence of the conversation. In our data however, the organizational function of the exchange is ignored (by the speaker herself). We therefore treat it as having been 'pushed down' to the level of an ordinary Inform exchange. The only unit that cannot be 'pushed down' is the *framer*, which is lexically defined, but it must be noted that in normal circumstances a *framer* cannot realize the pre-head of a move at I in any but a Structuring exchange. Because it has been 'pushed down', then, we do not consider the exchange as incomplete. (Sinclair and Coulthard (1975:35) apply the concept of 'pushing down' at act level only; here we have extended it to the exchange and thus to all ranks lower than the exchange.)

Leaving these apparent anomalies aside, then, we may turn to instances of exchanges where an unrealized element is 'heard' as being present. The exchange structure of the first example has been altered in accordance with the decision discussed above (p. 146).

Example 38	act	e.s	move	e.s exchange
T: What's this?	inq	h	eliciting	I Elicit
P: It's a saw	i	h	informing	R/I
T: ∅	(rec)	h	(acknowledging)	R
— — — — — — —	— —	—	— — — — —	— — — — —
T: NV	inq	h	eliciting	I[b] Re-initiation
P2: A hacksaw	i	h	informing	R/I
T: Yes it's a hacksaw	rec	h	acknowledging	R
(mid key)				

Note: We choose *receive* as the implied act here simply because, as a mid-key item, it can be seen as encapsulating the concept of 'acknowledging'.

In this example, then, the lack of an acknowledging move in the first exchange is heard as a negative evaluation, which in turn implies that the question is recycled. We may therefore say that the R part of the first exchange is 'there' although it is unrealized. (The exchange would not, of course, have been considered incomplete in any case, since it is followed by a bound exchange.)

In an Elicit exchange initiated by a primary knower, then, the third part of the exchange will be taken as present, even if it is unrealized, if the institutional situation allows this. The classroom situation is a classic example. Whether the unrealized acknowledging move is heard as representing positive or negative evaluation will depend on teaching style and on the utterance following the unrealized move. In some classrooms the pupils are wrong unless told they are right, in other classrooms vice versa. In the following example the obligatory but unstated evaluation at the end of the first exchange is clearly positive:

Example 39

	act	e.s	move	e.s	exchange
T: What kind of bonding does it have	inq	h	eliciting	I	Elicit
P: Ionic	i	h	informing	R/I	
T: 0	(rec)	h	acknowledging	R	
T: Will it conduct	n.pr	h	eliciting	I	Elicit
P: Yes	i	h	informing	R/I	
T: Yes (mid-key)	rec	h	acknowledging	R	

This argument, that an obligatory element of exchange structure may be coded as present, although unrealized (unless what follows contradicts this interpretation), has already been used in our discussion of the guide and the tourist group (Example (21)) and of 'Oh hold on I've got to get the extension hold on' (Example (24)). It is interesting to speculate how much further this principle of implied elements of exchange structure may be taken. The following examples occurred in our students' data:

Example 40

(A customer (A) is attempting to negotiate a lower price with a shop assistant (B))

	act	e.s	move	e.s	exchange
B: Actually the cost price for this it should be ten seventy we selling you see actually we don't earn much from the customer we need to have more customer	i	h	informing	I	Inform
A: 0	(rec)	h	(acknowledging)	R	
A: Then how is it NTUC is selling at fifty you see	inq	h	eliciting	I	Elicit
B: No because for the meantime ah they calling in more you see	i	h	informing	R	

Example 41
(Two students are discussing their experiences while taking part in a procession)

	act	e.s	move	e.s.	exchange
A: My lorry was in very bad condition know got a hole in the centre know y'know there was a hole in the centre	i	h	informing	I	Inform
B: Ø	(rec)	H	(acknowledging)	R	

B: Mine mine was the passenger lorry not the actual float	i	h	(informing)	I	Inform

Example 42

	act	e.s	move	e.s	exchange
Child: Mummy can I put my shoes on?	n.pr	h	eliciting	I	Elicit
Parent: Ø	(i)	h	(informing)	R	

Parent: What your big ones?	m.pr	h	eliciting	I	Elicit
Child: Yes (high key)	conf	h	informing	R	

It seems, then, that there are certain circumstances in which a missing, obligatory element of structure is implied or 'understood'. Those suggested so far are:

  (i) the acknowledging move in a primary knower initiated Elicit exchange;
 (ii) the answering move in a Structuring exchange;
(iii) the acknowledging move in an Inform exchange;
(iv) the informing move in an Elicit exchange where the head of the eliciting move is realized by a *neutral* or *marked proposal*.

The advantage of the 'implied element approach is that it concurs with the intuition that nothing is missing in the exchanges cited above (Examples (38)–(42)), without involving the resort to double labelling (see pp. 149–52 above) to show the coherence of a conversation. It is of course necessary to allow, however, that a certain coding may be tentative until confirmed or contradicted by what follows. The unrealized elements are 'understood' *if and only if* what follows in the discourse is consistent with that interpretation.

This principle of 'consistency' is a useful one for discourse analysis. In addition to the points made above we have also suggested that a *framer* will indicate a transaction boundary if and only if what follows is consistent with this interpretation (see p. 128 above where the *framer* is defined, and pp. 139–40, where transactions and their boundaries are discussed). Such tentativeness seems to us to reflect the negotiable status of any discourse category. Whatever act or move an utterance appears to realize, it is always subject to reclassification in the light of subsequent contributions by other participants. This indeterminacy in turn reflects the ambiguous position of the discourse analyst, who is neither A nor B, and who stands both inside and outside the conversation.

We leave the reader with two concluding points, the first of which is that many of the concepts we have discussed above remain sadly undeveloped: the concept of information-transmission as being the defining property of an exchange (and the consequent problems raised by Structuring and, crucially, Direct exchanges); the question of dual function and double labelling; and the whole area of inexplicitness raised by the positing of implicit elements of exchange structure. All these areas are in need of further clarification.

Our second concluding point is that this article is not intended to be definitive. The system of analysis described above is flexible; new acts, moves and exchanges can be added as the need arises, so long as such new additions are sufficiently generalizable and so long as the basic theoretical principles of Sinclair and Coulthard (1975) are adhered to. Much work also needs to be done on the ranks above the exchange. If, however, the reader as analyst wishes to abandon these theoretical principles (for example the rank scale, following Wells *et al.* (1981)) we suggest that he/she needs to think in terms of constructing an alternative description which would account for the data of everyday conversation in a more satisfactory way. We are not claiming that it cannot be done. All that we can say is that while the Sinclair–Coulthard system has its critics, very few of them have attempted to suggest viable alternatives. To suggest, as some do, that everyday conversation cannot be subjected to linguistic analysis is not a solution.

SAMPLE ANALYSIS: A TELEPHONE CONVERSATION

Note: The first column headed 'e.s' gives the element of move structure realized by the preceding act, and the second column headed 'e.s' gives the element of exchange structure realized by the preceding move. The last two columns number the exchanges and the transactions respectively. A single line indicates an exchange boundary, a broken line indicates that the next exchange is bound-Elicit, and double lines indicate a transaction boundary. Pauses are timed in parenthesis; (#) indicates a pause of less than one second. Laughter is shown by (la).

line of dialogue		act	e.s	move	e.s	exch	ex	tr
1	(telephone rings)	sum	h	opening	I	Summon	I	1
2	A: Hello	re-sum	h	answering	R			
3	B: Hello	gr	h	opening	I	Greet (incomplete)	2	
4	A: Oh hold on I've got to					Structuring	3	
5	get the extension hold on	ms	h	opening	I			
6	B: ∅	(aqu)	h	(answering)	R			
7	(20)							
8	A: Hello?	gr	h	opening	I	Greet (incomplete)	4	
9	(1)							
10	A: Hello?	gr	h	opening	I	Greet	5	
		gr	h	opening	I			
11	(1.5)							
12	B: Yeah hello	re-gr	h	answering	R			
13	A: Hello?	gr	h	opening	I	Greet (incomplete)	6	
14	Oh (#)	m	s	informing	I	Inform	7	
15	no we were just	i	h					
16	leaving actually							
17	B: Oh (mid key)	rec	h	acknowl	R			
18	Why (#)	s	pre-h	eliciting	I	Elicit	8	
19	did you wake up late today	n.pr	h					
20	A: Yeah pretty late	qu	h	informing	R			
21	B: Oh dear	end	h	acknowl	F			
22	A: So I've got to get	i	h	informing	I	Inform (incomplete)	9	
23	him off to school							
24	How are you anyway Danny[5]	inq	h	eliciting	I	Elicit	10	2
25	B: All right	i	h	informing	R			
26	A: You all right	ret	h	eliciting	I[b]	Clarify	11	
27	B: Uh-huh (mid key)	conc	h	informing	R			
28	A: Yeah?	ret	h	eliciting	I[b]	Clarify	12	
29	B: Mm (mid key)	conc	h	informing	R			
30	A: You got home all right? (#)	s	pre-h	eliciting	I	Elicit	13	
31	you weren't too tired?	m.pr	h					
32	B: Well er (2)	m	s		R			
33	I got up pretty late myself	i	h	informing				
34	I mean I – I was	com	post-h					
35	supposed to get							
36	up at about seven o'clock							

37	A:	What d'you mean	ret	h	eliciting	I[b]	Clarify	14	
38		you were supposed to							
39	B:	Well I had the alarm	i	h	informing	R			
40		clock on for seven							
41	A:	Hah (low key)	ter	h	acknowl	F			
42		Well	m	s	eliciting	I	Elicit	15	
43		your alarm clock doesn't							
44		seem to work	m.pr	h					
45	B:	No it did	rej	h	inform	R			
46		I think I turned it off	com	post-h					
47	A:	Mm (low key)	ter	h	acknowl	F			
48		It's you that doesn't work	com	post-h					
49	A:	Hey Danny	sum	h	opening	I	Summon	16	3
50	B:	Yeah	re-sum	h	answering	R			
51	A:	You know we bought Ben that	ms	h	opening	I	Structuring	17	
52		helium balloon							
53	B:	Yeah	acq	h	answering	R			
54	A:	Why doesn't it float any	inq	h	eliciting	I	Elicit	18	
55		more (1.5)						(incomplete)		
56		It doesn't float any more	i	h	informing	I	Inform	19	
57	B:	What do you mean	ret	h	eliciting	I[b]	Clarify	20	
58		it doesn't float						(incomplete)		
59	A:	I mean you know it's not	i	h	informing	I	Inform	21	
60		(la) important it's just er								
61	B:	What do you mean it	inq	h	eliciting	I[b]	Re-	22[6]	
62		doesn't float any more						initiation		
63		a peculiar physical fact that								
64		helium yesterday was lighter than								
65		air and today it's heavier								
66	B:	Really?	m.pr	h	eliciting	R/I			
67	A:	Yeah (high key)	conf	h	informing				
68		isn't that weird	com	post-h				R		
69		I mean nothing could have	i	h	informing	I	Inform	23	
70		happened to it (high ter)						(incomplete)		
71		(3)								
72		But i-						(incomplete)	24	
73	B:	Well	m	s	eliciting	I	Elicit	25	
74		unless they *weren't* using	m.pr	h						
75		helium								
76	A:	They were	rej	h	informing	R			
77		I saw them fill it	com	post-h						
78	B:	It was written helium that	m.pr	h	eliciting	I	Elicit	26[7]	
79		he -er that was what was								
80		written on the um &								
81	A:	No	rej	h	informing	R			

82		but I mean –		(uncodable)					
83	B:	& on the tank or something							

84	A:	Well what *was* it then	inq	h	eliciting	I	Elicit	27

85	B:	Sorry?	L	h	eliciting	I^b	Repeat	28
86	A:	What *was* it then	inq	h	eliciting	R/I		
87	B:	I don't know you know	s	pre-h	informing	R		
88		I mean I'm just trying to						
89		work out and see I I mean it						
90		could be *anything* wh-						
91		helium doesn't get converted	i	h				

92	A:	What?	L	h	eliciting	I^b	Repeat	29
93		I can't hear you at all	com	post-h				
94	B:	Well helium doesn't get	i	h	informing	R		
95		converted erm you know lying						
96		just lying around						
97	A:	That's what I would have	end	h	acknowl	F		
98		thought too						

99	B:	I mean unless you're thinking about something	i	h	informing	I	Inform	30
100		that undergoes a reaction						
101		and er you						

102	A:	What?	L	h	eliciting	I^b	Repeat	31^8
103	B:	Well the only possibility is	s	pre-h	informing	R/I		
104		(#) I don't know er er unless						
105		it's some (#) some gas that	i	h				
106		undergoes a reaction and						
107		is converted to something						
108		else I mean er er &						
109	A:	Obviously must be	end	h	acknowl	F		
110		cos it's now converted +	com	post-h				
111	B:	& but I can't figure						
112		out what it could be						
113	A:	+ into something heavy						

114	B:	Why i-it's not floating	m.pr	h	eliciting	I	Elicit	32
115		at all						
116	A:	No (mid key) (#)	conc	h	informing	R		
117		It's lying on the floor	com	post-h				
118		like any old balloon						
119		(1)						

120	B:	It's a bit *strange* you know	obs	h	informing	I	Inform	33
121	A:	Yeah interesting (#)	ref	h	acknowl	R		

122		Anyway look	fr	pre-h	informing	I	Inform	$34^9 4$
123		I have to be off OK (#)	i	h				

124		Did you enjoy last night (high key)	n.pr	h	eliciting	I	Elicit	35 5
125	B:	Er well	m	s	informmg	R		
126		it was pretty good exercise	qu	h				

127	A:	(la) What do you mean	ret	h	eliciting	I[b]	Clarify	36
128		good exercise it						
129	B:	(la) I mean walking round	i	h	informing	R		
130		looking for the fair was						
		exercise						
131	A:	Yeah my *feet* hurt	end	h	acknowl	F		

132		Looking for the what?	ret	h	eliciting	I[b]	Clarify	37
133	B:	Looking for the fair	i	h	informing	R		
134	A:	Mm	(eng)					
135	B:	the trade fair or						
136		whatever it was						
137	A:	Mm	(eng)					
138	B:	autumn something fair						
139	A:	Yeah (mid key)	rec	h	acknowl	F		

140		We we don't walk enough	obs	h	informing	I	Inform	38
141		my feet really hurt (2)						
142	B:	Mm (low key)	ter	h	acknowl	R		

| 143 | | Yeah bit of a let-down | obs | h | informing | I | Inform | 39 |
| 144 | A: | Mm (mid key) | rec | h | acknowl | R | | |

| 145 | | Still Ben had a nice time | obs | h | informing | I | Inform (incomplete) | 40 |

146	B:	Especially when the Chinese opera	obs	h	informing	I	Inform	41
147		turned out to be (#) er a						
148		group of Chinese madrigal						
149		singers or something						
150	A:	If it was	ref	h	acknowl	R		
151	B:	(la) Wh-whatever	end	h	acknowl	F		

152	A:	OK	fr	pre-h	opening	I	Structuring	42 6
153		Danny I must go	ms	h				
154	B:	∅	(acq)	h	(answering)	R		

155	A:	Look	m	s	eliciting	I	Elicit	43
156		I'll – can I talk to you	m.pr	h				
157		later on this morning						
158	B:	Yeah OK (mid key)	conc	h	informing	R		
159		sure (low key)	conc	post-h				

| 160 | A: | Is that OK | ret | h | eliciting | I[b] | Clarify | 44 |

| 161 | | Hah? | p | h | eliciting | I[b] | Re-initiate | 45 |

162	B:	Sorry what was that	L	h	eliciting	I[b]	Repeat	46
163	A:	Can I –	m.pr	h	eliciting	R/I		
164		I'll talk to you when I						
165		get there						
166	B:	Yeah (mid key)	conc	h	informing	R		

| 167 | A: | I must go now | ms | h | opening | I | Structuring | 47 7 |
| 168 | B: | OK | acq | h | answering | R | | |

| 169 | A: | Bye-bye | gr | h | opening | I | Greet (incomplete) | 48 |

| 170 | B: | Well have a nice day | gr | h | opening | I | Greet | 49 |
| 171 | A: | Thank you | re-gr | h | answering | R | | |

| 172 | | Bye-bye | gr | h | opening | I | Greet | 50 |
| 173 | B: | Bye | re-gr | h | answering | R | | |

NOTES

1 It also seems possible that Structuring, Greet and Summon exchanges may contain the elements of structure R/I and F. Since we have not encountered an example, however, we simply state this as a possibility.

2 It qualifies as a transaction in spite of the fact that it has no exchange realizing the M element, which we have categorized as obligatory. It is possible that a sub-class of transactions, consisting of those which open and close whole conversations, is needed. These would have no obligatory M element.

3 It is possible that Hasan's (1984) concept of GSP may offer a way of representing the structure of an Interaction.

4 The concept of the exchange as a unit for the transmission of information seems to us to be far from unproblematic. For example, in some Direct exchanges a directing move predicts a behaving move, which is analogous to an eliciting move predicting an informing move. In other Direct exchanges, however, the directing move predicts an acknowledging move, no equivalent of the informing move being needed, (see pp. 135–6).

5 We see 'anyway' as an embedded framer; the identification of a transaction boundary on this basis is reinforced by considerations of topic.

6 Exchange (22) is enclosed in this way to capture the fact that B repeats his *inquire* in almost identical words (Re-initiation exchange bound to exchange 20). A, however, has already initiated a new free exchange (Inform, exchange 21) and she ignores B's contributions in exchanges (20) and (22) completely. We therefore have to see the participants as not communicating with each other at this point, creating an awkward problem for linear analysis. What eventually happens is that B abandons his question, and contributes to exchange (21), which is a complete exchange.

7 The sign '&' at the end of l.80 and the beginning of l.83 indicates that this is seen as a continuous eliciting move by B. B finishes his neutral proposal after A has spoken, but the exchange is heard as complete because A has anticipated the end of B's move and has supplied an appropriate informative at 'No' (followed by 'but I mean' which is itself uncompleted and therefore uncodable).

8 Here we have used two symbols: '&' at the end of l.108 and at the beginning eliciting move by B l.111, to indicate that this is seen as a continuous informing move by B; and '+' at the end of l.110 and the beginning of l.113, indicating a continuous acknowledging move by A. The situation is similar to that described immediately above: again the exchange is heard as complete. A and B are speaking simultaneously (a fact that we have not been able to indicate in the analysis): B is finishing his informing move while A, taking his point and anticipating its conclusion, is supplying an appropriate acknowledging move.

9 For the unusual coding of this exchange see the discussion of a similar exercise on p. 151 above.

'Analysing everyday conversation' was first published in Coulthard (1987a) *Discussing Discourse*, 107–48.

8 Inner and outer: spoken discourse in the language classroom

Jane Willis

In 1979 and 1980 I set about recording a variety of classrooms where English was being taught as a foreign language. My purpose was to develop a method of analysing and describing the language used in foreign language lessons in such a way as to enable objective comparisons to be made between the discourse resulting from different classroom activities and different teacher styles. This research, based on an adaptation and extension of the Sinclair and Coulthard (1975) model, is fully reported in J. Willis (1981). In this chapter, I shall concentrate on one basic concept in that research, which I hope will help to shed light on how language is used by teachers and students in language teaching classrooms. Implications and adaptations for the more 'communicative' classrooms of the 1990s are also discussed.

CONTENT LESSONS AND LANGUAGE LESSONS

Most classroom researchers would agree that the classroom talk of language lessons is more difficult to analyse and describe than the classroom talk of 'content' lessons. Despite the fact that there are many different ways of teaching language, most language classrooms have one thing in common: language is used for two purposes; it serves both as the subject matter of the lesson, and as the medium of instruction. It is precisely this dual role that makes language lessons difficult to describe.

The model devised by Sinclair and Coulthard (1975), later revised by Sinclair and Brazil (1982) (and outlined in this volume, Chapter 1), can be used to analyse most typical 'content' classrooms. It preserves the flow of the interaction and reveals its structure, highlighting common patternings and revealing breakdowns. As it stands, however, it does not handle the two-level structure of the mainstream language classroom.

In order to produce a clear and useful description of the structure of language-classroom discourse, it is necessary to have an analytic model which can distinguish and separate out these two uses of language, but at the same time, preserve the flow of the interaction and reveal the relationship between the two.

OUTER AND INNER

In seeking to separate out the two uses of language, and thus to clarify this two-level structure, I adopted the terms Outer and Inner, at the suggestion of Sinclair (personal communication), later described in Sinclair and Brazil (1982:23):

> The 'Outer' structure is a mechanism for controlling and stimulating utterances in the 'Inner' structure which gives formal practice in the foreign language.

In other words, the Outer structure provides the framework of the lesson, the language used to socialize, organize, explain and check, and generally to enable the pedagogic activities to take place. In some classrooms, more usually in countries where the target language is not the medium of instruction, all or most of this Outer language is in the learners' mother tongue.

The Inner language consists of the target forms of the language that the teacher has selected as learning goals. These are generally phrases, clauses or sentences, presented as target forms, quoted as examples, repeated and drilled or otherwise practised by the class, often as discrete items, the sequence of utterances bearing little or no resemblance to possible sequences in 'normal' discourse. Once they have been presented as target forms, no matter how meaningful the original illustrative situation was, they are devoid of their normal communicative value and are seen as samples of language. Widdowson (1980) alludes to this Inner discourse as 'pedagogically processed' as opposed to 'natural' language. (The Outer would be 'natural' in this sense.) It is obvious that none of this Inner level language could be in L1. If you look at Example 1 below you will see where the discourse switches from Outer to Inner and back again.

The examples that follow are taken from a lesson based on a page of pictures from Unit 17 of *Kernel Lessons Intermediate* (O'Neill *et al*. 1971). The students are adults, all quite recently arrived in Britain from a variety of countries in Africa, Europe and the Far East, and there is one married couple from Eastern Europe. In the transcript, the students speaking are referred to by the first letter of their name and the teacher by 'T'. The first example comes from the beginning of their second lesson of the morning.

The numbering of the exchanges follows the original numbering in the transcript included in J. Willis (1981), so that cross reference can be made easily. Also you can see clearly from the numbers where I have occasionally omitted an exchange; this is to avoid undue repetition, unnecessary complications or overlengthy examples.

Example 1

Outer	Inner
1 T: Let's go on where we were, shall we? On erm, page . . .	
2 T: What page is it? M: Page 98. C: Page 98. T: Page 98, yes.	
3 T: We were looking at Fred, weren't we, in bed, Fred in bed, mm.	
4 T: Erm. Let's have a look at the questions by the picture. Don't look at the writing. OK? (Non-verbal response)	
6 T: Erm, can we make the question by the picture? Look at Fred. Can you make the question, Socoop? Would you like to try that?	When Fred army
7 S: Erm. Erm. Picture number three? T: Yes.	
8 T: Look at the question by the picture.	
10 S: Erm. T: That's right.	When did Fred joined army.
11 T: Only Say it again. S: T: Yes.	When did Fred join the army When did erm Fred joined the army.

Here we see the lesson beginning on the Outer level, the teacher finding the page and establishing the picture, setting up the activity, the student checking that he has got the correct picture – all this is Outer and forms the framework for the Inner level; it is all naturally occurring language, and truly interactive.

Normal exchange structure occurs throughout: after the initial Boundary exchange (1), there is a Teacher-Elicit exchange (2), with the typical three part move structure of Teacher Initiation, Student Response, Teacher Follow-up. A further Boundary move (3) is followed by a Teacher Directive exchange (4) – an Initiation followed by a non-verbal Responding move as the students find the words by the picture.

At this point, (6), Socoop is asked to make the question, and the teacher gives him the cue words, quoted from beside the picture in the book; these cue words are an example of an utterance on the Inner level. After checking he has the right picture in (7) which is a Student Elicit, on the Outer, as it is a real question, Socoop finally responds to the teacher's Directive and forms the question – back again to the Inner.

The teacher's Follow-up 'That's right' is Outer again, but then she re-initiates, (11), correcting him, by going into the Inner, repeating the sentence, laying emphasis on the target word, 'the'. He replies on the Inner, inserting the 'the', and the teacher shows her acceptance with a Follow-up 'Yes' on the Outer.

Notice how, in (11), we have on the Inner level, as a Responding move, a form of words that looks like a question, which would usually be an Initiation, but which in fact acts as an answer. Normally, if a question is asked, in class, an answer is expected. This is certainly the case with any Initiating move on the Outer. The question here, though, in its position on the Inner, does not predict an answer; we merely expect the teacher to evaluate it as a form of words. This is one of the ways we can recognize and distinguish the Inner structure. The question that Socoop forms has no propositional content; and it is only interactive in that Socoop has complied with the teacher's directive to form a question using those words. The teacher's Follow-up, 'That's right' – when in fact the question is wrongly formed – can only be explained by understanding 'Yes, you've responded correctly by making a question, you have carried out my directive.' Her Re-Initiation beginning, 'Only when did Fred join the army' tells him there is something wrong after all, but that his mistake is an Inner mistake. He complies with her directive to say it again, and she completes the exchange with a 'Yes' as Follow-up.

Note that if you read down the Inner column, the utterances on the Inner do not form any coherent discourse on their own. They are only interactive in so far as they are related to the rest of the exchange on the Outer. They are completely dependent on the moves on the Outer for their existence. The Outer, on the other hand, can and does exist on its own, as we see from the first four exchanges in this lesson.

If you look at the exchanges which go from Outer to Inner, there is a very definite lack of propositional coherence. In real life, if someone says to you 'Look at the question by the picture', you can answer in a variety of ways: 'Yes, but why?' or 'Wow! I didn't realize it was like that' or 'No, I can't do that one either', but it would be very difficult to think of a situation where you would answer 'When did Fred join the army?' and hear the other person replying 'That's right'. In other words, the only way to make sense of such exchanges in the language classroom is to see them in terms of Outer and Inner.

This type of teacher-initiated exchange where the teacher asks the student to say some words, repeat something, make a question, all involving language used as Inner, I have labelled 'Direct:verbal' (DV for short). It is more akin to the Sinclair and Coulthard 'Teacher Direct' type of exchange (which in a content classroom would predict a non-verbal response) since it 'directs' a verbal performance from the student, whereas the 'Teacher Elicit' predicts an informative, message-oriented response. Both require a Teacher Follow-up move to complete the exchange successfully.

TWO TYPES OF INNER: DEPENDENT OR INDEPENDENT?

In addition to choral repetition and teacher controlled language practice of the type described above (Inner), some teachers ask students to do 'question and answer' type drills in pairs. Whereas the examples of Inner language above were quite definitely non-interactive on their own, and dependent on the Outer layer for their existence, in the following example we have some question and answer pair-work which is not Outer because the focus is still on the form of the words. It doesn't really matter whether the student tells the truth when replying; the important thing is that he/she gets the form correct and yet the two students are taking turns to speak and interacting in a fashion which I would call 'pseudo-interactive'. While this 'pseudo-interaction' is actually in progress, it can be temporarily independent of the Outer structure; the two students together can complete the required exchange or series of exchanges independently without teacher intervention, until they finish, at which point the teacher's Follow-up move takes the discourse back to the Outer. Sometimes, though, the teacher will offer a Follow-up move after each student move, even after the Initiation.

So now we have a system with both Inner Dependent and Inner Independent Columns (see Example 2 on p. 167).

The fourth exchange below, (45), is a very clear example of the type of exchange that ensues when the teacher asks one student to ask another student a question. In this type of exchange two responding moves are predicted, on the Inner; one in the form of a question and the other in the form of an answer. This resulting pair-interaction forms a two-move exchange on the Inner Independent, followed by a teacher Follow-up move.

This type of teacher initiated exchange I have called a 'Direct:verbal exchange', DVX for short, to show the difference between a 'Direct:verbal' which predicts one Responding move and this one, which predicts two Responding moves from two different students, a question and an answer, jointly making an exchange in its own right.

Example 2
At this point, they are practising the pattern 'like X-ing . . .'

Outer	Inner	
	Dependent	*Independent*
42 T: Ask er Constantine er	living in Cheltenham.	
43 A: (question intonation)	Cheltenham?	
T:	Cheltenham.	
That's his town.		
44 A: Er		Do you like living in Cheltenham?
C:		Yes, I do.
T: Um hm. Good.		
45 T: What about erm – ask your wife – (laughter)		
C:	washing the dishes.	Do you like -er doing dishes?
T: Mm		
V:		No I don't like, wash er dishes.
T:	doing or washing.	
Mm. (falling intonation)		
46 V: But I have to, every time!		
T: Yes, that's quite right. In fact you hate washing the dishes, but you have to do it.		

The first attempt at a DVX here, (42), broke down because Antonio did not know what the word 'Cheltenham' meant, so he initiated, repeating the word form (Inner) with a questioning intonation which gave it the inter-active force of 'Please can you explain this word?' (Outer). The teacher explained, and Antonio re-initiated himself, independently of the teacher and Constantine replied 'Yes I do'; the teacher's final Follow-up 'Um hm. Good' (Outer) shows that both have completed their part in the exchange successfully.

Exchange (45) between husband and wife on the topic of 'washing the dishes' is fair proof that the message is secondary to the form of the response; Constantine certainly did not need telling that his wife did not like washing up.

Notice that their exchange on the Inner Independent is a two-part exchange, (I R), although in real life one would have expected Constantine to make some sort of Follow-up move, perhaps just an 'Oh!'. The fact that he doesn't, underlines even more strongly the lack of real propositional content; they are producing the correct sentence forms, not actually exchanging information, so there is nothing to provoke an 'Oh!'.

With a DVX, in fact, it is expected that the teacher will regain control after the students have responded by holding their brief interaction on the Inner. It is typical that only the teacher has the right to the final Follow-up move which judges the success or otherwise of the exchange, not the student.

Exchange (46) is a good example of a student-initiated Inform type exchange, on the Outer. Here is Virginia making conversation, reacting to the topic of washing the dishes. She is not just repeating patterns of words directed by the teacher, on the Inner. She really means what she says and wants to share her ideas with the rest of the class. She goes on:

Example 3

Outer	Inner	
	Dependent	*Independent*
48 V: But in England, many husbands help er in er kitchens. T: Yes. M: Oh!		
49 V: in my country, er.		

Notice how here we have a student Follow-up move; once the discourse has moved onto the Outer with a student initiation, the rules have changed. Whereas any type of DVX requires Teacher evaluation, to judge the correctness of the form produced on the Inner, here, in a Student Inform exchange, on the Outer, there is a naturally occurring Follow-up move which reacts to the propositional content of the Informing move. Mohavi is quite obviously surprised to learn that husbands in England wash up.

And the discussion continues, the teacher using every opportunity she can to get the students to use verbs with '-ing' forms, for example drilling the pronunciation of the word 'helping', while the students are keen on escaping from the control imposed by the teacher's attempts to return to practice on the Inner.

Another example of an activity in which student interaction is coded on the Inner Independent is the interaction following the exchange type 'Direct:verbal activity' (DVA). An example follows:

Example 4

Outer	Inner	
	Dependent	*Independent*
263 T: Just have a look at the pattern on the top here. We've already been practising this.		
	Would you mind sitting there. Would you mind coming in.	
264 T: Just ask the person next to you some of those questions, could you?		
265 T: Just ask for practice, and you can answer,		
	No, not at all,	
or		
	I don't mind.	
All right?		

(Massed pair-work begins here and only two groups are recorded.)

268 S:		Would you mind coming in?
T:		No, not at all.
269 T:		Would you mind drinking tea?
S:		Not at all.
272 M:		Would you mind waiting for me?

273 A: Pardon?

    M: Would you mind
waiting for me?

    A: No, not at all.

    T: That's right.

274 T: Yes, now, . . .
       The next one. Let's
       look at the next one,
       now we've we've
       practised that.

Here, the teacher's Initiations in exchange (264), and again in (265), (266), (267), predict a whole series of exchanges, with the structure IR Exchanges such as these are called DVA because they predict a whole activity (in this case a series of Listing exchanges) on the Inner Independent. Teacher Follow-up is often withheld until the end of the series or activity, unless she happens to be listening in to one pair as they finish an exchange, as in (273). But in fact here, her Follow-up immediately precedes a Boundary exchange (274) where she draws this activity to a close to start something new.

This conversation-drill activity here is a very controlled activity. A role-play activity could be less tightly controlled, but would still be on the Inner Independent, since normally in a role play the students are given their parts, are told what they have to do, both the content of the utterances and the turn-taking system are controlled by the cues or prompts, and the outcome is often predetermined. So this too is 'pseudo-interaction' despite a surface semblance of real life. No real communication is happening, and no worlds are being changed by it.

TYPICAL PATTERNS IN LANGUAGE TEACHING SEQUENCES

Using this three-column display system, then, it proved possible to examine more closely the relationships between the Outer and Inner levels of discourse, and to identify typical patternings that occur in language teaching classrooms.

Four main patterns emerged. These I will now summarize. There are sections of lesson (in my data a 'section' was anything from 1½ minutes to 4 minutes of lesson) where:

1 Only the Outer column is used, which denotes focus on the topic and information conveyed, rather than the language itself. (This would also include organization, etc.) This of course involves interactive and communicative use of language, 'natural' (Widdowson 1980), 'truthful' (McTear 1975). In my data, but not exemplified here, there is a long discussion of the

kinds of work a chairman does, and whether schools have chairmen in Britain, as they do in America (exchanges 200–31); the teacher participates only as chairperson, not as language teacher. This is all in the Outer; no attempt is made to switch the focus to language *per se*.

2 Mainly the Outer column is used, with the brief sortie into the Inner Dependent. This denotes the occasional teacher correction or the supplying of an appropriate word or phrase to help the discourse advance. Again the emphasis is on the topic, as in (1) above, but the teacher is acting in the role of linguistic adviser as well as chairperson. This is what happens in the 'Women's work' discussion which begins in Example 2 above. (See also the following paragraph which describes how the discussion continues.) This would also be the pattern if a teacher was explaining or talking about a comprehension passage; here the focus would be mainly on the meaning; of course words would inevitably be quoted from the passage in the process and these words would be recorded as Inner.

3 Stretches of the Inner Dependent column are in fairly regular use. This reveals a focus on the language, perhaps drilling or other ELT practice techniques in action; activities which are of a non-interactive nature sometimes described as 'mechanical'. In the above lesson, there was a long section where the teacher was getting each student in turn to practise the pronunciation of the word 'months'. Each time the word 'months' was, of course, on the Inner (J. Willis 1981, exchanges 14–22).

4 Stretches of the Inner Independent column are in use, together with the Outer, and occasionally the Inner Dependent column. This shows controlled but interactive practice, 'pseudo-interaction', with the odd teacher correction or suggestion for a word or phrase. This is exemplified above, in Example 4, exchanges (265–73).

Very often a Boundary exchange, or a series of nearly consecutive Boundary exchanges, will show the division between sections such as these. No matter how 'free' the interaction gets during the course of an activity, the teacher is always empowered to produce a Boundary exchange, to terminate one activity, and to start another. Exchange (274) is a good example of a Boundary exchange (see Example 4 above).

Sometimes teachers will try to disguise a Boundary to preserve the surface cohesion of topic, while still aiming to change the direction of the lesson. An example of this presented on p. 172 comes after twenty-eight exchanges' worth of discussion on 'Women's work' which is still going strong among the students and has now got on to the subject of men being lazy; students have been trying to ignore the teacher's interruptions on the Inner, with corrections of language items, so she has to find a way to get back into the interaction. She finally does this by focusing on topic and seeming to continue the discussion:

Example 5

Outer	Inner

76 T: I think Fred is the same.
⎡Look at Fred! (high key)
V:⎣Yes.
    T: He says 'I don't like washing dishes,'
       don't you? (low termination)
77 T: Let's look at the next one . . .

Other paralinguistic features also come into play during Boundary exchanges (Kendon 1973). The teacher, who has been mostly leaning back in her chair during the discussion, now inclines her body forward towards the class and picks up the book which, during the discussion, has been lying to one side. Intonation, too, plays an important part; there is low termination in exchange (76) and high key at the beginning of (77).

Instances have also been noted of teachers regaining control by introducing Follow-up moves of an evaluative nature, in situations like discussions where students would expect at most an acknowledging type of Follow-up from the teacher. For example, a 'That's right, good, well done' ending a student-to-student exchange on the Outer, had the effect of stopping the student discussion fairly abruptly.

SOCOOP'S DILEMMA

One important question is: how can students tell whether the teacher's Initiation is intended as a Direct:verbal, i.e. a directive to use a particular form of the target language in the response, or as an Elicit, i.e. a genuine question which requires an informative, and normally truthful, answer? In other words, should the response be on the Inner or the Outer?

There is a story of a very important British Council visitor being shown round an impressive language laboratory in the Middle East. All the students are practising in their booths, and the visitor, on being shown how the teacher-console works, asks if she can listen in and talk to a student. So she puts on the headphones, presses a button, and says to the student, 'Hello, do you enjoy working in the language lab?' The response comes, 'Hello, do you enjoy working in the lang . . . er?'

So a short answer to the question above is, that sometimes students can't tell whether to answer on the Inner or the Outer. This apocryphal student had been repeating things on the Inner for so long that he did not recognize the visitor's question as being Outer . . .

The following extract from my data is particularly revealing of the sort of breakdowns that can occur when students are not sure of whether they are to reply on the Inner or Outer. The class is doing some practice with the verb 'like', and Virginia has just said that she likes being a learner of English/learning English. Follow Socoop's conversation (34) and notice the teacher's reaction (35). What is the reason for it? And how does the series of exchanges finally end?

Example 6

Outer	Inner	
	Dependent	*Independent*
34 T: Ask erm Socoop, Socoop, Can you ask him? V: Er yes, er yes.	being erm a father. Being a father.	
		Do you like er being a father?
T: Um hm. S:		Yes, I
(pause) (proudly) I am er father of four children. T: Yes. (referring tone)		
35 T: Listen to her question, though. Say again. Say it again. V:		Do you like er being a father?
T: Um hm. S: (No response)		
36 T:		Do you like being a father? Do you like being a father?
S:		Yes I like being to be . . .
T: Um hm. S: (No response)		
37 T:	Yes I	
S:		Yes I like . . . being
T:	Yes I do. Yes I do. I like being a father.	
Mmm		

So what went wrong? Socoop understood the question, and offered 'Yes, I am er father of four children' as proof of his enjoyment of being a father, as one might in a normal conversation. The teacher was not satisfied because she had expected a response which practised the form of 'like' with verb in '-ing'. The teacher's reaction, getting Virginia to repeat her question to him, baffled Socoop, who thought he had already answered it rather well. Finally he half-heartedly repeated the words 'like being', then thought perhaps it should be 'like be', whereupon the teacher gave up and answered the question herself. (Which must have worried her students somewhat since she was quite definitely a woman.)

So basically what happened was this: the teacher required a response on the Inner, to practice 'like' with a verb, and Socoop responded on the Outer. And in normal conversations, one does not repeat the words of the question in the answer, so he was merely applying (quite correctly) the rules of natural conversation.

Many other classroom researchers have recorded similar breakdowns (see McTear 1975, Long 1979), and anyone who has taught a foreign language to elementary students will have had similar experiences.

Sometimes students deliberately react to a DVX in a meaningful way just for fun; one class I was observing was practising polite requests with 'Would you mind . . .' followed by 'No, not at all'. They got to the cue: 'Would you mind lending me 50 cents?' One student's partner answered, loudly, 'Yes, I mind.' And then added for the benefit of the teacher and the other students, 'He never pay back!'

SO HOW DO STUDENTS TELL INNER FROM OUTER?

Close analysis of classroom data in the light of the Hallidayan concept of 'situation', consisting of 'tenor', 'mode' and 'field', (see J. Willis 1981:124), suggested that students perceive different types of clues from the general 'situation' to help them distinguish what is wanted.

Firstly, they may recognize the current role of the teacher (tenor): if the teacher is encouraging an open discussion, what is required will almost certainly be Outer. If the teacher is in the role of instructor, and the 'field' is largely concerned with language *per se*, the likelihood of an Inner requirement is higher. See Example 4 above, which illustrates the teacher's role about to change in this way. Most teachers use explicit Boundary exchanges followed by a series of Direct and Inform exchanges, which tell students what to do and how to do it. In the language classroom, they are often explicitly given the words to do it with. (See Example 4, 263–5.)

Secondly, if there are no explicit Boundary exchanges, students may deduce from the preceding series of exchanges, paying special attention to the teacher's Follow-up moves, how they are to respond. After one or two DVXs, it is highly likely the next will also be a DVX, and require an Inner response, unless the teacher signals in some way that it is not; for example, by adding the word 'really' to the question, and changing the stress.

Thirdly, the structure and length of the Initiating move itself is revealing, and likely to make students pay more attention to form.

The structure of the typical Initiating move in Teacher Elicit exchanges in my data is very simple, consisting of head act *elicit* followed by a verbal or non-verbal *nomination*. However, the structure of Initiating moves in DVXs is often far more complex, see exchange (6) in Example 1, which has six acts, and exchange (34) in Example 6, which consists of five acts: *starter*, *NV*, *nominate*, *starter*, *direct*, *clue*. The reason for this is clear. At the beginning of a new transaction, for a DV Initiation to be successful, the language needs to be modelled, students need to know who speaks to whom, and attention is drawn to visual aids or book cues. As the transaction progresses, DV Initiations tend to get simpler because students already know the basic requirements.

Fourthly, paralinguistic features, intonation and kinesics can give a lot of clues. If a teacher says something slowly and deliberately, it is likely to be Inner. This often involves a teacher breaking an utterance up into more tone units than would be usual in normal conversation, and using a different stress pattern. I quote an example from exchange (5) (layout as in Brazil *et al.* 1980, whose discourse intonation system I have used throughout):

// WOULD you MIND // NOT LOOKing // at the WRITing //

In most real-life situations this would be one, at the most two, tone units. (If it were three, it would be very rude!) And also, here, a complete pitch sequence happens in the one sentence, starting on high key, going to mid key, and ending in low termination, which seems to give it the status of a title or an announcement. Most students would recognize this as something out of the ordinary, and to be taken account of as Inner.

The whole exchange actually slots into Example 1 on page 164. I omitted it originally because it is an example of a move which seemed to have a dual role: it seemed to act both on the Outer, as a directive, to stop the students looking at the writing, and on the Inner, as a sample of the language structure that is going to be taught later.

As the teacher actually said this, she leant much further forward towards the class, used a large hand gesture, and looked very pointedly at each student, as if to say, 'Take note!'. She had to repeat the same words a second time so as to include all the class in her gaze while she was speaking. It was an obvious change from Outer to Inner, but still retaining a relevant message – a rare occurrence.

FOCUS SWITCHES: FROM OUTER TO INNER AND BACK AGAIN

We have already seen in Examples 1 and 4 how a teacher will go from Outer to Inner. In Examples 2 and 6, however, we see the students going from Inner to Outer; Virginia talking about husbands washing up, and Socoop talking about his children. This is very typical; students escaping from teacher-imposed control, and teacher trying to bring the focus back to language form.

Interestingly, there are no examples at all in any of my data of a teacher switching straight from a series of DVXs (Inner) to an Elicit exchange (Outer) with no intervening exchange. There is always at least a Boundary, or an Inform, or a Direct in between; and significantly these are all exchange types which require no verbal Responding move from the students. We can only surmise that this is to prepare students for the switch from the requirement of an Inner response to an Outer response. By contrast the students tend to switch from Inner to Outer with no warning at all, and at the slightest excuse.

A summary of the normal patterns for focus switches is given below.

Teacher-initiated switches
OUTER TO INNER
Common
Correction of error.
Supplying new words.
Beginnings of drill or practice sequences: normally marked by Boundary exchanges.

INNER TO OUTER
Rare
Usually at end of transaction.
If elsewhere, always marked in some way; normally as a result of student's misunderstanding, e.g. of instructions.

Student-initiated switches
OUTER TO INNER
Rare
Queries about the pronunciation or meanings of words or structures.
Requests for confirmation, though normally the latter only occur if already on the Inner level.

INNER TO OUTER
Common
Either deliberately escaping from formal constraints imposed by teacher, or non-recognition of them through misunderstanding. Requests for explanation or further information.

There are of course many switches from Inner Independent to Inner Dependent. Where the reverse occurred, and this was rare, there tended to be confusion. As we have seen, some confusion and humour can be generated by students switching from Inner Independent to Outer.

Examples of switches following these patterns can be found in many other classroom data, for example McTear (1975), where he comments on the complexities of FL classroom exchange structure; when his data is re-analysed, separated into Outer and Inner, these complexities largely disappear. Ellis (1984:109–11) talks about 'medium-oriented' and 'message-oriented' interactions, and quotes an example of data from Allwright (1979) to which the application of Outer and Inner may well prove enlightening. A student, Igor, introduces and pursues the topic of taxis in Moscow at the expense of the teacher's focus on vocabulary building: another student escaping from Inner to Outer. It is also interesting to note what Ellis has to say about the suitability of certain types of lessons and styles for aiding natural language acquisition, and to interpret his advice on providing 'learning opportunities' for students in terms of Inner and Outer, but this is beyond the scope of this chapter.

INNER POVERTY

When examining utterances that occur on the Inner, and comparing them with utterances on the Outer, there are striking differences, both in exchange structure and move structure.

At the level of exchange, Elicit exchanges on the Outer typically consist of three moves, I, R and F (Initiating, Responding, and Follow-up.) On the Inner Independent, only two moves: I and R; as we have seen the F move belongs to the teacher and is almost always evaluative.

At the level of move, it was evident that one-act moves were the norm on the Inner, whereas on the Outer, Initiating moves consisted of up to six acts, the norm being two or three. One would expect the teacher's Initiations to be more complex; for one thing, she has a native-speaker competence, for another, she has complicated interactions to set up. However, student moves also sometimes consisted of more than just the head act when on the Outer. Words like 'Erm', 'Ah' and 'Eh?' abounded as *signal*, *pre-head* and *post-head* acts on the Outer and served to keep the interaction going. This finding, too, has obvious implications for language learning and teaching.

THE 'COMMUNICATIVE' CLASSROOM: CITATION, SIMULATION AND REPLICATION ACTIVITIES

The lessons that I recorded and analysed were typical samples of English Language Teaching at the time, at the elementary and intermediate level. The system of analysis that I developed for these lessons would need to be extended and refined before it could handle some of the kinds of communicative activities which are becoming more and more common in classrooms today. Sinclair and Coulthard chose the classroom as the setting for their original analysis because the clearly defined roles of teacher and pupil and the teacher's responsibility for control offer a stark and comparatively simple discourse structure. But it is precisely because the tight control in the sort of lessons I analysed fails to reflect the complexities of discourse and language use outside the classroom that teachers are turning towards communicative activities in their lessons.

The distinction that (J.) Dave Willis (1990) makes in his book *The Lexical Syllabus* between three different types of classroom activity is useful here. I quote:

> The first two, *citation* and *simulation*, both focus on language form. The purpose of *citation* activities is to model target utterances for the learners. Teachers have a range of devices for this. The important thing, as we have seen, is that students are required to respond to a teacher elicitation with an utterance which is appropriate in form. So Socoop's perfectly acceptable sentence:
>
> 'Yes, I am, er, father of four children'
>
> was rejected by the teacher because it did not display the form the teacher wanted, a verb with a gerund as object. Any of the following would have been acceptable:
>
> 'I love/like/enjoy/dislike/hate/can't stand *being* a father' irrespective of whether it happened to be true or not.
>
> (p. 57)

Following the system of analysis detailed in this chapter, the 'citation language', i.e. the target utterances, would be classified as Inner.

Simulation activities include activities such as role plays, and writing activities such as letters of complaint, where students pretend or imagine themselves to be characters in a given situation, and act out a situation or produce a piece of writing that bears a resemblance to reality but is not in actual fact informing anyone of anything new, or communicating in the true sense of the word. To quote again from the same source:

> I call activities of this kind *simulation* activities because, although there is an appearance of communication, the real purpose is to display control of language form. Students adopt for example the roles of doctor and patient simply in order to show that they have 'learned' expressions like:
>
> 'What's the problem?'
>
> and
>
> 'I've got a pain in my back.'
>
> (p. 58)

Role play activities like this could be considered as 'pseudo-interaction'. This interaction would be classified for the most part as Inner Independent and would most likely follow one or more DVA exchanges. Student and teacher language used while setting up, organizing, commenting on or even digressing from the activity, e.g. deciding how to play a role, reacting to the way someone was acting, would be classified as Outer.

The third type, *replication* activities, focus on outcome rather than form. To quote further:

> They are called *replication* activities because they replicate within the classroom aspects of communication in the real world. There is a wealth of activities already accessible to teachers involving games, problem solving, information gathering and so on in which learners use language for real communication. In these activities, they ask questions because they need to know the answers in order to solve a problem or win a game, not simply to show they can produce question forms in English. The forms of the language they use are in no way predetermined. They can use whatever language they wish in order to achieve the desired outcome quickly and efficiently.
>
> (p. 59)

The 'discourse activities' as described and analysed in Warren (1985), the chaired and unchaired student group discussions in Singapore classrooms as reported in Davis (1987), and the oral communication tasks analysed and described in Bygate (1988 and 1991), are examples of replication activities. Implicit in all this is the belief that, in terms of discourse structure, the conditions for almost any form of language use can be reproduced in the classroom. Replication activities also form the basis of the *Collins Cobuild English Course*, Levels 1 to 3 (Willis, J and Willis, J.D. 1988–9).

An example of a replication activity in the form of an extract from the data recorded by Bygate (1988) follows. The students, Peruvians, in groups of four, are about to play a game of 'Twenty Questions' where they have to guess the name of the country written on the card picked by one player.

I have added numbers and analysed the exchange types below according to J. Willis (1981).

Example 7

1 S12:   am I am I supposed to er ask questions
   S9:   Yes

2 S10:   we're going to ask you questions and you will answer them so we

3 S9:   [yeah] one player takes a card / ? / – the others try to guess what country
   S10:   yeah

4 S9   so you turn
   S10:   OK

5 S10:   I where which continent is that country
   S12:   s south america
   S11:   ehm south america

6   S11:   is it eh the north part of south america or at the south part of
            south america south america
     S12:   it's in the ahm – middle yes in the middle
     S11:   the centre
     S12:   the centre
7   S9:   so perhaps erm – is it a big one – or is it erm – is it bigger than
            our country
     S12:   no, it's shorter
     S9:   it's shorter

	Exchange type	Move	Act
1	Elicit (check)	Initiation	elicit (check)
		Response	reply
2	Boundary	Focus	metastatement
3	Direct:VA.	Initiation	starter, directive:VA
4	Direct	Initiation	directive
		Response	acknowledge
5	Elicit	Initiation	elicit
		Response	reply
		Follow-up	acknowledge
6	Elicit	Initiation	marker, elicit
		Response	reply, comment
		Follow-up	acknowledge
		Follow-up	acknowledge
7	Elicit	Initiation	marker, starter, elicit
		Response	reply
		Follow-up	acknowledge

So here we find normal three-part exchanges, with students not only handling Initiating moves quite competently, but also naturally supplying the third, Follow-up move. In the absence of the teacher, their interaction becomes far richer, at the level of both exchange and move.

The question is, should such replication activities be classified as Inner or Outer? There are arguments both ways; but intuitively one feels that since they too are language learning activities, students still approach them with a language learning 'mental set' and as such they should be on the Inner. But they are certainly not Inner Dependent, and neither could they be classified on the Inner Independent as 'pseudo-interaction'. From initial, informal observations, and analysis of replication activities such as the one in Example 7 above, it seems that they are far freer, and richer in move structure, than the present 'pseudo-interaction'. One solution might be to introduce a fourth column, subdividing the Inner Independent into 'Pseudo' and 'Free', which would then give us:

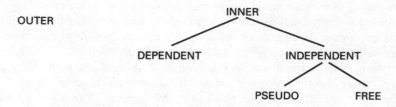

One would expect that the Free column would be even far more complex than the Outer in exchange and move structure; with no central teacher control, the students in the group need to negotiate roles and control of turn-taking and topic among themselves. The Free column might possibly be far more heavily used in a lesson based on communicative activities than the Outer, or indeed the other Inner columns.

Different again from the activities described by Willis and Warren (1985) above is the type of lesson taught during the Bangalore Project, following what Prabhu terms a 'procedural' syllabus (Prabhu 1987). This consists solely of tasks of different types, that students work on individually after an initial run-through with a similar example with the teacher, very much in the same way as a maths teacher introduces a new type of maths problem. Here there is no explicit focus on language at all at any stage; the resulting interaction resembles that of a 'content' lesson and would be coded as Outer.

IMPLICATIONS FOR LANGUAGE CLASSROOMS OF THE FUTURE: WHAT SHOULD CLASSROOM OBSERVERS BE LOOKING FOR?

In the 1990s, as students become even more aware of the need to become fluent in English and to cope with the flow of natural speech, there is likely to be a greater demand for replication activities to allow learners to practice communicating in the classroom, not simply at utterance level, but at discourse level, taking responsibility for their own turn-taking and negotiating their own way through a complete interaction. Even so, the majority of lessons I have observed over the last year (1990–1) have contained more citation and simulation activities than replication. In some cases students are left free to carry out a task on their own in groups (replication, classifiable as Inner Independent Free), but during the subsequent 'reporting back' phase are expected to produce utterances conforming to a pre-set structural pattern, which turns the activity back into a citation activity, on the Inner level.

If, as Hatch (in Hatch 1978) suggests, learners acquire grammar through discourse, we should be perhaps hoping to see lessons with rich interaction in the Outer and Inner Independent. Dick Allwright (Allwright and Bailey 1991) talks of lessons with 'learning opportunities' – it would be worth considering how these might be characterized in terms of Inner and Outer.

One very real possibility arising from this system of analysis is that of the *real-time coding* of interaction in language classes. Informal experiments suggest that it is quite possible to record easily at the rank of exchange. Observers simply note down, in a column in an abbreviated form, the types of exchange as they happen, since these are identifiable from their Initiating move. There is time to identify the speaker (T or S), the moves (I R F) and sometimes also time to add a few more details, such as some words or phrases. Arrows across to the four Inner columns could be used to show the type of Inner in use. The resulting protocols could be used for teacher development, and if combined with an audio recording, for action research projects.

The analysis of group work/replication activities where no leader is appointed or emerges as the dominant speaker within the group, is currently beyond the scope of this system for analysis. Several researchers have looked into this problem (Cheung 1984) and have come up with their own findings.

Other research reported in Davis (1987) deals largely with the added complexities of analysing the kind of discourse structure which occurs during less controlled multi-party interactions. Davis argues that the Initiating move is crucial in controlling propositional development, and it is only when students are free to develop the discourse for themselves that they are obliged to explore the resources of the language.

We have come a long way since 1979. The 1980s saw an increase in the use of authentic texts and a growing awareness of the need for 'real' English and more opportunities for real communication in the language learning classroom. There has been a growing interest in 'Action Research' projects undertaken by the teacher in the classroom. In 1991 the IATEFL Research Special Interest Group was founded and this should provide an ideal forum for the discussion of research methods and ways to analyse increasingly challenging types of classroom interaction.

'Inner and outer: spoken discourse in the language classroom' is a modified and explained version of the article of the same name published in Coulthard (1987a) *Discussing Discourse*, 1–19.

9 Intonation and feedback in the EFL classroom

Martin Hewings

We still have very little idea of what goes on in a [language-teaching] classroom in terms of interaction.

(Cook 1982)

INTRODUCTION

The research described below is an attempt to come to a better understanding of what does go on by applying the system of ascribing communicative significance to intonation outlined in Brazil, Coulthard and Johns (1980) and Brazil (1985) to a corpus of recorded data. A very limited aspect of interaction is considered: the provision of feedback by a teacher following and relating to a student's response in language pattern drills in the EFL classroom.

In the teaching exchange (Sinclair and Coulthard 1975), consisting of initiation–response–feedback, most interest in pedagogical research has focused on the first two parts. Considerable work has been done, for example, on the type of initiation that makes a response more or less 'meaningful' or 'communicative'. Rather less attention has been given to the form of feedback given by the teacher and a consideration of its possible influence on language learning. This, perhaps, is surprising in view of the fact that in each such three-part interchange, feedback may well constitute one-third of the total language produced. A recognition of this imbalance was the primary motivation for the research reported here, a more extensive description of which can be found in Hewings (1985).

FEEDBACK

The notion of feedback derives from analysis of the manipulation of systems in which part of the output from the system is returned to it as input, modifying its characteristics and, consequently, its subsequent output. An analogy can be drawn between this procedure and a common event in the second language (L2) classroom. A student is provided with a stimulus to produce a sample of the L2. His/her performance is then matched against some standard of achievement or the degree of approach to some target set up by the teacher, who then assesses or corrects the performance accordingly. Typical classroom exchanges illustrating this are:

1*　T:　What does Fred do at seven o'clock?
　　　S:　He gets up.
　　　T:　Good.

2*　T:　What did Ali do on Thursday evening?
　　　S:　He went to cinema.
　　　T:　Okay. He went to the cinema.

(Constructed examples are denoted by an asterisk. Unless otherwise stated, all others come from the recordings analysed in Hewings (1985).)

The repeated production of language samples by learners and their assessment by a teacher is a well-documented feature of a behaviourist approach to language teaching (see, for example, McDonough 1981:ch. 2), and typified in activities such as pattern drills and question–answer sequences. The understanding implicit in giving feedback in this way is that the learner's subsequent linguistic behaviour will approach a target: in the short-term this might be the ability to, for example, respond to a picture prompt with a particular utterance with acceptable fluency and pronunciation; in the long-term it might be near native-speaker competence.

Feedback is, of course, a complex phenomenon, to which a number of physical and psychological factors contribute. It is conveyed not only through spoken, but also through non-verbal channels. Aspects of paralanguage, kinesics or proxemics, for instance, may be of significance: an intake of air between clenched teeth or the raising of eyebrows to draw attention to an error, or a pat on the head to indicate approval. In aiming towards the eventual understanding of the interaction of the various parameters of feedback, it is necessary to isolate each in turn. In this chapter, attention will be focused on the linguistic realizations and in particular on the part that intonation plays in providing information about the acceptability and quality of a learner's performance in the L2. So it will be asked, for example, whether the pragmatic function of 'Good' in (1) above, in the sense of what it communicates about the quality of the student's performance of 'He gets up', would be different if it were spoken with a falling as opposed to a rising tone.

The examples of classroom interaction used as illustrations below are taken from a corpus of recorded data collected in EFL classrooms in Malaysian secondary schools during 1983 and 1984. The teachers are all British, and the students are at a fairly elementary level. In all the examples cited there is a verbal realization of feedback although non-verbal parameters may also have been operative. The examples presented are typical of exchanges in L2 classrooms where learners are at a low level of ability, and English is the language predominantly used, in that the teacher is more likely to make students aware of an error by giving an acceptable version him/herself or by prompting another student to produce a response, than by presenting in English a formal explanation of the nature of the error, which students may not be able to understand. Consequently, much of the feedback with which I am concerned here is realized linguistically by a small set of items including 'Good', 'Fine', 'Right', 'OK' and 'That's right' (Sinclair and Brazil's 'Closed items' (1982:28)) and/or a repetition of all or a part of the student's response.

CLASSROOM EXCHANGES

Before examining the categories of information conveyed through intonation in feedback, it will be useful to establish precisely what is the purpose of this type of three-part exchange in the L2 classroom. Consider first:

3* T: Where did I put the blackboard duster?
    S: In the cupboard.
    T: Thanks.

4* T: Where did I put the blackboard duster?
    S: In the cupboard.
    T: Good.

Exchange (3) is intended as an example of an act of 'genuine communication', the teacher cannot remember where he has put the blackboard duster, whereas (4) is an exchange from a drill where the teacher places the blackboard duster in various places around the classroom and instructs students to tell him where he has put it. Here the information sought by the teacher is not in reality the location of the blackboard duster, but whether the student can produce an utterance of a form within the standards of acceptability he has himself, implicitly or explicitly (by, for example, providing a 'model' utterance) laid down. In this second type of exchange two expectations need to be fulfilled:

(a) the student is expected to respond to the teacher's initiation;
(b) the teacher is required to give an assessment of the student's response, the purpose or business of the feedback being to 'inform everyone whether (the student's) contribution is acceptable to the teacher or not' (Brazil 1981:181).

Consequently, once (b) has been achieved, the exchange is at an end: the business is complete. Only informationally 'empty' items, such as a repetition of the assessment, can occur subsequently within the same exchange. Anything else is considered as functioning in a new exchange.

The notion of 'acceptability' in the L2 classroom needs further clarification at this point. Consider the exchanges:

5   T: Why would you want to be strong?
     S: To make muscles.
     T: To make muscles. Yes.

                    (data from Brazil, Coulthard and Johns 1980:151)

6   T: This one here, Afizah.
     S: Some potatoes.
     T: Good.

Exchange (5) is taken from an L1 classroom, (6) from an EFL classroom. Both exchanges share at least one of the characteristics of much of classroom discourse which distinguishes it from non-classroom verbal interchange: the participant who elicits the response already knows what information to expect in the response. Furthermore, if the information supplied in the response does not match his expectations, he is in a position to re-initiate the exchange until an acceptable response has been given. However, the type of response elicited in (5) is rather different from that in (6). In (5) the student selects from a limited but not predictable range of responses. In (6), however, the student's response is totally predicted by the situation in which it is given, a language pattern drill. Thus, the third part of exchange (5) contains an assessment of the meaning or communicative value conveyed in the response. In (6) the assessment is of the performance of the form of the response. This point is further illustrated in (7).

7*   T: This one here, Afizah.
      S: Well, it looks to me like some potatoes.

While the communicative value of the response is essentially the same as in (6), in a drill where the elicited response is expected to be 'some potatoes', it would be inappropriate, going beyond the bounds of acceptability imposed by the teacher, of what is permissible linguistically at this particular time.

THE FUNCTIONS OF INTONATION IN FEEDBACK

Given that an assessment of the acceptability of a response is a necessary part of this type of exchange, in providing feedback after the response, the teacher has three options open to him/her:

   (i) to give a negative assessment – that is, to reject the response, indicating it was unacceptable;
  (ii) to withhold the assessment until some later stage of proceedings, or to give a partial acceptance;
 (iii) to give a positive assessment – that is, to indicate that the response was acceptable.

In what follows I address myself to the role of intonation in enabling a student to decide which of these three options the teacher has selected. Each option will be considered in turn.

Negative assessment

The nature of the classroom activity being investigated, carefully structured and rehearsed pattern drills and question–answer sequences, means that the number of unacceptable responses compared with acceptable ones is small. Outright rejection normally only follows a student's misunderstanding of what is required of him leading to an inappropriate response, as in:

8   T: //o the NEXT one please //
      S: //p he's SLEEPing //
      T: //o NO //o NO //p THIS one //

After an appropriate but in some way unacceptable response, the usual procedure adopted by teachers in the corpus is to re-initiate the exchange, attempting to elicit a corrected response either from the same or a new student. In such cases intonation is often significant in conveying the teacher's expectations for the subsequent response.

9   S: //p she COOK a CHICken //
      T: //o SHE //
      S: //p COOKED a CHICken //

In this example, the teacher provides an incomplete quotation of the student's response in feedback, selecting o tone (level or neutral tone). The established classroom convention is that the student should complete the quotation, making necessary modifications. The significance of tone selection becomes apparent if alternatives to o tone are considered.

10 S: //p she COOKED a CHICken //
      T: //r+ SHE //

Here the feedback is likely to be heard as an indication that 'she' is the item in need of correction, and result in a second response such as:

11 T: //r+ SHE //
      S: //p HE cooked a chicken //

Brazil (1985:147) suggests that one reason for a speaker selecting r+ tone is that the lexical matter of the tone unit is in some way in need of reactivation. The echo of 'she' in (10) indicates to the student that he should reconsider this word in his response; in other words, it is marked as unacceptable. A similar result is achieved with selection of p+ tone in:

12 S: //o GREEdy TOM //o is GO to EAT //
    T: //p+ is GO //
    S: //o is GOing to EAT //

p+ tone, Brazil (1985:148) suggests, may be selected in order to mark matter as new to both hearer and speaker. By indicating that 'go' is also 'new' to himself, the teacher marks the word as an unexpected choice: that is, not the one he was hoping to elicit and, therefore, inappropriate in this context. Choice of r tone is illustrated in:

13 S: //p she PLAYed FOOTball //
    T: //r HE //

where the feedback might be glossed as 'not she, but he'. The r tone carries the implication that this is something the student knew already. By selecting it the teacher indicates that he perhaps sees 'he' as a slip rather than an error in need of correction. Unlike in previous examples, no further response is required from the student in order for the exchange to be complete.

From these illustrations it can be suggested that while it is the incompleteness of the quotation in such feedback that results in a further response from the student, it is tone selection that provides an indication of where the error was located in the response. r+ and p+ tone focus on the word in which the error occurs, leaving the student to correct it, while r tone focuses on the corrected word. However, o tone, by far the most common tone selection for such items in the corpus, leaves more for the student to consider, locating the error only as occurring somewhere after the repeated section.

Withholding of assessment

The second possibility to be considered is feedback giving neither positive nor negative assessment: that is, in which assessment is withheld. In the corpus this withholding of assessment is normally achieved by selection of o tone as, for example in:

14 T: //r+ HOW did they GO to the JUNgle //p HOW //
    S1: //p they WENT by BUS //
    T: //o by BUS //o AND //o BY //
    S2: //p VAN //
    T: //o VAN //o and BY //
    S3: //p TRUCK //

T: //o TRUCK //o or LORry //o GOOD //o and BY //
S4: //p CAR //
T: //p CAR //p alRIGHT //

One of the meanings Brazil attaches to selection of o tone is that it occurs when tone unit boundaries do not fall at 'points of potential completion' (1985:205ff). In the context considered here 'completion' represents an indication that an assessment of a response has been given. Selection of o tone withholds assessment. This is well illustrated in (14). The teacher wishes to elicit a list of relevant means of transport and only produces a proclaiming (i.e. informing) tone when this list is completed to her satisfaction. Items such as //o by BUS //, //o VAN //, //o TRUCK // and //o GOOD //, then, represent an acknowledgement that the response has been noted, but refrain from giving an assessment.

Sinclair and Brazil (1982:125) consider the selection of r+ tone in the following example taken from the L1 classroom:

15 T: Where do we get tea from?
    S: China.
    T: //r+ CHIna //

Here the teacher acknowledges a shared understanding that tea does indeed come from China, but selection of referring tone will be heard as conspicuously not indicating that the response was (all of) what the teacher wanted. While acknowledging the truth of the response, the teacher is also indicating that he wants the pupil to go on and say more, or that he wants someone else to offer a response. A possible continuation might be:

16 S: China
    T: //r+ CHIna //
    S: India
    T: //r+ INDia //
    S: Sri Lanka
    T: //p SRI LANka //

where the proclaimed Sri Lanka signals the 'achievement' of the business – here, the elicitation of a list. Although different tones are selected for feedback in examples (14) and (15/16) the same function appears to be realized: the withholding of an indication of the satisfactory completion of the interchange until more responses have been given. While selection of r tone here is not represented in the corpus it is possible to imagine a context in which it might occur:

17* T: Where do we get tea from?
    S: China.
    T: //r YES //

A possible paraphrase of this feedback could be 'We know that tea comes from China – but where else?' Alternatively, we might hear

18* T: Where do we get tea from?
   S: Sainsbury's.
   T: //r YES //

where the implication is 'We do indeed get tea from Sainsbury's – but that is not the answer I wanted!'

o tone in feedback occurs in other types of interaction than in the elicitation of a list of items. In (19) for example,

19 S: //o EVery WEEK //o GREEdy TOM //p EATS RICE //
          //p EATS SOME RICE //
    T: //o EATS SOME RICE //   (a)
          //p oKAY //   (b)

the student, by correcting herself, in effect produces alternative responses for the teacher to assess. In selecting o tone for 'eats some rice', the teacher effectively says 'This is the alternative I choose to assess', before going on to make an assessment with //p oKAY//. We see here a switch from what Brazil terms oblique orientation to direct orientation. In (a) the teacher quotes a sample of language originally uttered by the student, adopting no position on its accuracy or acceptability. In (b), however, he returns to an interactive stance and the negotiation of a positive or negative evaluation.

Positive assessment

The third and by far the most common option is to give a positive assessment.

20 T: //o number TWO //o ROSlan //p READ it //
    S: //p RUN aWAY from SOMEwhere //o MEAN
          //p EScape //   (a)
    T: //p oKAY //o   (b)
          //o THREE //p HENG CHIN //   (c)

In the example above (a) labels the student's response, (b) is feedback relating to that response and (c) is the initiation of a new exchange. Of interest here, then, is the item

    T: //p oKAY //

In the L2 classroom data studied the majority of items of feedback, either those of a single tone unit, as in (20), or the final tone unit of longer items such as in (21),

21 S: //o CAPtured MEANS //p MADE PRISoner //
    T: //o GOOD //o CAPtured MEANS //p MADE PRISoner //

are proclaimed – that is, p or falling tone is selected. This, however, is not surprising when the function of such items is considered: the assessment of the student's performance.

The primary distinction within Brazil's system of tone choice is between rising (R) tone and falling (P) tone. The significance attached to choice of rising tone is that the speaker, by its selection, projects both himself and the hearer as belonging to that group of people who already share the information carried by the lexical and grammatical content of the tone unit. In this way it can be said to be 'integrative' or to be projecting a state of convergence between speaker and hearer. Selection of proclaiming tone, on the other hand, is 'divisive' or projecting a state of divergence, in that the speaker marks the hearer as not belonging to that group of people who share such information. One specific aspect of this general invocation of the convergence/divergence relationship is that the speaker, through tone selection, is able to mark the content of the tone unit as either 'shared' or 'new' knowledge. By selecting proclaiming tone the speaker may, for instance, indicate his expectation that what he is saying is something the hearer didn't already know. In offering his response as a performance, the acceptability of which is so far unnegotiated, the student presents it to the teacher for approval or rejection. The evidence suggests that while positive assessment is proclaimed, some other tone choice is made for negative assessment or a withholding of assessment.

While proclaimed feedback such as in (20) and (21) can be seen simply as an indication of the acceptability of the response, the teacher can, of course, indicate a great deal more than this if he chooses, and we will now consider repetitions of all or part of the student's response as, for example, in:

22 S: They were listening to the radio.
    T: Yes. They were listening to the radio.   *or*
    T: Good. Listening to the radio.

In particular, attention will be focused on segmentation into tone units and key selection. An acceptance followed by a repetition can often be glossed either as 'Yes, that's acceptable but it could have been improved in this way', or 'Yes, that's acceptable, and notice in particular this.'

In the following example the teacher gives a positive assessment (b) and then repeats the response (c).

23 S: //o NOW //o abdul HAFfis //o is CLEANing //p the
        BOARD //   (a)
    T: //p oKAY //   (b)
        //o NOW abdul HAFfis //p is CLEANing the BOARD // (c)

The hesitancy of the student's response (a), with frequent tone unit boundaries being realized by short pauses, apparently reflects the more general observation that the planning and pre-coding of 'chunks' of language in tone units by non-fluent speakers of English advances in shorter steps. The teacher, in his repetition, opts to distribute tone unit boundaries differently. A possible interpretation of his decision to repeat the response and to segment it in this way is that he hopes to provide a model which he considers to be more fluent and, therefore, more representative of the target language.

In (24), a rather different reason for repetition and re-segmentation seems to occur:

24 S: //o GREEdy TOM //o had EATen //p a DUCK //
    T: //p GOOD //

     //o GREEdy TOM HAS //p EATen a DUCK //   (a)

The teacher, although indicating the response as acceptable with //p GOOD // wishes to focus attention on the student's error 'had''. On the subject of segmentation Brazil (1982a:287) proposes that

> one reason for ending a (tone) unit and beginning a new one is the need to select afresh in one of the three systems (tone, key and termination). If a motive exists for doing this, then boundaries may occur anywhere.

The teacher's motives in this case for creating a tone unit boundary between 'has' and 'eaten' appear to be twofold. Firstly, he wishes to make 'has' prominent. By this means he presents it as being selective in the 'existential paradigm' (Brazil 1985:41). In other words, 'has' is selected as opposed to 'had'. Secondly, he wishes to select high key for 'eaten' (see below). The result is that what one might predict to be the intonational characteristics of (24a) in a different discourse setting (that is, 'has' and 'eaten' in the same tone unit with 'has' being made non-prominent or non-selective), are modified in response to certain pedagogical considerations.

Use of high key as a way of drawing particular attention to a word is a common feature in feedback in the corpus. One example was in (24) above. Another is in:

25 S: //o siti HAwa //o is GOing to WATCH //p TElevision //
    T: //p GOOD //

     //o siti HAwa //o is GOing to WATCH //p TELevision //

where high key is selected for 'going'. Attention is focused on 'going' here, not because of some error in the student's response, but because this is the part of the pattern the teacher wants the students to pay attention to. The general communicative significance of high key, according to Brazil (1985:67–74) is to mark the matter of the tone unit as in some way 'contrastive'. In examples (24) and (25) the teacher invokes the 'particular-izing' function of high key where the implication is that 'going' is selected rather than all other alternatives that the students might consider accept-able. In other words, 'going' is heard to be carefully selected and, there-fore, worthy of particular attention. Similarly, in:

26 S: //o YUsof CAME //p from a VERy imPORTant FAMily //
    T: //p YES //

//o it SAID he CAME //p from a ^{ROYal} FAMily //
//p so an imPORTant FAMily //

'royal' is selected with high key, focusing attention on the statement in the text being used that Yusof's was a royal (as opposed to a 'non-royal') family.

DISCOURSE STRUCTURE AND INTONATION IN FEEDBACK

The positive assessment of a response, we have argued, closes the exchange. As an indication of this closure the teacher might simply move on to initiate a new exchange. S/he may also, however, choose to give an intonational marker of the completion of a section or unit of the discourse, and we now turn to this discourse structuring function of intonation. In the following extract, for example,

27 S: //o AHmad and ZAIdi //p WENT to the CINema //
    T: //p GOOD //   (a)
       //o and the NEXT one //   (b)

the teacher selects low termination (strictly speaking low key and low termination in this minimal tonic segment) for the item 'good' (a), which is his indication of assessment, before going on to initiate a new exchange with (b). It is suggested that this selection of low (rather than high or mid) termination serves to indicate the closure of the exchange.

Brazil (1985:178–99) identifies a phonological unit which consists of all the tone units occurring between two successive low terminations and labels it the *pitch sequence*. Its boundaries coincide with the beginning and end of an 'intuitively significant' section of the discourse. Each choice of low termination, therefore, represents the close of such a section. The precise significance that can be attached to pitch sequence closure can only be discovered by reference to local meaning within the discourse, but generally speaking, with reference to classroom discourse, it may be stated that pitch sequence closure coincides with the end of a perceived stage in a lesson. Being the dominant party in classroom discourse this perception is usually that of the teacher and it is primarily his/her prerogative to select low termination. It is proposed, then, that a pitch sequence boundary, that is, a choice of low termination, occurring in an item such as 'good' is a marker of the closure of the exchange. In other words it indicates that the business of the exchange has been completed to the teacher's satisfaction, and that the assessment is finished.

It would thus seem reasonable to suggest that in selecting low rather than mid or high termination for 'good' in (27) the teacher wishes his students to perceive a more significant boundary in the discourse than would otherwise be the case. Once again it is necessary to consider the context in which a low termination choice is made in order to establish its precise significance. In the following extract, in response to each picture prompt showing a person performing a particular action and the question 'What did he/she do yesterday?', the student produces 'He slept', 'He washed his face', etc. in order to practise the simple form of the past tense of various verbs.

28   T: //p WHAT did he do YESterday //
     S1:   //p he SLEPT //
     T: //p SLEPT //p GOOD //
           //o aFENdy //p WHAT did he do YESterday //
     S2:   //p he WASHed his FACE //

     T: //p his FACE //o GOOD //
           //p what did SHE do yesterday //
     S3:   //p she DRANK //
     T: //p she DRANK //p WHAT //
     S3:   //p SEVen up //
     T: //p she drank SEVen up //p GOOD //
           //p WHAT did HE do yesterday //
     S4:   //p he MENded the CAR //
     T: //o he MENded the CAR //o YES //   (a)

           //o but can ANybody think of aNOther word //   (b)
           //p beginning with R //
     S5:   //p rePAIRED //   (c)
     T: //p rePAIRED //p YES //   (d)

           //p husSEIN //o WHAT did he do YESterday //   (e)

The first few initiations result in acceptable responses to which the teacher provides feedback consisting of proclaimed repetitions or a proclaimed 'good'. At (a), however, the student produces the response 'he mended the car'. 'Mended' is apparently not the verb the teacher wishes to elicit as she opens an exchange at (b) intended to elicit 'repaired'. Once this is achieved (c), she gives a positive assessment (d), ending in low termination, and continues with the drill (e). It is common in the corpus that such departures from the drill, in order to elicit an acceptable response, to add information or to provide a 'model' performance, are often closed by the selection of low termination, marking them as in a sense separate from the main subject of the discourse, the pattern drill.

The argument that a low termination choice represents a boundary in the discourse gains further credibility when occurrences of two consecutive low tone units, each having low termination, are investigated as, for example, in:

29   T: //o THIS one HERE please //o siti noRAIN //
     S: (some rice)
     T: //p RICE //p ºKAY //p SOME RICE //

Developing the model of classroom discourse outlined by Sinclair and
Coulthard (1975), researchers (reported in Coulthard and Montgomery
1981:ch. 1) saw evidence for an additional unit between exchange and
transaction to which the label *sequence* was given. Sequences represent
stretches of discourse in which a formal pattern is maintained above the
level of the exchange. In the classroom, for example, a sequence

> arises when a predictable routine is begun – perhaps a number of similar
> questions, or repetitive commands, or anything that participants recog-
> nize as forming a distinctive set of exchanges, with a beginning, middle
> and end.
>
> (Sinclair and Brazil 1982:52)

A drill, for example, eliciting responses of a particular syntactic pattern,
would constitute such a 'predictable routine'. The ends of such sequences
in the corpus are often marked by the production of two consecutive low
termination tone units as in (29). This pattern is frequently followed by a
change of topic or activity, introduced, for example, by 'Right. Let's look
at the next set of pictures now' or 'Can you take out your exercise books,
please'. The item

//p SOME RICE //

has the status of a discrete pitch sequence: that is, an intuitively significant
section of the discourse. Its local significance appears to be that it marks a
more significant boundary, that is a boundary between two elements of a
higher rank in discourse structure, than that between two exchanges. As an
item of feedback, while the first low termination tone unit,

//p ºKAY //

marks that the exchange has been completed to the teacher's satisfaction,
the second indicates that the sequence is similarly complete.

While this pattern is most often found at the end of a clearly defined
sequence coinciding with the beginning and end of a drill, it is also common
at the end of a section in which the fluency of the drill has been seriously
disrupted. In example (30) the teacher accepts (b) a student's response (a)
and it is then pointed out to him that the response was inappropriate (c).

30   Sl: //o GREEDy TOM //o HAS EATen //p a DUCK //   (a)
     T: //p a DUCK //   (b)
     S2:   //p a CHICken //   (c)
     T: // o SHE //   (d)
     S2:   //p SAY CHICken //

T: //o SHE //   (e)
S2: //p SAID //   (f)
T: //p said a DUCK //p SORry //p i MISsed that //   (g)
    //p oKAY //p FINE //   (h)
    //o THIS one HERE then //   (i)

After initiations (d) and (e) which finally elicit the correct verb form (f), the teacher acknowledges his own error (g) and then closes this 'deviant' section of the discourse by intonationally marking it as separate from the rest (h), going on to initiate the next exchange in the drill (i). In this way the teacher indicates to the students the boundary between what he sees as separate stages of the lesson – the drill proper, and digressions from it.

CONCLUSION

The above presents some of the main observations made in an exploratory descriptive study of the role of intonation in the organization of classroom interaction. I have tried to show that by drawing upon selections from the intonation systems of prominence, tone, key and termination, the teacher is able in feedback to show his/her approval or disapproval of a particular response, withhold an assessment of it, draw the student's attention to particular aspects of the response and mark the termination of units of discourse. More generally, it can be argued that without analysis of the intonational characteristics of any utterance in discourse, the ability accurately to interpret its pragmatic function is much reduced.

'Intonation and feedback in the EFL classroom' was first published in Coulthard (1987a) *Discussing Discourse*, 221–35.

10 Interactive lexis: prominence and paradigms

Mike McCarthy

This chapter is in two parts. The first part attempts to place Brazil's (1985) view of prominence within the context of studies of stress and tonicity, especially where such studies seem unable to resolve difficulties and anomalies in data. This is done in order to juxtapose a series of views on the relationships between salient intonational phenomena such as accent and nucleus placement, and attempts to explain such features in terms of 'given' and 'new' information, with Brazil's own view, which is seen as a unified response to such phenomena that removes anomalies. This is a necessary exordium to the second part of the chapter, which will demonstrate, with real data, that Brazil's view of prominence as a realization of significant choice not only dissipates anomalies and red herrings but offers a powerful model for the analysis of the negotiation of lexical meaning in real-time discourse. The chapter will support Brazil's view that when speakers choose their words, they do so within a projection of a context of interaction, and that prominent and non-prominent matter represents the speaker's choice whether to label items as non-selected common or shared ground or as open-ended, selected matter, yet to be established as common ground. The data referred to will underline the interactive dimension of lexical meaning rather than its inherent or stable features which semanticists have traditionally fixed upon. The data will, it is hoped, show that prominence is a major vehicle for realizing these interactive meanings.

PART I: TONICITY AND PROMINENCE

Prominence is central to Brazil's systematic account of intonation in English, both as the domain in which tonicity operates and as the realization of the existential paradigm, which will be further discussed in Part II. For Brazil, prominence is the feature attached in speech to 'syllables that a hearer can recognize as being in some sense more emphatic than the others' (1985:18). Prominence, though attached to syllables, gives significance to words in any discourse and the implications of prominence are explored on the basis of 'words having or not having a single prominent syllable' (1985:38).

There is, of course, nothing new in attributing importance in verbal messages to those words uttered with prominent syllables. Sweet spoke over a century ago of 'the principle of emphasis, which gives the strongest stress to the most important word' (1875–6), already making the link between prominence and word significance. Equally, the whole of the long debate on 'sentence stress' functions necessarily within the arena of the variable statuses which words (and by extension, lexical items) have in sentences. Certain features of the debate on nuclear stress placement are relevant to the present concern, for Brazil's account of prominence subsumes and neutralizes apparent dichotomies and irregularities by providing an explanation of prominence independent of the issue of nucleus placement.

The syntax-dominated position of the transformationalists (Chomsky and Halle 1968) and later restatements (Chomsky 1972:*passim*), including re-orientations accepting semantic and discourse constraints (Jackendoff 1972:243), created problems difficult to resolve with regard to sentences anomalous to the general account of surface stress in terms of deep structural prescriptions. Wells and Local (1983) observe that the debate as epitomized in Bresnan (1971) and subsequent semanticist attacks on the syntax-biased position, never really freed itself from 'the purview of syntax and semantics'. Theories which see sentence stress as somehow fixed to a neutral 'right-placed' position have to confront an enormous number of utterances where a good deal of matter in clause-final position is not stressed, even where lexico-syntactic, semantic or 'textual' reasons would seem to suggest it ought to be. Thus anomalies are no less apparent in the 'textual' approach of Halliday (1967, 1970), in which a neutral or unmarked position for the main stress of a sentence is central to the theory.

The transformational approach saw the marked version as derivable from the neutral deep structure; the textual approach sought explanations in notions such as contrastiveness or givenness (Halliday 1967:23). Both approaches have been cogently criticized in recent years (Schmerling, 1976; Culicover and Rochemont 1983; Oakeshott-Taylor 1984, provide succinct overviews). Base rules which attempted to generalize nuclear stress to right-placement, or to the last lexical item in a sentence, failed to explain numerous counter-examples where stress seemed to fall on, for instance, pronouns, or penultimate lexical items. Crystal discusses such inconsistencies and entertains the possibility of the final lexical item in a sentence being one 'assumed by the speaker to be familiar or obvious' (1975:26) and thus not to be stressed, an echo of his earlier assertion that it is 'up to the speaker' which word is stressed most strongly (1969:263). Bolinger (1972a) attacked inconsistencies from a semantic point of view, accusing the syntax-based school of 'attributing to syntax what belongs to semantics'. He looked at examples where right-placed lexical verbs are not stressed, as in 'I've got no CLOTHES to wear' and some where they are, as in 'I've a point to EMPHASIZE', and accounted for such variability as dependent on semantic 'richness' of the verbs involved, and whether it is 'things' or 'processes' that are being talked about. Bolinger admitted a pragmatic dimension, though, in accepting 'enough mutual understanding' between speaker and interlocutor as sufficient condition for a non-prominent verb, even in situations where the verb is semantically 'rich' and unpredictable (as the verb *emphasize* could be in certain situations). Nonetheless he still concluded that 'semantic and emotional highlighting' not syntax, were the main determinants of stress.

The problems in handling anomalies encountered by linguists whose view rests on a marked/unmarked distinction is a predictable corollary of the inherent slipperiness of the definitions of 'given' and 'new' information. 'Given', defined as that which has already formally occurred in a discourse (i.e. repeated words, etc.) cannot be necessarily relegated to non-prominence on re-occurrence, as Oakeshott-Taylor (1984) demonstrates in discussing (apparent) anomalies such as:

1   A: What d'you think of JOHN?
    B: Oh, JOHN's all right

Conversely. Brown *et al.*, who accept Halliday's position partly but reject the notion of an unmarked placement for 'new' information, observe that new 'is not merely a question of formal occurrence either, but may be any element not recoverable in the discourse, or a mood shift' (1980:160). Nor are there fewer difficulties, it would seem, in non-formal approaches to the given/new question. Chafe, recognizing the limits of equating given and new with old and new knowledge, prefers to talk in terms of matter 'already activated' and 'newly activated' and moves towards a broader, almost mentalist position where speakers and hearers share 'the perception' of given and new, and where givenness is a status decided on by the speaker and therefore 'it is fundamentally a matter of the speaker's belief that the item is in the addressee's consciousness, not that it is recoverable' (1976:32). The difficulties phonologists have in reconciling a label for discourse content such as given/new with anomalous data is paralleled by a lack of a clear tradition of thought, outside of strictly phonological studies, on a number of overlapping questions such as theme/rheme structures (both as formal and content issues), propositional structure and cognitive questions (e.g. speech planning), a situation that has reigned for well over a quarter of a century, and which is usefully summarized in table form in Allerton (1978).

The entanglement of the various notions that cluster round the question of given and new and its relation to tonicity is attacked and somewhat clarified by Taglicht (1982), who sees the question as a wider one encompassing the placement of all accents in tone groups, not just nuclear ones. Tone groups consist of 'focal' items (marked by accent, after O'Connor and Arnold 1973) and 'residual' items (no accent). This is the 'intonation structure' of tone groups. What is 'new' (i.e. being presented as 'newsworthy') is now 'part of the total pragmatic import of the message, arrived at by extracting the "new" information from the set of "focal" items'. For the listener, nuclear accents signal 'new' information, while non-nuclear accents attach to 'potentially new' items whose interpretation depends on the listener's 'assessment of the total context'.

Taglicht acknowledges that Brazil (1978a) perceives newness as relating to 'something like accent rather than to tonicity alone or to tonicity plus syntax' and Taglicht's separation of intonation structure from the pragmatics of information assessment to a certain extent moves the given/new issue (as an aspect of information-status) to its rightful place as a feature of context of situation, by virtue of including non-nuclear accentuation in the debate. This partially echoes Brazil's unified approach to accent placement which deals with notions such as given and new under more generalized headings. These headings account for choices of accent placement independently of the choice of nuclear tone and so no nuclear placement need be anomalous since the two features represent choices made within different systems; the system of tone choice will be one thing, the system of accent placement (within the tone group, not word accent), what Brazil calls prominence, will be another. It is prominence which is at the higher level: prominence is the domain within which tonicity operates; the rules of prominence subsume all rules of givenness and newness. Brazil puts it succinctly: the last prominent syllable in the tone unit is where tone choice (i.e. choice of nuclear tone) operates and these 'tonic syllables are to be understood as constituting a sub-set of prominent syllables' (1985:21). This clearly and unambiguously separates the question of prominence from syntactic or lexical concerns. In short, the difficulties inherent in the tonicity/given–new debate arise because explanations of one set of phenomena (nuclear tones) are being sought in features which belong to an independent level of choice (prominence) and vice-versa, and anomalies are created.

This last point is best illustrated by returning to examples similar to those highlighted by Bolinger (1972a). The apparently anomalous:

2   I've got some BOOKS to sell

(uttered, for example, at a bring-and-buy sale) is not problematic if we tackle *sell* as a choice of non-prominence within the prominence system. If we can explain this non-prominence without recourse to syntactic or lexical structure (as Brazil's work does) then the tonic placement is not anomalous to any norm and is dealt with in terms of its internal choice of, say, a falling tone rather than a fall–rise, and not in terms of tonic placed on *book* rather than *sell*. The converse utterance (by a customer in a bookshop):

3   I've got some books to SELL

now need only be considered in relation to a positive choice of prominence on *sell* rather than *book*; the question of tone choice is identical with that in

(2). When the two issues are clearly separated in this way, it can be seen that many of the covering remarks made by analysts attempting to explain tonic segments are glosses for a variety of features connected with prominence and tone choice which need clearly to be distinguished. Terms such as 'contrastive' and 'emphatic' (Crystal 1975:8–10), or tonic placement reflecting 'the decision of the speaker' on what is given and new (Halliday, 1967:27), Crystal's reference to matter 'assumed by the speaker to be familiar or obvious' (1975:26), Bolinger's 'every peak is semantic' (1961), his 'semantic and emotional highlighting' (1972a) or his reference to matter 'worth getting excited about' (1972b:24), Pike's earlier allusions to intonation as 'an indication of the attitude with which the speaker expects the hearer to react' (1945:21), Newman's (1946) remarks around the same time on 'expressive accents', and some of the statements earlier quoted in this chapter, are all examples that can lead to a confusion of the significance of two distinct intonational choices.

PART II: PROMINENCE AND THE LEXICON

Bolinger (1961) had hinted at what Brazil was later to formulate rigorously when he said: 'in a broad sense every peak is contrastive', reiterated by Schmerling's (1976) remark that 'there is a sense in which anything meaningful is contrastive'. Both unconsciously echo Trier's dictum (1931, cited in Lyons 1977:270) that anything we utter implies its opposite, a statement seen by Lyons as 'more relevant to the construction of a theory of language-behaviour than it is to the analysis of a language system' (ibid.). These quotations serve not merely to underline difficulties associated with notions such as contrastiveness in relation to stress (what is there which is not contrastive?) but also provide a background to Brazil's view of the matter.

Brazil says that prominent syllables embody 'speakers' choices from known alternatives' (1985:53); the corollary is that non-prominent items represent no selection and a situation where no alternative is relevant. This generalization will have to be expanded later, but it does, for the present, enable us to see the breadth of Brazil's definition and the essentially interactive nature of prominence. Questions such as 'given' versus 'new' in terms of old and new information (whether formally or propositionally recoverable in a discourse), 'emphasis' and 'contrast' of items in a discourse, focal or thematic centres, or 'information centres' (after Grimes 1975:280ff) now become subordinate to a speaker's perception or projection of a context of interaction in which he/she may choose to realize an item as though it were a 'given' in terms of negotiated, shared meaning, or to realize it as 'new' in the sense of discourse-forwarding, unnegotiated, matter-yet-to-be-fixed (or indeed something in need of re-negotiation). By this definition, since it is a social projection of a context (Brazil 1985:47), prominence will not be explicated with reference to truth-conditions, factuality or 'textual' rules. The assumptions made by the speaker in the choice of prominence may be challenged by the listener; the world projected by the choices will be a half-way house in terms of the overall patterns inherent in any discourse: the varying convergence and divergence of the speaker's and listener's worlds. Any proper explication of such choices will be a pragmatic one.

This last remark would seem, on the face of it, to leave Brazil's theory somewhat deflated: if all prominence choices can simply be attributed to the speaker's decision to project things as 'choices from known alternatives', then, so what? Yet it is precisely here that the most powerful link between the interactive and the linguistic is seen by Brazil. All language is indeed choice from alternatives, but prominence choices represent not selections within the general paradigms inherent within the fixed, stable, shared language system as a global whole, but within a narrow, ever-changing set of paradigms whose limits are discourse-internal, fixed by the interaction of the participants themselves and shifting in real time. These paradigms are existential paradigms, they represent 'that set of possibilities that a speaker can regard as actually available in a given situation' (Brazil 1985:41). They are sets of choices imposed by the real world and the interaction of the moment. This view can be seen to operate in Oakeshott-Taylor's example at (1) above and repeated here:

4   A: What d'you think of JOHN?
    B: Oh, JOHN's all right

John is projected by the speaker as a selection from a list of possible candidates towards whom he/she has positive or negative feelings; that list does not have to be realized in the discourse; it may be, but it is essentially a projected world. One of Brazil's own examples amply illustrates the converse:

5   Q: who sent you away?
    A: an insolent ofFICial

where non-prominent *insolent* is projected as no selection, from no putative list of alternatives (i.e. what else do you expect officials to be?). In the two cases illustrated, the paradigms are distinct: *John* is not a selection from the system-paradigm of 'all proper male adult names' and *insolent* is not one from the 'open class of adjectives relating to manner or behaviour' in any real sense. John is from a projected paradigm of real-world candidates; insolent is from a paradigm with only one member. Yet clearly, in the last example, *insolent* could be substituted by *cheeky* or *bolshy*, for example by a speaker reiterating another speaker's use of *insolent*, a feature that occurs often in conversation. If the reiteration is non-prominent it will pass with minimal disturbance to the message. Brazil's explanation for this represents another key concept in his overall theory: that the 'slots' amenable to prominence or non-prominence are not word slots (in the sense of item slots) but *sense* slots, and that any item substituted for another in a non-prominent slot will be projected by the speaker (and, crucially, perceived by the listener) as largely synonymous with the item substituted. The existential paradigm is not a set of linguistic items but a set of 'mutually incompatible senses' (Brazil 1985:56). Thus, in (6), the alternatives are synonymous.

6   Q: Who sent you away?
              insolent
    R: A(n) cheeky ofFICial
              bolshy

The three choices are 'equally available words not representing sense choices' (ibid.). If there is anything to choose between the items (e.g. a different age group or social group's preference) then these will be choices of 'modes of expression' rather than sense choices (ibid.:58) and they further underline the shifting, social nature of the paradigms.

Logically, if speakers project items as being selective or non-selective from paradigms, then we should expect occurrences where items are signalled as non-synonymous, where it is semantic distinctions that are important, and anticipate utterances such as:

7   he WASn't merely CHEEky, he was DOWNright INsolent

Such an utterance sounds quite uncontroversial, and indeed this deliberate search for precision, the rejection of an item as inadequate to one's meaning and the clear signalling of the increment of meaning that one item can offer over another, has informed the debate on 'metalinguistic negation' which is addressed in Kiparsky and Kiparsky (1971) and, latterly, Horn (1985).

Naturally occurring discourse may therefore be predicted to contain, by virtue of the interactive nature of the paradigms, not only the conventional lexical relations inherent in a decontextualized description of the language but existentially valid relations, including relations 'not necessarily [those] customarily thought to inhere in the abstract lexicon of the language' (Brazil 1985:55). Lexical studies needs must take such a dimension into account and (a) examine large amounts of data to ratify the implications of Brazil's theory, and (b) incorporate categories into lexical theory that can accommodate the singular nature of lexical discourse relations which cannot easily be captured by the tools of conventional lexicology and lexical semantics. One does not in fact have to look far for substantiating data. The remainder of this chapter will refer to conversational data from the Survey of Spoken English (hereinafter SSE) available in published form in Svartvik and Quirk (1980) and in Crystal and Davy (1975). The samples are representative of a larger collection extracted from some 17,000 tone units of SSE data, a full report of which has been published elsewhere (McCarthy 1988). The existential level of lexical relations observable in the data can broadly be characterized as creating relations of equivalence, opposition and inclusion (with obvious parallels in the synonymy, antonymy and hyponymy of semantics) and subcategories of scalability, reversibility, etc. No special claim is made for the terminology proposed here: the data largely speaks for itself and the labelling is secondary. The realization of these existential relations is clearly observable where relexicalization takes place in the data, i.e. any occasion where content is repeated (including identical lexical form), whether prominently or non-prominently, together with surrounding evidence in the discourse.

It was stated above that central to Brazil's theory of prominence is the notion of projection of context and signalling of selection or non-selection paradigmatically. SSE data bears this out: as well as the many non-prominent 'grammar-words' which are found in any discourse, we find non-prominent relexicalizations of lexical items where second occurrence is signalled as synonymous with the first. In a discussion of a lecturer's timetable we find:

8   A: are THEY in fact **conducted** by HIM
    C: HE **does** this five fifteen on a WEdnesday one . . . . . .
    C: HE **gives** some of them in this ROOM

(143:882–8)

(Relevant reiterated items are indicated in bold; the letters before speakers' turns are those used in Svartvik and Quirk (1980); reference figures refer to page numbers, then to tone unit numbers; dotted lines indicate intervening tone units.)

What is significant in this example is the way that a second speaker relexicalizes an item and then re-relexicalizes the item signalling re-occurrences as synonymous by making them non-prominent. The kind of equivalence that occurs is discourse-internal; semantic potential that may be exploited in other situations to create differences of meaning is not realized. Semantic and discourse synonymy can coincide:

9   A: AGatha CARter of WHOM you may have **HEARD**
    A   CLARKE **knows of** HER SHE's a meDIEvalist

(90:437–40)

Hear of and *know of* are componentially near synonyms. Examples such as (8) and (9) reveal the need to separate the structural-semantic account of synonymy from pragmatic relations of equivalence. *Conduct*, *do* and *give* might not be predicted to occur adjacently in a thesaurus and operations to 'squeeze' them into a componential account of meaning would have to be laborious and analytically counter-productive.

'Scalable' adjectives are also an area where data yields rich illustrations of the significance of prominence in the signalling of lexical relations. Items such as *want*, *pleased*, *willing* and *longing* (to do something) are not necessarily used in the straightforward scale-of-intensity way in which dictionary definitions might suggest:

10 A: NOW HE has SAID that HE and his TEAM are **WILLing** to come
   to any NOT **WILLing** they **WANT** to come to Every dePART-
   ment . . . . . .

A: i DO hope that the department will co-OPerate on this and
   WHEN by co-OPerate **WILLing** to SPEND some TIME WITH
   him and his STAFF who are **LONGing** to come and TALK to the
   dePARTment

B: we'd be VEry **pleased** to do THAT preSUMably

(837–9:551–687)

A's first use of *willing* is subject to 'contradiction negation' (Horn 1985) A
seeks a more intense term – and the newly-chosen *want* is then reiterated
prominently as *longing* and non-prominently as *pleased* (B). Meanwhile
willing has re-occurred quite unproblematically (with its original 'neutral'
meaning?) in A's second turn. What might seem remarkable is that such
shifts in lexical items hardly ever seem to cause problems of meaning for
listeners; the overlay of phonological prominence removes all potential
ambiguities and conflicts. Such items as occur in (10) belong classically to
scales whose norms are negotiated rather than absolute; their points of
reference have to be agreed upon among speakers but this is part of the
discourse process, and disagreement does not occur. Speakers are aware
both of the potential for discourse-internal scaling and intensification:

11 E: you'd be **prePAREed** to TEACH and **HAppy** to . . .
   B: YES **keen KEEN** to in fact YEAH

(874: 181–8)

Here, as one might expect, the intensified relexicalizations are prominent,
and, once again, they occur not just in one speaker's turn but over speaker-
boundary. Adjective sets such as *appalling/terrible* (819:876) and *amazed/
surprised* (130:155–7) occur also in interesting prominence patterns which
suggest that decontextualized attempts to fix them on scales of intensity
miss much of the interactive negotiability of such items in real-time speech.
Perhaps of greater interest is the way in which adverbial intensifiers are
often signalled as equivalent (by non-prominent relexicalizations) in ways
which decontextualized semantics might not predict:

12 A: but he's SO BUsy
   B: M
   C: you KNOW
   D: yes he's **VEry** busy at the MOment
   E: YES well he's ALways **frantically** BUsy

(101:1055–61)

Frantically is to be heard as equivalent to *very* which in turn is an intensification of *so*. The reverse order occurs too:

13 A: she's **TErribly** SErious **very** SErious girl

(104:1207–8)

Such intensifiers are necessarily on a negotiated scale of meaning and speakers project assumptions of their usability to describe situations, so much as to say 'for our purposes I am assuming *very* to be on the same level as *frantically* or *terribly*'. Equally, if the existential paradigm permits a range of equivalence or discourse synonymy for items, then relations of oppositeness ought to reveal the same awareness and negotiability of sense and the 'limits of the moment' within which items are to be understood.

Antonymy in discourse is slightly less straightforward than the relations of sameness or synonymy. This is recognized within semantics. Lyons talks of speakers drawing attention to the precise terms of reference for gradable adjectives by clearly defining the relationship of an adjective to its potential antonym. In the pair: 'Is X a good chess player?' 'No, but he's not bad either' the second speaker needs to avoid the implicature which would be suggested by a simple 'no' (Lyons 1977:278). This type of signalling may be interpreted as speakers clarifying the precise nature of the existential paradigm within which notions of oppositeness (or potential oppositeness) are operating. SSE data has examples of this. Opposites occur not merely gratuitously but clearly as mutually defining terms within paradigms; the mutually exclusive senses are 'publicly exposed':

14 A: //r he's a **THOUGHTful** man, //r he's NOT a **HASty** man //

(44:597)

Hasty is not a repetition of any previous occurrence. Here the referring tones (fall–rises) project an assumption that the two extreme points are shared points of reference or 'common ground' (Brazil 1985:109), further reinforcing the view of the paradigm as an act of negotiation. (14) is, again, not an isolated example: *grow* and *diminish* elsewhere occur in an almost identical 'paradigm-framing' operation (156:247–9), and on other occasions speakers reveal their awareness of the need to specify the position of an item within the paradigm by paraphrasing with synonymy rather than antonymy. Taglicht (1982) has observed the importance of oppositeness as a 'textual pragmatic concept', making a distinction between primary (inherent) opposites and secondary (discourse-circumstantial) opposites, but the functions of oppositions of the kind alluded to in the present data need more research; they clearly operate within paradigmatic bounds conditioned by the context of interaction and play a key role in the fixing of lexical meaning in discourse.

The last of the major lexical relations alluded to, inclusion, or discourse hyponymy, has a significant role in the 'packaging' of unfolding information in talk. Speakers may reiterate entities either in the form of a term of greater specificity for which previously a superordinate term has sufficed, or may do the reverse, renaming an entity or entities by an item of broader or superordinate reference. Allerton (1978) has referred to the phenomenon where an item is reiterated by a superordinate form and has pointed out the apparent irreversibility of hyponymous realizations; (15) is typical, (16) is odd:

15 A: d'you drink WHISky
    B: i'm afraid I don't TOUCH spirits at ALL

16 A: d'you drink WHISky
    B: i'm afraid I don't LIKE bourbon

This is explained by the fact that whereas the hyponym entails the superordinate, the reverse is rarely true. Generally speaking this is so, and superordinates (and more especially the class of general noun) operate cohesively within and over speaker turns to encapsulate previous items:

17 A: we DON'T seem to have very much **WOOD**
    B: YES THAT's a POINT YES M
    C: well i supPOSE if we went into the PARK we MIGHT collect a few **STICKS** but it's NOT quite like having **LOGS** IS it . . . . . .
    D: BACK in the MIDlands we would KNOW if you KNOW WHERE we could GO and GET all these **things** from but
                        (Crystal and Davy 1969: 29:1141–8)

Wood is specifically relexicalized (prominently) as *sticks* and *logs* and then both are encapsulated in the inclusion-relationship realized by nonprominent *things*. This follows the entailment principles, though it is not inconceivable that a second speaker might project an assumption that *sticks* and *wood* are equivalent in a situation where *sticks* (and not *logs*) were the only obvious or appropriate kind of wood for the job:

18 A: we NEED some **WOOD** for the FIRE
    B: well there ARE some DRY **sticks** HERE

An example of this reverse entailment, which is really a projection of discourse equivalence between the semantic superordinate and its hyponym, is the following:

19 C: but I had TROUBLE GETting my **PApers** i eVENtually got a **work permit** after about a FIVE month deLAY
                                  (146:1060–1)

Here the 'papers' in question are projected as being discourse equivalent to the work permit. *Papers* is understood by the participants to be a usable term to refer to documents enabling the speaker to work in the USA.

What is to be included in a term, or what needs specifying, will be situation-bound and prominence choices will reflect speakers' projections of mutual understanding of the situation. Indeed all these discourse-bound lexical relations are concerned with 'use' rather than 'meaning'. It is thus more appropriate, perhaps, to look at the 'usefulness' of items in any discourse; the relational terms offered here (equivalence, contrast and inclusion) are intended to reflect just such a dimension.

The above data samples are presented as examples of the types of occurrences that should be included in an examination of the level of lexis in discourse. They are significant both as realizations of the negotiability of lexical meaning and as manifestations of the existential paradigms from which lexical selections are made in real time. Brazil's view of prominence as the phonological system that realizes the paradigms is an indispensable background to a discourse theory of lexis and as such is a major advance in the study of the relationship between semantic, formal and substantial levels of linguistic encoding.

'Interactive lexis: prominence and paradigms' was first published in Coulthard (1987a) *Discussing Discourse*, 236–48.

11 Listening to people reading

David Brazil

READING AND TALKING

Since the so-called 'Discourse Model' for the analysis of intonation was proposed (Brazil 1975), a considerable number of people have sought to apply its categories to what happens when we read aloud. Areas of interest have varied widely, from the intonation of native learners when they read out to adults in the very early stages of literacy to the performance of actors, poets and others when they read verse aloud. Among the matters investigated have been the different styles of reading that go with different kinds of public communication on radio, television and elsewhere; the possibility of using material read aloud as a means of identifying the special characteristics of the intonation that foreign learners of English use is currently being explored.

Personal contact with some of this work convinces me of the need to look systematically at the great variety of activities that common usage includes under the collective label 'reading aloud'. Evidently, we cannot get very far on the basis of a straight comparison between the intonation of speech and the intonation of reading. We need, first of all, some way of clarifying, in a way which is relevant to the task in hand, what readers are doing on a particular occasion when they read aloud. By relevant I mean that any typology that emerges should be capable of being mapped onto the intonation in some way. There are many ways in which one might classify the multifarious acts of reading aloud of which literate people are capable. In trying to contribute to the essential task of systematizing the diversity, I am concerned here with distinctions that have, or seem likely to have, regular intonational consequences.

The discourse-based description of intonation which is set out in some detail in Brazil (1985) was based upon the examination of a great deal of spontaneous, naturally produced, data of various kinds. Its categories are defined, moreover, in terms which make direct reference to the here-and-now state of speaker/hearer convergence that is assumed to provide the matrix for each successive increment in an interactive speech event. Its central organizing principle could be said to be the notion of a step-by-step progression, in which situationally appropriate discourse is generated by both parties to the interaction in response to the assumed communicative need of the moment. All of which is to say that it treats spoken discourse as a real-time 'happening', as a linearly organized sequence of events, the details of whose organization beyond the moment of utterance may as yet have not been determined by the speaker.

Now it is evident that there are problems in relating this set of concepts to the act of reading aloud. Most obviously, we read aloud from a prepared text, so there is no question of our being engaged in the generation of here-and-now appropriate utterances. The fact of working with such a text crucially modifies the open-ended nature of the speaker's activity: far from 'happening' piecemeal along the time dimension, the material we read and convert to speech 'exists' as an already completed object and, in certain acts of reading aloud at least, the reader's apprehension of its completeness – of the point to which everything is leading – must surely be one of the things that determines how it is read. Even more important for my present concerns is the more complex way in which the notion of a speaker/hearer relationship must be applied if it is to be useful in a discussion of reading. It is now quite usual to speak of reading as an 'interactive' activity, but what people seem usually to have in mind is some kind of 'interaction with the text', an idea which differs importantly from that of 'interaction with a listener'. Arguably, preoccupation with reading as a silent, private activity has favoured the former notion. I am not, at present, concerned with this. My starting-point is the observation that, in spite of the many differences between the circumstances in which spontaneous speech and reading aloud occur, both activities utilize the same repertoire of intonational options, and since these options correlate with aspects of the speaker/hearer relationship in speech, there is a strong case for exploring the nature of that relationship in reading.

It is this latter relationship that I propose to focus upon, and which I shall make the basis of the differences I shall try to point up among the various ways in which we can read aloud. In doing so, I shall make spontaneous interactive speech my point of comparison. Roughly speaking, I shall be seeking to identify different kinds of reading by asking how far they resemble speech in those respects which affect their phonological form. It may reasonably be objected that this procedure is flawed at the outset, for there are at least as many different ways of speaking as there are of reading aloud. Nevertheless, it is possible to work on the basis of a centrally conceived phenomenon called 'interactive speech' in which participants consistently and in good faith orientate to each other's supposed view of the relevant circumstances surrounding the communication – the 'common ground' of the Discourse Intonation conceptual framework. If we call this complex of circumstances the *context of interaction*, then we can call the speaker's propensity to take those circumstances into account his or her *engagement with the context of interaction*. In the unlikely –

perhaps impossible – event of a speaker proceeding with no regard at all for a notional communicative state of play between themself and a real or potential hearer, we should be justified in speaking of total disengagement. The central possibility that I set out to explore is that we can set up a working classification of acts of reading aloud by recognizing various *degrees of engagement*. I shall be trying to show that, by making comparison with the speaker's performance in interactive events:

1 we can postulate and justify a scale of degrees of engagement;
2 the placing of any bit of reading on that scale provides us with a useful working classification of performances;
3 and although there is considerable overlapping of the specific intonation treatments associated with the various types, each actually involves the reader in using the intonation system in a distinctive way.

The first part of the paper is concerned with what is involved in setting up such a typology. After that I illustrate its use by comparing three specimens of reading. Finally, I apply the procedure to a brief examination of the relationship between the metrical organization of verse and the way it is read.

ENGAGEMENT: 1

I will begin at one pole of what is probably best thought of as a continuum. Let us postulate a condition which we will call *minimal engagement* – Stage 1 along a notional scale, the other end of which is *full engagement*. It is a condition in which speakers have no concern with the communicative possibilities of what they read, over and above that which arises unavoidably from the apprehension that it is a sample of a language that they and those who hear them, know. Perhaps the clearest example is the act of word-citation. To read aloud a word randomly chosen from a dictionary is to make no assumptions about how it will fit into any discourse or impinge upon any hearer in anything more than a minimal way. And it happens, conveniently, that the institutionally fixed citation forms of certain words provide us with a clue to the intonation treatment of minimally engaged reading. Words which are assigned a secondary stress followed by a primary stress, e.g. ^2un ^1happy, and are customarily read out as two-prominence tone units,

   // UN HAPpy //

are usually recognizable as citations, because when these words are used in engaged discourse there is a very strong tendency for no more than one of the potential prominences to be realized. Thus the citation form contrasts with the various treatments that the same word might receive when it is used in interaction:

// a UNhappy exPERience //
// it MADE her unHAppy //
// a RAther unhappy TIME //, etc.

In the case of words like *unhappy*, a manifestation of minimally engaged discourse can, then, be recognized by the presence of 'extra prominences'. Much the same is true, in the reading of longer stretches of language: the normally observed maximum of two prominences per tone unit can be exceeded. Just as

// she said she was UN HAppy //

puts something like audible quotation marks around the word 'happy', so the allocation of three prominences to the second tone unit in

// she SAID she'd HAD // a RATHer unHAppy TIME //

puts them around 'a rather unhappy time'.

Examples like these do, in fact, represent what seems to be the most common reason why competent readers have recourse to a minimally engaged mode in performance: it enables them to separate off some part of what is read and present it as an assertion which the reader simply quotes verbatim. It is a means whereby readers can limit themselves to reporting a form of words and stop short of implicating themselves in questions concerning the truth, the sincerity, or perhaps the present significance, of what is read.

Noting this enables me to make a general point about the kind of enterprise I am undertaking. Speaking of different kinds of reading which correlate with degrees of engagement might suggest a procedure for classifying whole events, say the reading-out of a public announcement or of a paragraph from a book. Probably, in most cases, readers do sustain the kind of consistent stance that would make this possible. We must be prepared, however, for fairly frequent changes of stance in the course of some readings: in principle, the degree of involvement can change at the end of any tone unit.

We can think of the examples we have just discussed as instances of readers exploiting the system: of making use of the opportunity to withdraw temporarily from a higher level of engagement, and of making clear that they are doing so, in order to attach particular communicative implications to a part of the text. But minimally engaged reading does occur in other circumstances. One such is in the inexpert or unsympathetic reading aloud of a line of verse:

// i WANdered LONEly AS a CLOUD //

Another can sometimes be heard when young learners read aloud in class or elsewhere:

// it was VERy GRAND to KNOW SOMEbody who
OWNED a CIRcus //

Both of these demonstrate the reader's strictly limited involvement in the material being read. Both readers – though for different reasons – see their task as to 'say what the text says' without being concerned with what its potential communicative implications might be.

The lack of engagement that such reading represents can, in fact, be fairly easily related to the categories of the Discourse Intonation model and to the significances attaching to them. Among the decisions that an engaged speaker must make there are two kinds that are evidently interdependent. They both concern the way linguistic items realize, or do not realize, existentially significant *selections*.

Firstly, there is the matter of how *prominence* is distributed. In a minimally engaged reading, this kind of decision is made simply on the basis of whether the words are perceived as 'content words' or not, a distinction we can provisionally think of as being inherent in the language system. In any engaged use of language, prominences occur as a result of decisions over and above those that result in the use of particular words; they are, in effect, decisions about the communicative status of the item in a particular conversational nexus. The maximally disengaged reader avoids making such decisions by regarding prominence as something which is already assigned in the citation form of the word.

Then there is the matter of division into tone units. In interactive discourse, a form of words like 'It was very grand to know somebody who owned a circus' might be divided in various ways, for instance

// it was VERy GRAND // to know SOMEbody who owned a CIRcus //

or

// it was VERy grand to KNOW somebody // who owned a CIRcus //

The decisive questions for the interactant concern how the selections realized by the various prominences combine, so as to articulate oppositions of a larger kind, and therefore mesh with present communicative needs. Doubtless an engaged reading of the context would provide a reader with grounds for selecting one of these versions or the other. The minimally engaged reading, however, is made without benefit of the kind of information which would incline the reader towards any particular way of assigning tone unit boundaries. The fairly common one-tone-unit-per-sentence arrangement that we find in such a reading can be thought of as arising from a reliance, once more, on the reader's recognition of a linguistic item, this time the 'sentence'; but it is worth noting that other considerations might tip the balance: in the case of the disengaged reading of verse, for instance, one-tone-unit-per-line is probably more common, something that reinforces the impression that the end result is a rather arbitrarily chosen fall-back position, arrived at in the absence of those situational factors on which speakers usually rely.

Finally, we may note the probability of there being a *proclaiming tone*.

This seems to follow naturally from the inbuilt ambiguity of this tone: a falling tone serves to mark the tone unit as the vehicle of unshared information, but this includes both now-relevant information about the world and information about the piece of language that is being quoted.

For one further example of minimally engaged reading, consider the case of someone idly reading out the titles of the books on the shelf in front of her (a comparatively rare instance of a reading activity to which no communicative purpose seems necessarily to accrue!).

//p the SOUND PATTern of ENGlish //
//p ENGlish phoNETics and phoNOLogy //

These forms can be compared with probable conversational forms:

Q: Where did you read that?
A: //p in the SOUND pattern of ENGlish //
(*or*)　//p in ENGlish phonetics and phoNOLogy //

ENGAGEMENT: 2

One consideration that probably limits the incidence of the kind of disengaged mode I have just described in actual reading is that it depends on the reader being able to process and verbalize the entire length of the tone unit without hesitation or cognitive hold-up. The mechanical fluency and exaggerated rhythmicality of the remembered line of verse is evidence of the way tone units are pre-packed and articulated as a whole. In spontaneous speech, the need for time to assemble each consecutive increment can be seen to impose limitations on the length of tone units. Obviously the cognitive needs of a reader are different from those of the speaker, but they are no less likely to impose constraints. Instead of being involved in the complex business of assembling an original utterance in real time, the reader has the equally complex task of decoding – also in real time – an already assembled text.

Depending upon their skill in doing this, and also on the familiarity of the text, we can expect the performance to exhibit the feature that commonly accompanies hesitation pauses, *zero* (i.e. '*level*') *tone*:

//o it was VERy //o GOOD to KNOW //o SOMEbody who
OWNED //p a CIRcus //

This example need only differ from the multi-prominence version we examined earlier in that the reader lacks the facility to deal with the printed item at a single bite. The number and distribution of prominent syllables remain as they were, and could be the result of a similar, non-listener sensitive, choice procedure. The tone unit boundaries are the only difference, and if these arise from cognitive need, they will indicate no necessary engagement with the kind of contextual projection that would motivate them in interactive discourse. This kind of *oblique* presentation would seem, therefore, to differ from the minimally engaged reading we placed at Stage 1 above only in so far as decoding and planning delays interfere with the smooth articulation of the (uninterpreted) language sample. In practice, it most often occurs as a switch to *oblique* orientation when obstacles are encountered in the course of an otherwise *directly* orientated performance.

The matter is complicated, however, by the fact that the same zero tone is exploited in a style of reading in which there are no decoding problems, a style which we can describe as in some sense *ritualized*. As in spontaneous speech, the tone unit with zero tone may occur in two different circumstances: it can, as we have said, mark a temporary departure from an otherwise hearer-sensitive stance in order to allow the reader to focus upon some matter of linguistic interpretation which is currently creating a problem; or it may be used consistently for the whole of some deliberately delineated portion of a text or even for the whole of the text. Its effect in the latter case is to mark the matter of the reading as *not* an attempted dramatization of a situated and person-to-person communication, but as an explicitly non-interactive presentation of whatever the content may be.

There is a difference between the two, however, for in the case of the ritualized presentation, we can expect that some of the intonational features it would have if it were part of a hearer-sensitive reading will be retained. This last expectation can be illustrated if we compare two possible readings of a stanza from Keats's 'Meg Merrilies'.

1 //r Her APPles //p were swart BLACKberries
   //r her CURrants //p POD'S o' BROOM
   //r her WINE //p was the DEW of the wild white ROSE
   //r her BOOK //p a churchyard TOMB //

2 //o her APPles //o were swart BLACKberries
   //o her CURrents //o POD'S o' BROOM
   //o her WINE //o was the DEW of the wild white ROSE
   //o her BOOK //o a churchyard TOMB

In the first version, the referring tone in the first tone unit of each line projects an assumption that hearers, having been told that Meg lived upon the moors, will naturally want to know how she managed for apples, currants and so on. The proclaimed tone units tell them. This is to say the reading is hearer sensitive. The lack of prominence in *swart* and *churchyard* reflects the likelihood that these will not constitute existential selections, since edible blackberries are normally swart and, at least in the world of Keats's poem, tombs are normally found in churchyards. These last details of the reading and certain others may be open to debate, but the point is that *an acceptable ritualized reading will follow an acceptable fully engaged reading in all matters except that tone differences are levelled under zero tone*. We can make this clear by comparing an oblique reading that an unprepared or unskilled reader might have produced:

3   //o her APples were //o SWART //o BLACKberries
　　//o her CURRants POD'S //o o' BROOM //, etc.

While the phonological shape of (3) can be presumed to arise largely from decoding or other problems that the reader happens to have along the way, that of (2) results from a partial meshing of the reading with a projected interactive context. While (3) is thus an involuntary consequence of something that has nothing to do with speaker/hearer relationships, (2) can reasonably be regarded as a result of a filtering out, on the part of the reader, of those distinctions that speakers customarily realize by choices in the proclaiming/referring system.

The kind of reading that makes use of level tones in this latter way can, therefore, be thought of as taking us one step away from the minimally engaged end of the continuum: it is hearer-sensitive in the way that it assigns prominence and tone unit boundaries, but, perhaps intentionally, not so in its choice of tones. The kind of ritualistic performance that results is fairly easily recognized in, for instance, much of the reading that forms part of religious observance. It is also frequently heard in the reading aloud of poetry, a fact that we shall return to later. It is worth noting in passing that these are both likely to be, to a large extent, rehearsed readings, based upon prior consideration of the implications of the subject matter: that is to say prior consideration of what the communicative value of the material might be if it were spoken instead in a conversational context.

In practice, it is not always possible to distinguish readings of the two kinds we have compared. If the phonological shape of a particular reading of, say, 'I Wandered Lonely as a Cloud' comes about accidentally, as it were, as a result of the chance encounter with decoding problems, there is a considerable likelihood that it will coincide with a perfectly acceptable ritualized version, deeply pondered and carefully executed. Often, there is not much room for variation and, for reasons that we need not go into here, places where decoding difficulties occur may well be those places at which, in probable discourse contexts, tone unit boundaries would be indicated. In analysing a particular reading, therefore, we may often have no way of knowing whether what we have is just the consequence of disfluency or of discoursically significant choices. The distinction is, nevertheless, one that must be recognized if we are to get a clearer picture of how degrees of engagement are manifested in performance. We will say that ritualized oblique reading represents Stage 2 on our scale.

ENGAGEMENT: 3

Stage 3 on the continuum can be represented by a kind of encounter with the written word that may seem, at first sight, to merit no consideration at all in the working out of an interactive theory of communication: the reading aloud of an uncontextualized sentence.

A study of this activity (Brazil 1984b) led to two observations, the interpretation of which does have an important bearing upon present concerns. When subjects were asked to read out lists of sentences presented to them simply as sentences:

(a) there was a high measure of conformity among the performances of various readers when they were confronted with certain sentences, but great variation when they were confronted with others;
(b) when readers did agree, their performances could often be manipulated in an equally predictable way by making some small grammatical or lexical change in the item they were asked to read.

As an instance of (b), compare the preferred readings:

1 //r WHERE it CAME from //p is a MYStery //

2 //p WHERE it CAME from //r is the MYStery //

Differences in tone choice seem here to be dependent on whether a definite or an indefinite article is used. A similar alternation can be elicited by varying the adjunct:

3 //r preSUMably //p the WEATHer improved //

4 //p adMITTedly //r the WEATHer improved //

The initial temptation to ascribe the differences between (1) and (2) simply to the reader's apprehension of a grammatical change, and to seek correlations between intonation and grammatical constituency, has to be resisted for at least three reasons:

1 A similar difference can be elicited by a lexical change as in (3) and (4).
2 The choice of either definite or indefinite article does not actually compel a particular phonological treatment; discourse contexts can easily be invented in which the alternative versions of both (1) and (2) are perfectly natural.
3 Both these pairs and an indeterminate number of other pairs in which different kinds of alteration are made can be given identical explanations if we make direct reference to the context of interaction.

The explanation takes the following form. For readers, the material to be read is part of the context of interaction. When that material comprises uncontextualized sentences it is the *only* basis they have on which to construct a conversational setting for what they read out. Some details of the organization of the sentence can powerfully suggest – in terms of probability – what that setting would be like, and these suggestions may be pertinent to the choice of particular intonation features. Thus, the occurrence of *the* in (2) suggests that the idea of a *mystery* has already been introduced into the conversational setting that the reader shares with some (unidentifiable) hearer, and is thus available to be referred to. The change to *a*, on the other hand, suggests a different division of knowledge in which *mystery* will be proclaimed as matter not yet shared.

It is important to be clear that this is not a case of the intonation contrast merely duplicating the information represented by the *the/a* contrast. If it were, alternative permutations would be heard as anomalous. It is rather that the form of the sentence exerts sufficient pressure in the direction of assuming one or other of two possible sets of discourse conditions to incline readers towards differential readings.

Experiments with a range of other pairs of sentences, differentiated in other ways, and eliciting readings which varied with respect to other intonational variables, suggested that, at least under the test conditions appertaining, this tendency of the reader to construct some kind of rudimentary discourse context even for a single sentence is very general. Moreover, when sentences do not elicit anything approaching a consensus reading, it seems that this is because their form would allow them to be equally plausible contributions in a number of different contexts.

I shall take it, then, that the phonological forms in question represent a clear movement along the *scale of engagement*. They exhibit, in fact, the only kind of engagement that is available for readers performing this particular task: engagement with a hypothetical conversational nexus constructed *ad hoc* on the evidence that the sentences provides. As occupants of Stage 3 on the scale, they differ from Stage 2 cases in that, in addition to other features, the tones associated with an engaged reading are deployed.

Although, therefore, the reading out of sentences has little place in what we might regard as normal linguistic activity, and the kind of performance it elicits occurs only to a negligible extent when people read other material for non-experimental purposes, there are reasons why the kind of Stage 3 engagement they involve is worth bringing into focus. For one thing, it shows the very marked propensity readers have for placing what they read in an interactive context, even when the help they have in constructing that context is no more than vestigial. We might almost say that attaching some kind of interactive significance to linguistic items is the more natural way of dealing with them. Another reason is that it serves to underline the need for some differentiation among possible degrees of engagement like that I am attempting.

I can illustrate this by looking briefly at a matter that has attracted a lot of attention in the literature of Linguistics in recent years. Linguistic methodologies which take the sentence as their starting-point tend to rely heavily upon what is taken to be an already agreed 'citation form'. There would seem to be an obvious connection between the kind of reading activity I have just described and the act of 'citation' on which so much of linguistic argumentation depends. If we read aloud – or even articulate inwardly to ourselves – the examples that linguists 'cite' we usually have no alternative but to treat them as isolated sentences; indeed, it is often stated that it is in this capacity that we must view them. Unfortunately, though, there is little or no recognition in the literature that a 'cited' sentence might be performed in a way which corresponds with any one of the three stages of engagement we have postulated so far:

1 //p WHERE it CAME from is a MYStery //
2 //o WHERE it CAME from //p is a MYStery //
3 //r WHERE is CAME from //p is a MYStery //

This failure to be clear about just what a citation form is can seriously confuse any argumentation that takes that form as its axiomatic starting point, particularly when attention is being directed to explicitly phonological matters. Let us take the common practice of equating the 'citation form', either explicitly or implicitly, with an assumed 'normal', 'neutral' or 'unmarked' intonation for the sentence in question – a base line from which the discussion of the significance of other possible contours is expected to proceed. A much discussed observation is that, while for many sentences, the favoured reading – and hence the 'neutral' intonation – puts the tonic syllable in the last content word,

//p i'm COMing on FRIday //

the way some sentences are read provides reason for saying that 'neutral' intonation will place it earlier:

//p the POSTman's coming //

What is missing from the very considerable amount of discussion that this 'problem' has occasioned is any apparent awareness that, at least for the two examples cited, 'neutral' intonation results from what we have called Stage 3 engagement.

// i'm COMing on FRIday //
or
// i'm coming on FRIday //

reflect a reader's experience that Friday would probably be selective in a situated occurrence of the sentence: anyone's reason for saying such a thing is highly likely to be to specify when, out of a number of possible occasions, he is actually coming. There might well be divided judgements as to whether *coming* was also likely to be selective (and therefore to be made prominent) or not. In

// the POSTman's coming //

the phenomenon to be explained is the lack of prominence in *coming*, and hence the necessary occurrence of the tonic syllable in the preceding word; and the explanation is simply that, in no communicative situation that comes readily to mind, is there any likely alternative to *coming*. (If we move outside the bounds of common probability and imagine a situation in which there is an existential choice between *coming* and, let us say, *going*, then there will be good reason for presenting either of these verbs prominently.)

The question of which kind of reading we equate with citation is crucial in this kind of discussion. If we take it to be either of those discussed under (1) and (2) above, both of the examples will, indeed, have the tonic syllable in the last content word. It is the versions that exhibit Stage 3 involvement that display a difference in phonological treatment, a fact which arises because the form we start with is, in fact, already determined by extra-sentential considerations. Once this is recognized, there scarcely seems to be a problem to wrestle with.

It is worth pointing out, in passing, another minor source of possible confusion which arises from the way matters like this are commonly discussed: the terms 'citation' and 'citation form' have a quite different connotation from that which they have when used in connection with words, as, for instance, earlier in this chapter.

ENGAGEMENT: 4

Let us now suppose that

//p it was HARD to beLIEVE //r she was ONly TWENty //

represents the preferred version for the reading out of this single sentence. There is little doubt that a reading which retained this phonological shape when it was read as part of, let us say, this stretch of language would be heard as odd:

I had no reason to doubt anything else she said. It was hard to believe she was only twenty.

What we expect a reader to do is to relate the sentence, not to the skeletal world of presupposition that the sentence alone suggests, but to the state of speaker/hearer understanding that the material immediately preceding it has precipitated. After

I had no reason to doubt anything else she said

we might expect

//r (but) it was HARD to believe //p she was ONly TWENty //

since the notion of being – or not being – *hard to believe* is now already in play and the possibility of her being *only twenty* is presented as something not included in the already mentioned *anything else*.

We can, then, recognize a further stage of engagement, one at which the reader's intonation choices are in line with each newly created context of interaction that the progressive revelation in the text sets up.

To illustrate further the difference between Stage 4 and Stage 3 engagement, let us take the preferred single sentence readings of the following:

//p he COULDn't //r have been misTAken //
//r the BOOKS //p were still lying on his TAble //
//p it must have been PEter //r they had SEEN //

If these three sentences are presented as a text, and the reader's decisions are made on a sentence-by-sentence basis, taking in the situation that has been created by earlier sentences, we might expect something like:

//p he COULDn't //r have been misTAken //p the BOOKS
//p were STILL lying on the TAble //r it MUST have been
//p PEter they had seen //

In this version, which is probably only one of several that could be invented, the books are treated as the reason for saying that *he couldn't have been mistaken* and are therefore proclaimed; and the judgement made by *must have been* has referring tone since it reiterates that implied by *he couldn't*. It follows from this kind of argument that the first sentence retains its Stage 3 form. It would seem, indeed, that someone beginning to read a so-far unseen text, whose relationship to the known interests of the hearer is not yet determined, has little option but to adopt temporarily a Stage 3 stance.

At this point, two other areas suggest themselves as ones which might be fruitfully investigated. One arises directly from what was said at the beginning of this section. It seems not unlikely that, under the pressure of real-time decision-making that reading evidently involves, readers will sometimes find themselves in a state of indecision as to whether they are processing a text on a sentence-by-sentence basis – an essentially short-term business – or processing it as a continuing entity. When Stage 4 engagement favours a form which differs radically from that which would be favoured by Stage 3 involvement, they might well have difficulty in deciding between the two. Supposing there were such a problem, we might ask what effect it would have on the phonological shape of the outcome. One possibility would be a temporary movement down the scale of engagement to Stage 2 or even Stage 1. This, we have already suggested, is what commonly happens when either speakers or readers encounter cognitive problems. In the circumstances we have envisaged, such recourse would relieve readers of the necessity for choosing and allow them time to re-establish their bearings in the present state of speaker/hearer convergence. Of course, only an extensive study of intonational features in the neighbourhood of errors, hesitations, self-corrections and so on in a large amount of data would give empirical substance to this speculation. I include it here, not because I can prove it, but rather as an example of the kind of question the present approach enables us to bring into focus.

Much the same is true of the other area. In the first of the examples cited above, the intonation of one tone unit is related to a feature of the state of speaker/hearer convergence that is articulated in the tone unit *immediately preceding* it. But, in the longer example, the intonation of //r it MUST have been // is related to something that happened in the first tone unit, //p he COULDn't //, and three other tone units have intervened. Some interest would seem to attach to the question of how long the 'memory' of something read at one point in the text continues to be operative as a determinant of later intonation choices. Once a feature of the state of convergence has been established in the text, how long does it remain in play, as something that the reader will orientate towards?

This last question assumes, of course, that we are indeed dealing with a case of Stage 4 engagement: that in making intonational decisions the reader relies exclusively on what has gone before in the text. In reality, everything that has gone before, however remote it may be from what is being read now, merges with those extra-textual areas of shared background that play such a big part in shaping the intonation of spontaneous speech. In other words, the greater the span of influence of an earlier tone unit upon a later one, the closer we seem to be getting to the next stage on our continuum.

ENGAGEMENT: 5

Stage 5 brings us to the point where reading aloud most closely approximates to spontaneous interaction. We can think now of a kind of reading that replicates interactive speech: speech in which participants pursue conversational purposes taking into account the entire complex network of shared assumptions. Obviously, what is involved goes far beyond confronting a text and making phonological recognition of the relationships among its parts in the way we visualized for Stage 4. The reader now has to be credited with seeing the text as the embodiment of a speaker's viewpoint, with assimilating that viewpoint to his or her own, and with creating notional hearers for whom the expressed information has relevance and who have a distinctive viewpoint of their own. Apart from the fact that memorization is not involved, the situation is similar to that of an actor performing lines already set down for him as if they were an expression of his own conversational purpose *vis-à-vis* another character. It is different, however, to a greater or lesser degree, in that whereas the 'other world' (or 'worlds') upon which the speech will impinge is largely provided by the actor's understanding of his supposed relationship with other characters within the framework of the play, our reader is likely to have a less clearly delineated world to direct his message to.

It may be helpful to recall what the intermeshing of worlds means for the speaker before going on to consider the rather different position of the reader. For the speaker, the crucial background of shared assumptions originates, to an only limited extent, in what is objectively present in the language. It comprises, in fact, the entire set of shared experiences that participants bring to the interaction, whether these are shared by reason of their personal relationship, their participation in a common culture, their common interest in some area of human activity like a sport, an academic discipline, a trade or profession, or anything else that can be found in those parts of their respective biographies that overlap. In the extreme case, an informal conversation between intimates, the possibilities are endless and the fact of already negotiated ground all-pervasive.

The written material that a reader must assimilate to speech is likely to have been created in different circumstances. For one thing, the person who created the text probably had a far less detailed profile of the addressee. Most written texts are aimed at composite readerships. Moreover, the individuals who comprise that readership are less likely to be known personally to the writer. (A personal letter is, of course, the obvious exception on both counts and consequently makes its own particular demands upon anyone who tries to read one aloud.) If we confine our attention, for the moment, to the large body of broadly discursive prose, we can probably say that considerations affecting the common ground are largely those which derive from a shared knowledge of, and an interest in, the subject matter.

The presumed recipient is, in other words, a group, defined by interest, rather than an individual or individuals. The task of recreating an interactive version of the text which devolves upon the reader would seem therefore to be satisfactorily completed when this has been taken into account. Something of what this involves will emerge in what follows.

SOME EXAMPLES OF READING

In all I have done so far in this chapter, I have been making predictions about readers' behaviour on the basis of a more-or-less commonsense view of how particular circumstances are likely to affect their use of the intonation system. At this point it is perhaps helpful to examine some specimens of what readers have actually done, to try to relate them to those predictions, and, particularly, to see what light the proposed scale of engagement sheds upon the particular acts of reading aloud they are severally engaged in.

To make comparisons easier, three people were asked to read out almost identical texts. They were simulated reports of events at a football match. Reader 1 was asked to read his text as a sports columnist filing a report by phone on the assumption that a colleague was taking it down from his dictation. The second, taking the part of the colleague, was to read back what he had written for checking purposes. The third, acting as newsreader, then read the report as it would be included in the radio news bulletin that evening. Practised and confident readers were used so that, although their performances were doubtless affected by the fact that the activities were simulated, the resulting readings were sufficiently close to the real thing for the comparisons to be useful.

It helps in the examination of the outcome if we take the third version first.

//r+ at the NATional stadium in NIBlitz today //p supPORTers CLASHED //r when ENGland //p played their WORLD CUP match //r against the PRESent cupholders //p RURiTAnia //o ENGland //p had HELD //r+ the CHAMpions //p to ONE ONE //p until HALF TIME //r but SOON after play was reSUMED //p a PENalty //p was awarded aGAINST them //r acCORding to our reporter jim BULLock //r the deCISion //p CAUSEd UProar //r+ aMONGST a GROUP //p of ENGland FANS //r+ and THIS in TURN //r provoked an ANgry resPONSE //r from some opPOSing supporters //r in an adJOINing section //p of the STAND //

We might expect this reading to be at or near the end of the continuum which represents maximal engagement. The newsreader could be expected to anticipate in her performance the assumptions which she, as purveyor of the news, shared with those people in her audience who were interested in this particular item. For our present purposes, the situation differs from that of one person telling another conversationally about what happened at Niblitz principally in that the second party, even if its composition is narrowed down to that portion of the listening public who take an interest in football, is an enormous and diverse group. This last fact would lead us to expect the reader to err on the side of explicitness: not to take everything for granted that might, in a one-to-one conversation, reasonably be taken for granted. It will be a fully engaged presentation, but one in which engagement will be with a composite recipient: considerations of highest common factors and of how much can properly be taken for granted, will therefore be of some importance.

Taking tone choices first, we can say that the treatment of the first sentence is in line with these expectations. On the day when this item occurs in the news, it is sensible to assume a widely shared interest in what happened *in the National stadium at Niblitz today*, and therefore to present this part of the bulletin with a referring tone. The same applies to *when England* and *the present cupholders*. But the same might well be thought to be true of *played their World Cup match* and *Ruritania*. Surely the kind of involvement we are attributing to hearers would make both the special significance of the match and the name of the opposing side equally available in the common pool? We may, perhaps, attribute the fact that this availability is not acknowledged by the reader to her being less than one hundred per cent efficient; and in view of the complexity of the demands that the performance of such a task makes, we ought not to be surprised at occasional lapses from the intonation that a strict examination of the circumstances would lead us to expect. An alternative version, which associates referring tone with mention of *the World Cup match*, could certainly be said to be a 'better' reading if it is judged solely on the basis of its meshing with a likely listeners' world.

It would, however, result in a sequence of three referring tones; the consideration we have mentioned above of not taking too much for granted could plausibly result in the reader proclaiming more than was strictly necessary. Much the same applies later to;

//r the deCISion //p caused UProar //r+ aMONGST a GROUP //p of ENGland FANS //

A reasonable prediction would be that it would be England fans, rather than those supporting Ruritania, who would be upset by a questionable decision against England. There is therefore no obvious reason why the last tone unit should be proclaimed. But, once more, we notice that if every tone unit that could justifiably have a referring tone had one, there would be a lengthy series of them. So again, we find that departure from the 'expected' pattern is in the direction of taking less for granted.

It would be difficult to say why one tone unit in the sequence rather than another has a proclaiming tone rather than the expected referring tone; the choice could well be a random one. What we should expect, however, and what seems to be borne out in practice, is that substitutions are much less likely to be made in the other direction. The version

//r supPORters CLASHED //r when ENGland //p played their WORLD CUP match //

which substitutes referring tone for proclaiming tone in the first tone unit, amounts to a misreading of the item: it attributes to hearers the assumption that there was a clash of supporters somewhere, and assumes that their interest is in hearing where! However bad the reputation of football fans may have been at the time, the news item would scarcely have been addressed primarily to that interest.

If the tendency towards extra explicitness can be related to tone choice, it seems to be even more in evidence in the allocation of prominent syllables. In the kind of community of interest that the football world represents, the four tone units (and six prominent syllables) of

// when ENGland // played their WORLD CUP match // against the PRESent cupholders // RURiTAnia //

would, in reality, amount to an unnecessary indication of several of the selections. Probably, all that would be really necessary would be to remind hearers of the two teams. This would be achieved by a version which had just two prominent syllables:

// when ENGland played their world cup match against the present cup holders ruriTAnia //

which, for most people would amount to

// when ENGland played ruriTAnia //

The shared knowledge that the *England v. Ruritania* game was existentially equivalent to *World Cup match* and that *the present cupholders* was similarly equivalent to *Ruritania* eliminates the possibility of selection at three of the syllables that the reader has made prominent: WORLD, CUP, and PRESent.

Only slightly less transparent considerations would allow a reduction of

(and this in turn) // provoked an ANgry response // from some opPOSing supporters // in an adJOINing section // of the STAND //

to

// provoked an angry response from some opposing supporters in an adjoining section of the STAND //

In the context of a news item about a *clash* the response would hardly be other than *angry*, those making it would hardly be other than *opposing* supporters, and if they had not been in an adjoining section of the stand the consequences would probably not have been newsworthy.

There is no need to labour the point that – regardless of *post hoc* assessments of what might or might not have been made non-prominent – the 'higher than necessary' incidence of prominent syllables is helpful to the hearer rather than otherwise in the peculiar case of the news bulletin. It is a form of redundancy that is regularly found in this kind of reading, and, like other forms, it doubtless facilitates the decoding process. As with tone choice, the possibilities of substitution are unidirectional: selective significance can be ascribed redundantly to an item which, on a dispassionate view of the matter, is probably not selective, but, if an item really is selective in its given context, alteration will result in something that is either unintelligible in the context or makes the wrong point. Thus, at the opening of the bulletin

// in the NATional stadium at niblitz today //

would give the misleading impression that the ensuing item was about the 'national', as opposed to the other stadiums in that city. Omission of either of the prominences in

// supPORters CLASHED //

would miss the essential information that the item is about *supporters* (as distinct from players) and the fact that they clashed (as distinct from the other things they may have done).

A summary of the reader's behaviour with respect to tone choice and prominence assignment might, then, be represented like this:

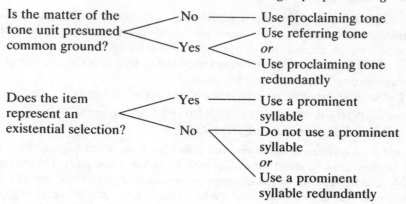

One further point can be made about this reading. It concerns the use of both tone choice and prominence, but in a rather different way. Notice, first, that the tone unit

//p until HALF TIME //

selects low termination and thus results in pitch sequence closure. Compare this with a later pitch sequence closure:

//r in an ADjoining SECtion //p of the STAND //

On the basis of the argument we have used above, *stand* scarcely qualifies for prominence – it could scarcely be an adjoining section of anything else. And even if it is given prominence redundantly as we have said it might be, a referring tone would seem more likely: if *an adjoining section* can be treated as coming within the area of shared understanding, *of the stand* could surely be as well. The apparent double anomaly is due, of course, to the need to close the pitch sequence. It is a general feature of the intonation system that, while prominence is most often used to indicate a sense selection, it can also be used to indicate a selection on one of the meaning oppositions that intonation choices themselves realize. In this case, the sole purpose of the last tone unit might be said to be to carry the sequence-closing combination of low termination and proclaiming tone.

The other sequence closure in the extract exemplifies another common way of bringing it about. We have:

. . . //r against the PRESent CUP holders //p RURiTAnia //

Here, the two-prominence form of *Ruritania*, that we have associated earlier with citation, is used to enable the reader to make separate choices in the key and termination systems: to bring about sequence closure while retaining mid key for the tone unit. It might be argued that this is unnecessary: that an appropriate reading would recognize the existential equivalence of *present cup holders and Ruritania* with low key:

//r against the PRESent CUP holders //p ruriTAnia //

The difference between the low and mid key choices is that the former attributes knowledge of the equivalence to the hearer while the latter makes no such attribution. Once more, the reading we have errs on the side of explicitness: it works against probability by not taking an aspect of speaker/hearer understanding for granted.

Let us now consider the first reading, the act of dictation.

//o supPORters CLASHED //o DURing PLAY //o at the
NATional STAdium //o HERE toDAY //

There is an obvious need to give the colleague time to take down the copy so the division into short tone units with level tones and pauses between is fairly predictable. If we focus upon prominence distribution, we find we have a performance of the kind we have associated with minimal engagement: all the content words, and only the content words, have prominent syllables. This version and the news item version are not identical in non-intonational ways, but we can make a comparison between

//o at the NATional STAdium //o HERE to DAY //

and

//r+ at the NATional stadium in NIBlitz today //

The journalist is not telling his colleague what happened but what to write down, and orientation towards language rather than sense reduces the likelihood of engagement as we have understood it. This stance is not consistently maintained, however:

//o WHEN ENGland //r played their WORLD CUP match
//o against the PRESent cup holders //p ruriTANia //

We can safely assume that the colleague knows, in a general way, what this report is going to be about. The change to what seems like fully engaged mode in the second tone unit of this extract is therefore not surprising. Notice that the referring tone implies that this part of the message will be predictable, and the allocation of prominence is in accordance with a tenable view of the state of understanding: two of the content words, *played* and *match* have their non-selective status acknowledged. The next tone unit has level tone. It is otherwise identical with the corresponding tone unit in the news item:

//r against the PRESent cup holders //

This represents a degree of engagement that we have called Stage 2: the speaker makes no decision with respect to the proclaiming/referring opposition, but distributes prominence in a way which implies an understanding about what will, and will not, be selective. There follows of stretch of minimally engaged speech:

//o ENGland //o had HELD the CHAMpions //o to ONE ONE
//o until HALF TIME //o but SOON //o after PLAY //o was reSUMED
//o a PENalty //o was aWARDed //p aGAINST them //

The return to engaged mode:

//r the deCISion caused UProar //o aMONG a GROUP
//r of ENGland FANS //

can be compared with the corresponding passage in the reading of the bulletin:

//r the deCISion //p CAUSED UProar //r+ aMONG a GROUP
//p of ENGland FANS //

If we ignore the differential treatment of *among a group*, we have here two engaged readings which differ principally in what they assume the hearer needs to be told. For the reporter – and he assumes for his colleague – uproar among fans following a decision against their team is not news. For the newsreader – and she assumes for her listeners – it is.

A similar assumption of insider understanding that there is nothing new in what is being reported underlies much of the rest of the extract:

//o and THIS in TURN //r TRIGGered //r an ANGry reSPONSE
//o from SOME //r opPOSing suPPORTers //r in an adJOINing SECtion
//p of the STAND //

When the colleague reads back the report for checking, he begins with referring tones, which, according to the criteria we have proposed, places the performance some way along the continuum towards full engagement:

//r+ supPORTers CLASHED //r+ DURing PLAY
//r+ at the NATional STAdium //p HERE toDAY //

It is noticeable, however, that all content words are given prominence, in what seems like a fairly mechanical way, without regard to how they may or may not indicate selection. An explanation of this might be that this is an interaction, not about the football world and what has happened in it, but about the language the reporter has just dictated. It follows from the general meaning attaching to referring tones that they are regularly used for making sure that a supposition is true. Within this general significance, we can separate out two uses to which they can be put. They are exemplified by:

Am I right in thinking supporters clashed?
Am I right in thinking that what you said was 'Supporters clashed'?

It is the second of these that seems most closely to parallel what is happening in the reading-back activity, and since the focus is language rather than sense, the factors which make content words non-selective are not operative. We have to include, in the data that we recognize as engaged *interaction about language*.

Once more, however, we find that the speaker is not consistent in his stance:

//o when ENGland PLAYED //o their WORLD //r+ CUP MATCH //p aGAINST the PRESent //r+ CUP HOLDers //p RURiTAnia //

In this extract it seems reasonable to say that the tone choices are motivated in different ways. Some of it resembles minimally engaged reading: *when England played their world*; some of it resembles engaged reading about language in which the reader is making sure that what he has taken down is correct: *cup match . . . cup holders*; in yet other tone units, he seems simply to be telling what he has written, presumably on the assumption that the journalist will tell him if he's got it wrong: *against the present . . . Ruritania*. The rest of the extract comprises predominantly 'making sure' tone units, interspersed with minimally engaged tone units having level tones.

//o ENGland //r+ had HELD the CHAMpions //r+ to ONE ONE //r+ until HALF TIME //r+ but SOON after play was reSUMED //r+ a PENalty //p was awarded aGAINST them //r+ the deCIsion //o caused UProar //r+ among a group of ENGland FANS //r+ and THIS in TURN //o TRIggered //o an ANgry resPONSE //o from SOME //r+ opPOSing supPORTers //o IN //o an adJOINing SECtion //p of the STAND //

Tone-unit-by-tone-unit speculation about what is going on in readings like these is clearly a risky business. We cannot pretend to know what the readers' intentions are from moment to moment; nor, indeed, must we be trapped into assuming that they necessarily know what they are themselves. We can merely try to give a generalizable explanation for their behaviour, and I have tried to do so by appealing to an analysis of some of the things which, on the intonational evidence, they might be thought to be doing. Although they give us reason for supposing that different modes of reading can be separated out and related to different uses of the intonation system, the second and third readings, in particular, show that we must be prepared for considerable variation in mode – for different kinds and degrees of engagement – in the same reading.

PROJECTING A CONTEXT

The notion of differing degrees of engagement is nowhere more necessary than when we seek to explore what happens when people read verse aloud. In this final part of the chapter I shall turn to this particular form of reading. There would seem to be good reason for doing so, for it is hard to see how a study of that feature which, above all others, is commonly taken to distinguish verse from other kinds of writing, *metre*, can be carried on without some recognition that it has potentiality for being realized as speech. And the foregoing suggests that readers, in the process of realizing metre, will be operating at one or more of the stages of engagement we have identified.

The study of metrical organization – of the conformity of the language of a verse to certain conventional patterns involving 'stressed' and 'unstressed' syllables' – has a long history, and suggestions that it can be aided by the kind of analysis linguistics provides have not always been welcomed. Nevertheless, it would seem unlikely that there is no describable relationship between the categories of metrical theory and those of such an analytical procedure as the one this chapter is concerned with. I shall try to go some way towards clarifying that relationship by seeing how far we can get, on the assumption that poetry is engaged communication.

Before doing so, however, I must consider briefly one way in which poetry differs from the kind of language that we looked at in the last section. We said there that the newsreader related her performance to assumptions about an audience, and in doing this she was dependent on her apprehension of a ready-made community of interest. She assumed that she knew what could be taken for granted and what needed to be told. She assumed, moreover, that members of the audience knew these things as well. The activity could therefore be seen as a co-operative matching of performance with expectation, something that is fairly apparent in the opening sentence: 'This is what I know you want to know about: this is what I have to tell you about it.' Readers of poetry have a different situation to operate in, and it is one which distinguishes very much of what we can informally speak of as *fiction*.

When a reader begins the first chapter of a novel like this:

//r NICHolas BUDE //r SIGNED his NAME //p at the BOTtom
of a page of NOTEpaper //

she addresses an interest in *where* a person of that name signed it. If she begins

//r NICHolas BUDE //p SIGNED his NAME //p at the BOTTom
of a page of NOTEpaper //

she addresses an interest in what he did *and* where he did it. Both assume that Nicholas Bude is known to the hearer. Now it is highly unlikely that any of these assumptions are based on the reality of the situation. The title of the novel *The Chinese Room* gives no prior indication of what the characters will be called; in fact both readings seem to be in line with a common authorial practice of introducing one character at the very beginning of the novel as if they were known, and as if their activities were an object of already negotiated concern. We can say, then, that in examining the reading aloud of fiction, the notion of *projection* is likely to be of considerable importance. Instead of matching their performances to an already existing state of understanding, readers must project such a state by *acting as though it existed*; and it is part of what is required of co-operative hearers that they accept the presuppositions that the projected state attributes to them.

If we return now to the two versions we proposed above, we can see that they project different states of understanding, and that the difference could have important implications for what follows. If we are told that Bude signed his name, the fact of his having done so might have later repercussions or require subsequent explanation. If it is assumed that we know he signed it, it is more likely to be where he signed it that will have later significance. A maximally effective reading of material like this will be anticipatory: it will take into account how the bit being read now fits into the subsequent development of the story. Instead of just acknowledging the existence of a context of interaction it will, to a large extent, create one in which the subsequent unfolding world of the fiction will be a determining factor.

VERSE AS CONVERSATION

Many poems fit quite easily into our understanding of what interactive speech is like. Some, indeed, are presented as representations of two-party conversations. Thus, it is hard to see how the opening stanza of W.H. Auden's 'The Quarry' could be seen as not partaking of the nature of a situated dialogue:

> O what is that sound which so thrills the ear
> Down in the valley drumming, drumming?
> Only the scarlet soldiers, dear,
> The soldiers coming.

What is less obvious is precisely what the situation is. A reading of the poem enables us to construct it in some important details (though not all of them may be acceptable to all readers). The first two lines are an interested enquiry by a woman about an unusual noise, the second two a rather dismissive explanation by a man. The latter is probably feigning unconcern, however, as it later becomes evident that the soldiers are looking for him. Their eventual breaking into the room and violently taking him away provides the climax to the poem.

We may ask how any of this will affect an appropriate reading. A dramatized reading might well suggest the relationship between the parties, their differing reactions to the sound, and any premonitions either might have as to its explanation in a variety of ways. Although much of this will involve vocal effects that do not fall within what I am now taking to constitute the intonation system, there is at least a possibility that it will affect the way the reader makes choices in that system. One possible, and justifiable, reading might sound like this:

> //p o WHAT is that SOUND which so thrills the ear //
> //p down in the VALLey //p DRUMming //p DRUMming //
> //r+ ONly the scarlet SOLdiers dear //
> //r+ the SOLdiers coming //

In this version, all the questions in the first two lines have a proclaiming tone. It seems important for subsequent developments that the speaker simply doesn't know what the sound is: it impinges upon her world as something in no way prepared for. A referring tone, with the 'making-sure' implications it has with questions - 'Is that what I think/fear/hope it might be?' – would suggest, too soon in the poem, that she heard the sound as threatening. By contrast, the referring tones in the explanatory lines imply that what she has heard is a perfectly routine matter: she knows about the soldiers – there's nothing unusual about what is happening.

The distribution of prominence is more complicated. The first line is treated in a way which parallels, let us say,

// WHAT'S that NOISE i can hear //

or

// WHAT'S that LIGHT that keeps flashing across the sky //

In either of these, the fact that the noise could be heard or that the light was flashing across the sky could be taken to be self-evident to speaker and hearer alike and is thus justifiably presented as non-selective material. What makes this parallel slightly less convincing than it might be, however, is the verb *thrills*. The associated concept is so much a matter of subjective response that it is hard to imagine anyone using such a verb in that part of an utterance which is presented as self-evident background: as presuming, in other words, that the other's ear is thrilled also. But attempts to redistribute prominence and/or alter tone unit boundaries to remove this problem seem to result in versions with quite inappropriate situational implications. The most likely, and least odd, alternative,

//o WHAT is that SOUND //p which SO thrills the EAR //

does not, in fact, help, since *thrills* is still presented as non-selective. The problem is not so serious as it may seem, however. If we say that *thrills* is not likely to occur non-prominently in such a context in the real world, we are saying no more than that the poet has chosen, for his own purposes, to project an unusual set of conversational conditions. And as so often happens when everyday expectations are contradicted, the element that contradicts them takes on a special significance. It is arguable that the obviously ambivalent connotations of *thrills*, which subsequent events in the narrative expose, are given weight precisely because a properly moti-vated reading of the line denies selectivity to a word against our expectations.

There is a similar case in the third line:

// ONly the scarlet SOLdiers dear //

Here, the lack of prominence in *dear* causes no surprise: it accords with the way terms of address are usually treated when they come after the mess-age. There is no possibility of selection because there is no one else the speaker could have been speaking to. The content word *scarlet* may seem to be a different matter, however. The reason for not making it prominent is as follows. The dismissive explanation is essentially the equivalent of

//r+ ONly SOLdiers //

To say this is to say that *scarlet* is not selective. If it were part of the speaker's purpose to identify the soldiers by referring to the colour of their uniforms, to specify scarlet soldiers rather than, let us say, blue ones, we should expect prominence. If he did, indeed, do this, an understanding might be projected that *scarlet soldiers*, in particular, were no cause for anxiety, a projection which would be contradicted by what happens later.

My reading reflects the more likely circumstance that *scarlet* is a taken-for-granted characterization of soldiers (at a time, perhaps, when all soldiers wore red), and it is worth noting that the additional connotations that this emotive word take on in a retrospective revaluation of the line – *bloodstained*, perhaps, or *bloodthirsty* – are possible only if *scarlet* is presented non-selectively in this way: the *scarlet* which is existentially equivalent to *bloodstained* is, in this poem, as much a permanent characterization of soldiers as is the *scarlet* that refers to the colour of their clothes. And since it has the special importance in the poem that comes from this possibility of double interpretation, we can argue that its somewhat unexpected intonational treatment underlines that importance.

REDUCED ENGAGEMENT IN READING VERSE

Having thus proposed a reading for these four lines which seems to fit our expectation of how they would be said as engaged discourse in the particular context of interaction I have constructed, I must now recognize that there is at least one other way of reading them which hearers might regard as equally acceptable. Among a number of people who were asked to read them, several did, in fact, produce something like this:

//o o WHAT is that SOUND which so thrills the ear //
//o down in the VALley //o DRUMMing //o DRUMMing //
//o ONly the scarlet SOLdiers dear //
//o the SOLdiers coming //

This treatment corresponds to what I earlier called Stage 2 engagement. Tone unit boundaries and the allocation of prominent syllables within the tone units are exactly as they are in the putative fully engaged version. All that is different is that level tone takes the place of all the tones that have interactive significance. The result is a kind of ritualized, stylized presentation of the poem which is fairly easily recognizable as typical of a great deal of public verse-reading. In the case of 'The Quarry', which is so clearly intended to be a situated two-part dialogue, such a reduction in engagement might, perhaps, be said to result in a less satisfying performance. If the alternation of speaker responding to speaker is held to be part of the experience, then a close replication of the reported discourse may seem desirable. The usefulness of recognizing Stage 2 engagement as an option for the reader is more apparent when we look at poems in which conversation is less clearly suggested.

A possible reading of the first stanza of Yeats' 'Sailing to Byzantium' is:

//o that is NO country //o for OLD men //o the YOUNG //
//o in ONE another's ARMS //o BIRDS //o in the TREES //
//o those DYing generAtions //o at their SONG //
//o the SALmon falls //o the MACKerel crowded SEAS //
//o FISH //o FLESH //o and FOWL //o commend ALL summer LONG //
//o whatEVer is beGOTten //o BORN //o and DIES //
//o CAUGHT in the sensual MUsic //p ALL neGLECT //
//o MONuments of unageing INtellect //

It is no part of my purpose to comment on the merits of such a reading. It seems likely, in fact, to come more closely to Yeats's own declared views about how his work should be read than would one which used the text as a basis for constructing a (in this case one-sided) conversation, in the way I have suggested can be done with Auden's poem. There are greater difficulties in hearing some of Yeats's lines as if they were communication directed towards a hearer than was the case with Auden. Nevertheless, we find that the reading depends, in an important sense, on their having the potentiality to be so directed. If we try to express the thought of the last two lines communicatively, we are likely to say:

//r CAUGHT in the sensual MUsic //p ALL neGLECT //r MONuments of unageing INtellect //

or, to paraphrase very crudely

//r preOCCupied with the business of procreAtion //p Everyone igNORES //r the THINGS that don't CHANGE //

We can best explain the non-prominent treatment of *sensual* and *unageing* in both versions by saying that after the detailed references earlier in the poem no epithet incompatible with *sensual* could apply, and that whatever is opposed in the argument to 'whatever is begotten, born and dies' will be *ageless*. Earlier lines are in a similar relationship to possible communicative utterances, for instance:

//p that is NO country //r for OLD men //r (where) the YOUNG //r (are) in ONE another's ARMS //

The things then referred to as typifying 'that country' (birds, etc.) might then be presented with a referring tone unit for each, followed by:

//r FISH //r FLESH //r and FOWL //p commend ALL summer LONG //p whatEVer is beGOTten //p BORN //p and DIES //

In other words, the complete reading, as an example of Stage 2 engagement, projects a here-and-now context of interaction in every respect except that hearer-sensitive tone choices are not made.

One further step can be taken by examining a possible reading of the opening of Eliot's 'The Love Song of J. Alfred Prufrock'. It is a feature of the enigmatic opening of this poem that it is not readily fitted into a conversational setting, a fact which is more significant in view of its obvious conversational nature:

> Let us go then, you and I,
> When the evening is spread out against the sky
> Like a patient etherized upon a table;

The poem seems to provide no reason for preferring, for instance, any one of the possible readings of the first four words to the others:

> //p LET us GO them //
> //r+ Let us GO then //
> //p let US go then //
> //p LET us go THEN // . . ., etc.

It is perhaps this deliberate indeterminacy that encourages readings like:

> //o LET us GO then //o YOU and I //
> //o WHEN the EVening //o is SPREAD OUT //o aGAINST the SKY //
> //o LIKE a PAtient //o ETHerized //o upon a TAble //

What we have here is a minimally engaged reading, in which prominences are assigned more or less mechanically to content words, without regard for any selective potential they may have. In this way, and by using only level tones, the reader projects no recognizable context of interaction. If I am correct in making this assertion, and if, as I believe to be the case, the reading follows directly as a consequence of what the poet has written, then we must assume that there is verse which operates in a different way from interactive discourse.

I shall not pursue the last possibility further, but merely summarize by saying that there seems to be some verse which encourages readings which partake of the features of fully interactive discourse, some which have the reduced discourse implications I have associated with Stage 2 on the scale of engagement, and some which are minimally engaged. In passing, we should note that, although the reader may have a fair measure of discretion in choosing the mode, there is reason to believe that changes of mode within a poem are sometimes indicated: that this is one among the many variables that the poet is able, through the reader, to manipulate. This is something else that I shall leave unexplored. To conclude, I shall try to relate the various types of reading I have mentioned to a way of approaching metrical analysis.

METRICAL PATTERNING

Perhaps the best way to start is with the Eliot extract. It is not always easy to get agreement about how a line of verse should be scanned, but an analysis of these three lines that might win a fair measure of assent would be:

| Lèt ǔs | gò thĕn | yòu ǎnd | Ì |

| Whèn thĕ | evĕniňg | iš sprēad | òut ǎ | gàinst thĕ | sky |

| Like ǎ | pàtiĕnt | ethĕr | izĕd ǔp | òn ǎ | tàblĕ |

For the first of these, the alternation of stressed and unstressed syllables maps exactly onto the allocation of prominent and non-prominent syllables in the suggested reading;

// LET us GO then // YOU and I //

This is not to say, however, that there is a simple correspondence between the two. Syllables that count as 'stressed' in the metrical analysis are of two different kinds in the intonation analysis: *tonic* and *onset*. It is a difference which, in another tradition, would be expressed in terms of primary and secondary stress. Let us provisionally assign the number 1 (meaning something like 'maximum weight') to tonic syllables, the number 2 to onset syllables (meaning 'less weight') and 0 (meaning no prominence) to the remainder. We can then represent the first Eliot line as

| 2 0 | 1 0 | 2 0 | 1 |

a procedure which enables us to see the distinction that conventional scansion treats as a simple opposition between 'stressed' and 'unstressed' syllables as a matter of *relative weight* within the foot. Applying it to the second line,

// WHEN the EV(e)ning // is SPREAD OUT // aGAINST the SKY //

we get:

| 2 0 | 1 0 | 0 2 | 1 0 | 2 0 | 1 |

with a reversed unstressed/stressed pattern in the third foot.

The third line introduces a new complication. If we apply the procedure to:

// LIKE a PAtient // ETHerized // upon a TAble //

we get:

| 2 0 | 1 0 | 1 0 | 0 0 | 0 0 | 1 0 |

Here there are two feet, *-ized upon a-* in which all syllables are given weight 0, a result which does not accord with the trochaic character that we perceive in both of them. It is evident that we need to recognize a subdivision among the syllables we have designated 0, something that we can achieve in this case by appeal to the distinction between *protected* and *unprotected* vowels. Both *-ized u-* and *-pon a-* have one vowel which is usually reduced to something like /ə/ and one which is never so reduced. On this basis, we can recognize the additional degree of 'weight' we need and re-analyse the line as

| 2 0 | 1 0 | 1 0 | 3 0 | 3 0 | 1 0 |

A similar treatment of the proposed reading of the Auden stanza is carried out on the assumption that it comprises mainly a combination of iambs and anapaests.

| ŏ whāt | iš thăt soūnd | which sō | thrĭlls thĕ ēar |
| 3 2 | 0 3 1 | 0 3 | 0 0 3 |

| dŏwn ĭn | thĕ vāll | ĕy DRŪM | mĭng DRŪM | ĭng
| 3 0 | 0 1 | 0 1 | 0   1 | 0|

| ōn lȳ | thĕ scār | lĕt sōl | dĭers dēar |
| 2 0 | 0 3 | 0 1 | 0 3 |

| thĕ sōl | dĭers cōm | ĭng |
| 0 1 | 0 3 | 0|

This is only one among a number of ways in which this stanza – and indeed the whole poem – could be mapped into the 'feet' of traditional metrical theory. I do not wish to advance arguments in favour of doing it in this way rather than another. The point is rather that, whichever way we divide up a line into feet, reasons can be found in the reading I have suggested for identifying one syllable within the foot as the 'weightiest', and thus for providing a firm basis for the 'stressed/unstressed' distinction.

In saying this, I may well seem to be flying in the face of a widely held view about the nature of the metrical basis of a poem. Crystal sums up this view as follows:

> There is almost total agreement that metre, however defined, should not be identified with the psycho-physical analysis of utterance, as displayed in the reading of a text. Metre is held to be an abstraction, in some sense, and is not to be identified with performance.

(1975:105)

Many people have found it hard to accept the notion of an underlying psychological pattern of stresses that owe their definition to no regularities in the spoken version of the poem. And accepting it seems to be a necessary step towards going along with the further claim that a poem, as realized in speech, does not usually coincide exactly with this underlying pattern; it is because the former is heard in the light of expectations derived from the latter that metrical organization makes its peculiar contribution to the effect of verse. To entertain this notion of an actual performance being set over against a regular pattern whose reality is purely 'psychological' seems to require that readers must be, in some sense, aware of both, but there are real problems in saying whence awareness of the latter is derived. Perhaps the most fundamental question concerns the allegedly 'abstract' nature of metrical patterning. The strongest interpretation of 'abstract' in the literature seems to require that what is perceived by the sensitive reader of poetry must be totally independent of the spoken realization. This is not necessary. The method exemplified above provides us with a pattern which is abstract in another, perhaps more relevant, sense: it can never be identified with physical realization. This must be true if for no other reason than that the latter must be analysed in terms of at least four classes of syllable, while the former recognizes only two. Moreover, the only predictable relationship between the two is that tonic syllables coincide with 'stresses': otherwise the two sets of categories map into each other differentially, and in a way which is wholly determined by their environment.

Another question concerns the special effect which results from the superimposing of realization upon psychologically informed expectation. The necessary non-coincidence of the two is amply demonstrated by the fact that, for instance, a metrical iamb has a maximum of six different realizations when described in terms of the four kinds of syllable we have postulated. An anapaest has thirteen. Some much-needed precision might be given to discussions of the way metrical expectations condition our responses to particular lines of verse if they were conducted in the light of this kind of differential realization. For instance, the fact that the second of the three iambic feet in

| | Only | | the scar | | let sol | diers dear |
| | 2 0 | | 0 3 | | 0 1 | 0 3 |

has maximum difference in weight (0 and 1) while the feet on either side of it have minimal difference, might be thought to be of some significance in an examination of how the poem, as a whole, works.

I have admitted to the possibility of differing views about the metrical organization of either or both of the Yeats and Auden lines. It is necessary to make clear that I admit to the validity of other readings than those I have suggested as well. Both components of the analysis are open to negotiation. This, I take to be inherent in the kind of exercise I am engaged in. Nevertheless, it is possible – and, as it seems to me, necessary – to suppose that there exists an ideal reading, even though it may never be realized in practice by any reader. The task of the responsible reader is to get as near as possible to this; and the intonation of the performance then provides us with the means both of constructing the abstract underlying pattern and of exploring the effects of the differential relationship between that pattern and spoken reality.

It remains to examine the 'Sailing to Byzantium' lines. Applying the same method to the first two lines gives us:

That	is	no	coun	try	for	old	men	The	young
3	0	1		0	0	1	3	0	1
In	one	anoth		er's	arms	Birds	in	the	trees
0	2	0	3		0	1	1	0	0	1

Of the ten feet that this particular analysis recognises, five are iambic, four are trochaic and one has minimal weight in both syllables. If we continue through the stanza, we find little reason for saying that the predominant pattern is either the one or the other. In such a case, there would seem to be good cause for applying the alternative method that metricists have always known to fit some kinds of English verse. Abercrombie (1964) outlines an approach to verse structure in which he propounds the concept of a silent stress, or *silent ictus*. The idea is presented in the context of Abercrombie's belief in the isochronicity of languages like English, a belief that stressed syllables tend to occur at equal time intervals. Probably in any reading of the line:

That is no country for old men. The young

there will be a pause after *men*, and this pause will affect the overall timing of the line as if it were a stressed syllable. Furthermore, by assuming that there is a similar silent stress before *that*, we can represent the line as a sequence of five feet, each beginning with a stressed syllable and possibly followed by one or more unstressed ones. So:

// that is NO country // for OLD men // the YOUNG //

is scanned as follows:

| ∧ that is | no country for | old men | ∧ the | young

It will be noticed that the 'stressed' syllables in this version are those to which I have assigned prominence in the partially engaged reading I have proposed. This remains true when the procedure is applied to the rest of the stanza:

// in ONE another's ARMS // BIRDS // in the TREES //
// those DYing generAtion // at their SONG //
// the SALmon falls // the MACKerel crowded SEAS //
// FISH // FLESH // and FOWL // commend ALL summer LONG //
// what EVER is beGOTTen // BORN // and DIES //
// CAUGHT in the sensual MUSic // ALL negLECT //
// MONuments of unageing // INtellect //

is scanned thus:

| ∧ that is | NO country for | OLD men | ∧ the | YOUNG

in | ONE another's | ARMS | ∧ | BIRDS in the | TREES |

| ∧ those | DYing gener | A tions | ∧ at their | SONG |

| ∧ the | SALmon falls | ∧ the | MACKerel crowded | SEAS |

| FISH | FLESH or | FOWL commend | ALL summer | LONG |

| ∧ what | EVer is be | GOTTen | BORN and | DIES |

| ∧ | CAUGHT in the sensual | MUsic | ALL neg | LECT |

| ∧ | MONuments of unageing | INtellect |

The question of what counts as a stressed syllable for this mode of analysis is crucial. There are many content words in the stanza which do not count although they would have prominence in a minimally engaged reading. In the last four lines we have *commend*, *summer*, *sensual* and *unageing*. If they were all realized the rhythmic structure would be lost. The reader is evidently involved in making decisions as to which potential stresses to realize and which not to. On the very limited evidence of this fragment of verse, it would seem that those decisions are closely related to the way the lines would be said conversationally, except for the possible reduction of all the tones to *zero* in the way that I have characterized as Stage 2 engagement.

The patterned regularities revealed by this metrical analysis would appear, like those from the method of classical scansion, to presuppose a performance which takes account of the interactive potential of the language.

12 Forensic discourse analysis

Malcolm Coulthard

INTRODUCTION

Courts are increasingly calling on linguists to help in certain types of case and one can already see the beginnings of a new discipline, *forensic linguistics* – 1991 saw the third British conference of Forensic Phoneticians and 1992 the first British conference of Forensic Linguists.

Until recently most of the forensic work has been in the area of *substance*, i.e. comparisons of samples of handwriting (Davis 1986), and of tape-recorded voices (Nolan 1983; Baldwin and French 1990), where the methodology is already well developed. By contrast, *forensic discourse analysis* is a very new area and the methodology is still being developed *ad casum*. This chapter, which uses data from real cases,[1] is a contribution towards this new discipline.

THE FACTS

Forensic discourse analysis is, in the main, concerned with two kinds of text: handwritten contemporaneous records made by police officers of interviews with witnesses and suspects, and statements dictated by witnesses and suspects to police officers.

An *interview* is normally conducted by one, usually the more senior, police officer and transcribed by a second. It proceeds very slowly, usually at 20–5 words a minute, a pace which is basically governed by the officer's writing speed. Some time after the interview both police officers prepare a typed version of the interview, based on the contemporaneous 'notes'; these versions are identical, except for the reporting clauses: 'I then asked Power "what did you do next?"' as compared with 'Sergeant Jones then asked Power "what did you do next?"'

The text is supposed to be a complete record of what was said during the interview and thus it includes the *caution*:

> You are not obliged to say anything unless you wish to do so, but what you say will be put into writing and given in evidence. Do you understand?

the *request to caption*:

> You now have the opportunity of reading over these questions and answers and if you agree with them sign them as correct.

and any response to this request:

> I'll initial the mistakes, but I won't sign them.

or

> Its not that they're not right, you've been fair, but I'm not signing anything.

The text should be an accurate record, that is in the words used by the participants, although it need not be totally verbatim – thus, false starts and repetitions are ignored and, if a question has to be repeated or reformulated, this too need not be recorded.

Records of *statements*, by contrast, must be verbatim – they must include all and only the words used, in the sequence in which they were produced, and there must be no questioning by the police officers during the statement-taking; in other words, a dictated statement should be an unprompted monologue.

This system of taking evidence, with one party in total control of the production, safekeeping and subsequent delivery to Court of the textual record, is obviously open to abuse. Sadly for the discourse analyst, but happily for those who have needed to employ him, forensic discourse analysis is likely to have a comparatively short life. So much evidence has come to light in the past three years of police 'verballing', that is police fabrication of (parts of) interviews and statements, that most police forces are rapidly adopting as standard practice the tape-recording and in some cases the videotaping of interviews.

THE BRIEF

In essence, what the forensic discourse analyst is asked to do, almost invariably by the defence, is to take one or more interview records or statements and comment on their likely authenticity. In other words, the accused, or in many cases the already convicted offender, claims that police officers have fabricated a part or the whole of an interview or statement and is looking for linguistic evidence of this fabrication.

What the defence hopes is that the discourse analyst will be able to demonstrate that some or all of the *content* of the interview is untrue. Thus, the first task of the analyst is to point out that discourse analysis can say nothing at all about the truth of what is said *in* the disputed text, but can sometimes comment usefully on the truth of diverging claims made by both sides afterwards *about* the text. In most cases, in demonstrating the inaccuracy, unreliability or impossibility of a claim made about a text, the analyst is able to discredit the text itself as evidence.

Looked at from one point of view, what the analyst is faced with in a fabricated text is the work of an amateur dramatist, someone trying to create a convincing record of a fictional interaction. The analyst, from his knowledge of how real interactions, in particular authentic interviews and statements, are structured, and by comparison with other texts, both fabricated and fictional, sets out to detect non-authentic features. However, in most cases the evidence is not as clear as in the extract below where the incriminating utterances (7) and (8), totally lacking in coherence and cohesion both with what has gone before and with what follows, were added later to an otherwise authentic and apparently faithfully recorded interview.

1 Have you got a brother named Roy?
2 Yes.
3 On the 31st October 1986 you deposited £1,000 into the T.S.B. Where did that come from?
4 The sale of the GTI with 'Rabbit Injection' written on the back.
5 Will you sign an authority for us to look at your bank account?
6 No.
7 *I take it from your earlier reply that you are admitting been (sic) involved in the robbery at the M.E.B.?*
8 *You're good, Thursday, Friday, Saturday, Sunday and you've caught me, now you've got to prove it.*
9 Do you want to read over the notes and caption and sign them.
10 I'll initial the mistakes, but I won't sign them.
   (end of interview)

In this particular case the linguistic evidence of fabrication could be confirmed by ESDA, a machine for Electro-Static Deposition Analysis, which enables the analyst to read, from indentations, what was written on the sheet(s) above. ESDA analysis clearly showed that an earlier version of this text had been written on the page above, an earlier version that was identical, except for the absence of the challenged utterances (7) and (8).[2]

THE EVIDENCE

The kinds of mistake which a fabricator of interviews and statements makes can usefully be grouped under three headings which I will label *psycholinguistic considerations*, *quantity* and *discourse structure*.

Psycholinguistic considerations

There are several misconceptions about how the brain deals linguistically with the decoding, storing and recoding of information which can lead to identifiable mistakes in fabricated texts.

Firstly, there is a commonly held belief that people are able to remember verbatim what was said to them – everyday story-telling depends crucially for its vividness on this assumption:

and then I said . . .
and then she said . . .

However, this is just not true. Experiments show that it is impossible for participants successfully to remember, even immediately afterwards, what was said to them in a two-party conversation that lasted for as little as five minutes (Hjelmquist 1984). Participants can typically reproduce only 25–30 per cent of the ideas contained in their interlocutor's contributions and then only in a paraphrased form. Their ability to reproduce verbatim can be as low as 1 per cent.

Secondly, perhaps more surprisingly, speakers do not remember accurately even their own contributions; verbally transmitted information is not, in the main, stored in a verbal form in the brain. Thus, when they need to say again what they have already said, speakers encode the content linguistically anew, and, as a consequence, there tend to be small but important differences between the two utterings. These psycholinguistic facts can be of great significance when we come to examine disputed texts.

One of the functions of the traditional police interview record has been to provide the Court with unambiguous evidence of what was *said* – this left it to the Court to make the interpretative decisions about the *meaning* of what was said – a memorable example is the phrase 'let him have it' in the police evidence at the Craig and Bentley trial, where the prosecution alleged that the phrase meant 'shoot him' and the defence 'give it [the gun] to him'.

Although interviews used to be, in the vast majority of cases, recorded contemporaneously in handwritten form, there were occasions when, for a series of reasons, police officers wrote up a record of an interview after- wards *from memory*, in a 'verbatim' form; that is they claimed to remem- ber the exact words spoken and presented their record as direct speech within quotation marks. Indeed, in one case, where the notebook shows that the 'notes' were written up after the event, a fact never disputed at trial, the sergeant reports himself as saying, at the beginning of the interview, 'What we intend to do now is to interview you by way of a *contemporaneous* note.' It would appear that, in this context at least, 'contemporaneous' meant 'recorded later as direct speech' – unless, of course, he was 'remembering' what he would normally have said.

Such after-the-event verbatim records have, apparently, almost always been accepted by courts as reliable records of what was said. Indeed, there is no doubt that in most cases such records were made in good faith. The problem facing the discourse analyst is to demolish the common man's assumption and to demonstrate that verbatim recollection is impossible.

One obvious way of doing so would be to ask the policemen involved to repeat their feat under controlled conditions but, so far as I know, this has not yet been allowed by any court. So, in such situations there are two approaches open to the discourse analyst. Firstly, he can appeal to the experimental evidence about linguistic memory quoted above and argue that even an honestly produced after-the-event 'verbatim' transcript must be totally unreliable as a record of the exact words that were uttered and only partially reliable as an account of the content of the reported interview. Secondly, he can compare authentic with disputed texts in the knowledge that, although any forgery sets out to look like the real thing, the forger will make mistakes.

Pursuing this line the first thing to examine in a text which is claimed to be a 'verbatim' record produced after the event is length. Average speaking rates are 8–15 times faster than average writing speeds, and thus an accurate after-the-event record of a 30-minute interview which, by definition, had not been slowed down by note-taking, should be many times longer than a contemporaneous record of a 30-minute interview – indeed solicitors and barristers are now finding themselves overwhelmed by the length of transcriptions of tape-recorded interviews.

Usually we can demonstrate that the disputed texts are simply too short. For example, in one case currently going to the Court of Appeal the claimed after-the-event 'verbatim' record of a 38-minute interview, when read aloud at normal speaking rate, lasts a mere 11 minutes, which fits very well with Hjelmquist's claim that participants remember 25–30 per cent.

The question of verbal memory was of vital importance in the evaluation of claims made in the case of one of the 'Birmingham Six', William Power. Parts of the interview record and the subsequently produced statement are verbally identical. The police officers claimed that this was because Power had simply retold the same story in the same words; Power's explanation was that the second text, the statement, was in fact in part copied word for word by the police officers from their written record of the first, the interview.

In order to support Power's claim I needed to draw on the evidence that people do not remember even their own utterances verbatim and that, when they need to say the same thing on a different occasion, they encode anew. Power himself, interestingly, kept reminding the prosecution barrister of this at his trial, when he was asked to confirm that he had actually said certain things attributed to him:

> Power: Yes sir, some words to that effect . . .
>   I don't know the exact words, sir.
>
> (TBJ, p. 4)

By great good fortune part of the Birmingham Six trial was 'replayed' because, at one point, the defence disputed the admissibility of part of the prosecution case. So, for three days there was a 'trial within a trial' (TWT), at the end of which the judge accepted the admissibility of the evidence and then the same content was covered again for the benefit of the jury (TBJ).

As a consequence there are many examples of Power being questioned twice about the same events, once in closed session and once before the jury.

His replies are not identical, although the differences in content are usually insignificant; sometimes the verbal differences in his replies are small, as in example (1), sometimes more marked as in (2) but the crucial fact is that he is re-encoding his experience and not remembering his previous encoding:

1 Power: One of them shouted 'who is the sixth man?' . . . I said 'what sixth man?'

(TWT, p. 54)

  Power: **Somebody was** shouting 'Who **was** the sixth man, **who was the sixth man**?' . . . I asked 'what sixth man, **what sixth man**?'

(TBJ, p. 6)

2 Power: They told me there was a mob outside the house and my wife and children would be lynched, only for the Police who were inside ragging it, searching it.

(TWT, p. 49)

  Power: **He** told me there was a mob outside **my** house and **they were ready to lynch my wife and children and the only thing that was stopping them was because the Police were outside my house**.

(TBJ, p. 4)

As these examples show, even when 'saying the same thing' Power verbalizes in a different form. Therefore, what is striking, when we compare the Power interview with his statement, two texts which also purport to be separate recountings of the same events, is that there are so many utterances that are word for word identical. I give just three examples below with extracts from the interview first in each case:

3 and then **he** told Richard to give me one as well
  and then told Richard to give me one as well

4 Hughie said 'You're going to take them it's not only you that you've got to worry about'.
  Hughie said 'You're going to take them it's not only you that you've got to worry about'.

5 Hughie came back . . . said to me 'You have to take them to the pub at the side of the Rotunda.'
  Hughie came back **and** said to me 'You have to take them to the pub at the side of the Rotunda.'

There are far too many of these identical formulations for the two texts to be records of two separate tellings – no one, and certainly not Power, as we saw from the trial data, has this degree of accurate verbal recall; thus, in so far as these texts are identical, the only possible conclusion is that one of them must have been copied from the other. As the statement contains slightly more information than the interview record, it seems reasonable to conclude that, as Power claimed, the former was in part derived from the latter.

In an attempt to corroborate this claim further, I took the last third of the interview record and transformed it, as Power asserted the police officers had done, from a question-and-answer sequence into a monologue, adding only essential linking items and omitting anything that a fabricator would be likely to think might seem redundant from Power's point of view. Appendix 1, below, sets Power's alleged confession side by side with my 'composed' confession. The similarities are sufficiently striking to suggest that this is the way that the statement was created.

My colleague Michael Hoey (personal communication) used the same argument, that in real interaction speakers do not say the 'same thing' in the same words, to question the authenticity of another disputed text, this time an interview, in which a suspect was apparently confessing to a whole series of burglaries. He noted that no fewer than eleven replies to questions about breaking and entering seemed to be formed on the same pattern and could be accounted for by the following formula, where the bracketed items are optional choices:

$$
I \begin{Bmatrix} got \\ climbed \end{Bmatrix} in \begin{Bmatrix} through \\ by \end{Bmatrix} \begin{Bmatrix} the \\ a \end{Bmatrix} \begin{Bmatrix} (back) \\ (front) \end{Bmatrix} \begin{Bmatrix} (bathroom) \\ (louvre) \\ (lounge) \\ (kitchen) \\ (bedroom) \end{Bmatrix} \begin{Bmatrix} door \\ window \end{Bmatrix}
$$

In real life only orators can produce lexico-grammatical patterning of this order in real time.

Quantity

Grice (1975) in his seminal article 'Logic and conversation' observed that one of the controls on speaker's contributions was the *quantity maxim*, which he summarized as:

(a) make your contribution as informative as is required (for the current purposes of the exchange);
(b) do not make your contribution more informative than is required.

What Grice is concerned with here is the fact that all utterances are shaped for a specific addressee on the basis of the speaker's assumptions about shared knowledge and opinions, and in the light of what has already been said, both in the ongoing interaction and in previous interactions. This appeal to what Brazil (*passim*) has called 'common ground', makes conversations frequently opaque and at times incomprehensible to an overhearer, as we can see in the question/answer sequence below:

Pc: Why did you do it?
A: Well he told me if I didn't it would be worse for me . . .

We can now appreciate why truly 'authentic' conversation would be impossible on the stage: the real addressee of any stage utterance is in fact the overhearer, the audience. Thus, there has arisen the dramatic convention of over-explicitness, which allows characters to break the quantity maxim and to say to each other things they already 'know', and even things that are strictly irrelevant, in order to transmit economically to the audience essential information. This is a convention which Tom Stoppard parodies in the opening scene of *The Real Inspector Hound*:

> *Mrs Drudge* (into phone): Hello, the drawing room of Lady Muldoon's country residence one morning in early spring . . . Hello! – the draw – Who? Who did you wish to speak to? I'm afraid there is no one of that name here, this is all very mysterious and I'm sure its leading up to something, I hope nothing is amiss for we, that is Lady Muldoon and her houseguests, are here cut off from the world, including Magnus, the wheelchair-ridden half-brother of her ladyship's husband Lord Albert Muldoon who ten years ago went out for a walk on the cliffs and was never seen again – and all alone for they had no children.

When we come to consider the fabricator of forensic texts, we can see that he is in a situation directly analogous to that of the dramatist – he is creating his text with the overhearer, in this case the Court, in mind, and is anxious to make the incriminating information as unambiguous as possible. Thus, at times, the fabricator, just like the dramatist, will break the maxim of quantity, though rarely as extremely as in this extract from the beginning of a fabricated telephone conversation, where a convicted defendant is trying to incriminate one of the prosecution witnesses:[3]

A: Hello
B: Hello, can I speak to Mr A please?
A: Speaking
B: Are you surprised I've phoned you instead of coming down and seeing you as you asked in your message over the phone yesterday?
A: No I'm not surprised. Why are you phoning me here for? Why don't you come in to see me if you want to see outside?
B: Well you've dragged me through a nightmare and I don't intend to give you an opportunity to set me up again for something else or beat me up again and abandon me miles away as you did outside Newtown prison with the two detectives; and for your information, as you may know, I've filed an official complaint against you and the two C.I.D. detectives

A: The detectives and I beat you up and C.I.D. they denied, they didn't beat you up and you cannot do anything because you got no proof.

In a less extreme form we can see the same phenomenon of over-explicitness in the extract below, taken from a police interview which the accused claimed was totally fabricated; these particular utterances, as well as including an admission of guilt, introduce quite naturally to the Court otherwise inadmissible information about past misdemeanours:

K: I didn't mean to kill anybody you know. Fucking stupid to do it with my foot like it was.
Pc: You're talking about your injured foot?
K: Yes.
Pc: You alleged someone had shot you in a drugs deal sometime before this Dixon's job.
K: I don't know if I said that but I had my toes shot off in Newtown.

The second sentence of K's first contribution is at least formed in a convincing way – 'with my foot like it was' appeals to shared knowledge which is not made explicit. By contrast, the policeman's contributions are over-informative: if, as the text implies, the police officer already knew about K's problem with his foot, he would have been much more likely to agree with the first assertion, contributing something like 'It certainly was', or 'Why did you do it then?'; if, on the other hand, he really needed clarification about the significance of the foot in the murder, he would probably have asked 'What do you mean, your foot?' He does neither, but instead makes explicit the shared knowledge. The policeman's second contribution is even odder in the context; why should he tell K something they both know? These utterances are clearly, in Grice's terms, 'more informative than necessary' and the simplest explanation is that they were designed for the overhearer/Court and not the co-participant.

Over-explicitness can be realized at nominal group as well as at clause rank. In the Power confession already referred to, there was frequent reference to 'white plastic (carrier) bags':

Walker was carrying . . . two white plastic carrier bags
Hunter was carrying three white plastic carrier bags
Richard was carrying one white plastic carrier bag
Walker gave me one of the white plastic bags
Hughie gave J. Walker his white plastic bag

It is highly unlikely that Power would have used the phrase, 'numeral + white + plastic + carrier + bags' even once. Firstly, it represents a degree of detail we do not see in the rest of his statement. Secondly, the detail does not seem to have any importance in the story as he tells it, and it is very unusual for narrators to provide detail which has no relevance to their story. Thirdly, it is a noted feature of speech that speakers do not normally produce long noun phrases of this kind; rather they assemble complex information in two or three bits or bites. For comparison look at the way the information came out in the 'interview' with the police, which has a ring of authenticity:

Power: He'd got a holdall and **two bags**
Watson: What kind of bags?
Power: They were **white**, I think they were **carrier bags**

Even then there was nothing about 'plastic'.

As it is unlikely that Power would have used the full phrase even once in his statement, it is exceedingly unlikely that he would have repeated it twice and then gone on to say 'white plastic bags' twice more. The extract below shows clearly that, once a full form of a referring expression has been used, a speaker's normal habit is to employ a shortened version on subsequent occasions.

Mr Field-Evans: And did you say '*two white plastic carrier bags*'?
Power: Yes sir.
Mr Field-Evans: Whose idea was it that Walker was carrying **two white carrier bags?** Were those your words or the Police Officers' words?
Power: They were the Police Officers'. They kept insisting that I had told them that they carried **plastic bags** into the station.
Mr Field-Evans: Does the same apply to what Hunter was carrying?
Power: I don't know what you mean sir.
Mr Field-Evans: I am sorry. Whose idea was it that you should say that Hunter was carrying **three white plastic bags?**
Power: Well, sir, I said that.
Mr Field-Evans: But was it your idea?
Power: No. They kept saying that I had already told them that they were carrying **plastic bags** into the station. When I said that, they said 'who was carrying **them**? who was carrying **them**?' They threatened me. I said 'They were all carrying **them**.' They asked me how many were they carrying and I just said **one, two, three, one** and **one**.

(TWT, p. 60)

In the case of Bentley, the last man to be hanged in Britain, we are faced with a slightly different example of breaking the quantity maxim. One of the marked features of linguistic communication, whether it is spoken or written, is that the vast majority of clauses are positive; people do not normally produce negatives except when, as with the negative clause I have just produced, there is a specific communicative reason for doing so. As Pagano (1991) has demonstrated, negatives are a marked choice and only tend to occur in texts when the writer/speaker assumes that the addressee has some reason to believe the opposite, either from something in the immediately preceding text or because of assumptions made about the addressee's state of knowledge.

One of the surprising features of the Bentley confession is the large number of negatives:

Up to then Chris **had not said** anything. We both got out on to the flat roof at the top. Then someone in a garden on the opposite side shone a torch up towards us. Chris said: 'It's a copper, hide behind here.' We hid behind a shelter arrangement on the roof. We were there waiting for about ten minutes. I heard some more policemen behind the door and the policeman with me said 'I don't think he has many more bullets left' Chris shouted 'Oh yes I have' and he fired again. I think I heard him fire three times altogether, the policeman then pushed me down the stairs and I **did not see** any more. I knew we were going to break into the place. I **did not know** what we were going to get – just anything that was going. I **did not have** a gun and I **did not know** Chris had one until he shot. (The whole confession is reproduced in Appendix 2 below.) I now know that the policeman in uniform is dead.

Bentley is supposedly telling a narrative of how he came to be with Craig on the rooftop; then, after a series of unremarkable positive assertions he suddenly says 'Up to then Chris *had not said* anything.' There is no preceding justification, no subsequent take up, no apparent reason for him to deny this particular occurrence; there were a great many things Chris had *not* done up to that point. Shortly afterwards the negatives come thick and fast. What has not happened is rarely reportable in narratives; why, one wonders, should Bentley want to report that Chris 'had *not* said anything' and why should he subsequently, in what is a narrative text, produce five clauses in succession, four of them denials, all concerned with facts, not events? The simplest explanation is the one Bentley himself advanced, that the police asked him questions about things that were important to them, he replied in the negative and the exchanges were incorporated into the text as negative monologue sentences.

Discourse structure

The difficulty with evidence based on discourse structure is twofold: firstly, we have the acknowledged fact that nothing can be regarded as 'undiscoursical', i.e. anything *can* occur and so the analyst is forced to argue at best by appeal to probabilities; secondly, we currently lack a data base, that is a substantial collection of texts with which one can compare a suspect text.

However, it looks as though concentration on the the rank of *sequence*, that is the unit of discourse where topic is handled, is likely to yield the best results. One of the marked features in interviews which are acknowledged to be authentic is the occurrence of sequences of topic-linked exchanges, what others might characterize as a series of follow-up questions

Pc: I would like you to tell me about that red **Fiesta**
B: I bought **a car** from a breakers yard . . .
Pc: **The car** was stolen . . . are these the tools used in the burglary

B: No
Pc: When did you receive **the red XR2**
B: I registered **it** within a few days of receiving the **car**
Pc: How much did you pay for **the car**?
B: £500

Obviously, if an interview is being fabricated it will be difficult to produce follow-up questions as the necessary information will not be available; thus we can notice in disputed interviews a predominance of one and two exchange sequences, that is rapid topic shifts at points when to the analyst/ overhearer it is inconceivable that a follow-up question was not posed:

Ds: What about the guns?
B: Down to him
Ds: Were they real
B: Don't be a cunt, say they're fake
Ds: Did you stop anywhere on the way to the motorway
B: No, why ask that?
Ds: What about these other jobs
B: What about them
Ds: Lets get those out of the way
B: I ain't admitting those
Ds: What about the one in Wylde Green, the one where the car came from Barnett?
B: Let's just say I know about it
Ds: So it was you?
B: It was a London team
Ds: What about Hockley?
B: Is that the place by the flyover?
Ds: Yes, a GTi stolen from Harlow was used
B: London team again
Ds: You?
B: Maybe, look no more questions about those jobs I won't talk about them
Ds: OK That's all for now

CONCLUSIONS

I return to my initial observation: there is no doubt that some forensic texts are partially or totally fabricated, but linguistics does not yet have acknowledged and reliable ways of testing for authenticity. What I have tried to present here are notes towards an analysis of forensic discourse. As our insights into discourse structure deepen, so will our ability to distinguish the authentic from the falsified. Equally, in working on the non-authentic we should gain more insight into how the authentic is structured.

NOTES

1 All examples used are from real texts; where possible the source is indicated and real names used. Only where confidentially is still necessary have the names of people and places been changed.
2 I am indebted to my friend and colleague Tom Davis, a forensic handwriting analyst, for this information.
3 This extract was given to me by Peter French, a forensic phonetician, who is currently preparing an analysis of it for publication.

APPENDIX 1

A comparison of part of William Power's alleged statement (Text A) with a monologue version created from pages 11–15 of the interview (Text B).

TEXT A	TEXT B
Alleged statement, pp. 11–15	**Monologue version of pp. 11–15**
Walker gave me the overcoat to put on and then gave me one of the white plastic bags he had been carrying and then told Richard to give me one as well. So he gave me one. Hughie gave Johnny Walker his white plastic bag and then walked away with Richard leaving me Walker and Hunter together.	Walker gave me one of the carrier bags and then he told Richard to give me one as well. Then I saw Hughie give Walker his bag and then he and Richard walked away from us.
I think we all had two bags each. I certainly had two. Hill then joined us he was carrying a suitcase. Hughie then came back and we were standing all in a group.	It was about then that Hill joined us. He was carrying a small case. Then Richard and Hughie came back and we were all in a group together.
I said to them all 'I'm not taking these'. I just knew what they were. There were bombs and I didn't want to take them. Hughie said, 'You're going to take them it's not only you that you've got to worry about'. Richard then came back and called Hughie over to the side.	I said to Hughie 'I'm not taking these'; I knew what they were, I just knew, bombs. But Hughie said 'You're going to take them, it's not only you you've got to worry about.' Then Richard (and Hughie walked away)
They talked together then Hughie came back and said to me 'You have to take them to the pub at the side of the Rotunda.' He just said, to go round and put them in the pub. He said, 'It will be easy you've got half an hour or more and by then	then Hughie came back and said to me 'You've got to take the bags to the pub at the side of the Rotunda.
	It'll be easy, you've got half an hour or more and by then

you'll be on the train.' He
told me to go straight round
and do it so I started to
walk away. I went out of
the station and passed the
Taxi Rank.
I looked back
and saw Hunter and Walker
coming out behind me
carrying two bags each. I
walked straight round to the
Rotunda to the Mulberry
Bush. I walked in from the
left hand side as I came
to it. I turned right inside
and down a couple of steps
there were quite a few people
in so I walked over to
the bar and put the bags
down at my feet because I was
going to have a drink.

I changed my mind and picked
the bags up again because I
panicked and was going to take
them out. I started to walk
out and then I put the
two bags down by the Juke
Box and then I walked
straight back through the
other door and went straight
back to the station the way
I came. When I got back
there the others weren't there.
A few minutes later Walker
and Hunter came back again.
They weren't carrying anything
this time. Then Richard and
Hill came back in from the
other entrance. Richard was
carrying the holdall and
suitcase and Hill was
carrying a small case.
Hughie didn't come back at

you'll be on the train.
Go and do it straight away.'

So I went out of
the station past the
taxi ranks alone. When I looked

I saw Hunter and Walker
walking along behind me
carrying two bags each. I
walked round to the
Rotunda, into the Mulberry
Bush through the door on the
left hand side

and down a couple of steps
(into the bar.)
I walked over to
the bar and put the bags
down. I
was going to have a drink but it
was a bit crowded and I was afraid.
So I picked
the bags up

and then I put
them down again
and walked
straight out through the
other door and went straight
back to the station.
When I got back to the station
the others weren't there.
After a while Walker
and Hunter turned up.
They weren't carrying anything
this time. Richard and
Paddy Hill came back next.
Richard had
a holdall and a
suitcase and Paddy
a small case.
Hughie didn't come back at

all we all went to
platform nine together and
got on the train that was
already there. Soon afterwards
it moved out. There were
other people in the carriage
so we couldn't talk much.

We just had a game of
cards.

all. Then we all went to
platform nine and
got on the train.
After a while
it moved off

We didn't talk much
as it was quite crowded.
We just played
cards.

APPENDIX 2

Derek Bentley confession

I have known Craig since I went to school. We were stopped by our parents going out together, but we still continued going out with each other – I mean we have not gone out together until tonight. I was watching television tonight (2 November 1952) and between 8 p.m. and 9 p.m. Craig called for me. My mother answered the door and I heard her say I was out. I had been out earlier to the pictures and got home just after 7 p.m. A little later Norman Parsley and Frank Fasey called. I did not answer the door or speak to them. My mother told me that they had called and I then ran after them. I walked up the road with them to the paper shop where I saw Craig standing. We all talked together and then Norman Parsley and Frank Fazey left. Chris Craig and I then caught a bus to Croydon. We got off at West Croydon and then walked down the road where the toilets are – I think it is Tamworth Road.

When we came to the place where you found me, Chris looked in the window. There was a little iron gate at the side. Chris then jumped over and I followed. Chris then climbed up the drainpipe to the roof and I followed. Up to then Chris had not said anything. We both got out on to the flat roof at the top. Then someone in a garden on the opposite side shone a torch up towards us. Chris said: 'It's a copper, hide behind here.' We hid behind a shelter arrangement on the roof. We were there waiting for about ten minutes. I did not know he was going to use the gun. A plain clothes man climbed up the drainpipe and on to the roof. The man said: 'I am a police officer – the place is surrounded.' He caught hold of me and as we walked away Chris fired. There was nobody else there at the time. The policeman and I then went round a corner by a door. A little later the door opened and a policeman in uniform came out. Chris fired again then and this policeman fell down. I could see he was hurt as a lot of blood came from his forehead just above his nose. The policeman dragged him round the corner behind the brickwork entrance to the door. I remember I shouted something but I forget what it was. I could not see Chris when I shouted to him – he was behind a wall. I heard some more policemen behind the door and the policeman with me said: 'I don't think he has many more bullets left.' Chris shouted 'Oh yes I have' and he fired again. I think I heard him fire three times altogether. The policeman then pushed me down the stairs and I did not see any more. I knew we were going to break into the place. I did not know what we were going to get – just anything that was going. I did not have a gun and I did not know Chris had one until he shot. I now know that the policeman in uniform is dead. I should have mentioned that after the plain clothes policeman got up the drainpipe and arrested me, another policeman in uniform followed and I heard someone call him 'Mac'. He was with us when the other policeman was killed.

Bibliography

Abercrombie, D. (1964) *Studies in Phonetics and Linguistics*, London: Oxford University Press.

Allerton, D.J. (1978) 'The notion of "givenness" and its relations to presupposition and to theme', *Lingua* 17, 220–35.

Allwright, R. (1979) 'Language learning through communication practice', in Brumfit, C. and Johnson, K. (eds), *The Communicative Approach to Language Teaching*, London: Oxford University Press.

—— and Bailey, K.M. (1991) *Focus on the Language Classroom*, Cambridge: Cambridge Unversity Press, 22–3

Austin, J.L. (1962) *How to Do Things with Words*, London: Oxford University Press.

Baldwin, J. and French, P. (1990) *Forensic Phonetics*, London: Pinter.

Barik, H.C. (1979) 'Cross-linguistic study of temporal characteristics of different types of speech materials', *Language and Speech* 22, 116–26.

Barnes, D. (1969) 'Language in the secondary classroom', in Barnes, D., Britton, J. and Rosen, H., *Language, the Learner and the School*, Harmondsworth: Penguin Books.

Bellack, A.A., Kliebard, H.M., Hyman, R.T. and Smith, F.L. (1966) *Language of the Classroom*, New York: Teachers College.

Berry, M. (1980) 'A note on Sinclair and Coulthard's classes of acts including a comment on "comments"', *Nottingham Linguistic Circular* 8, 1, 49–59.

—— (1981) 'Systemic linguistics and discourse analysis: a multi-layered approach to exchange structure', in Coulthard, R.M. and Montgomery, M.M. (eds), *Studies in Discourse Analysis*, London: Routledge, 120–45.

Bolinger, D. (1958) 'Intonation and grammar', *Language Learning* 8, 31–117.

—— (1961) 'Contrastive accent and contrastive stress', *Language* 37, 83–96.

—— (1964) 'Around the edge of language: intonation', *Harvard Educational Review* 34, 282–93.

—— (1965) 'The atomisation of meaning', *Language* 41, 555–73.

—— (1972a) 'Accent is predictable, if you're a mind-reader', *Language* 48, 633–44.

—— (ed.) (1972b) *Intonation: Selected Readings*, Harmondsworth: Penguin Books.

Brazil, D.C. (1975) *Discourse Intonation*, Discourse Analysis Monograph no. 1, Birmingham: ELR.

—— (1978a) *Discourse Intonation II*, Discourse Analysis Monograph no. 2, Birmingham: ELR.

—— (1978b) *An Investigation of Discourse Intonation*, final report to SSRC on research project HR3316/1.

—— (1981) 'Intonation', in Coulthard, R.M. and Montgomery, M.M. (eds), *Studies in Discourse Analysis*, London: Routledge, 39–70.

—— (1982a) 'Impromptuness and intonation', in Enkvist, N.E. (ed.), *Impromptu Speech: a Symposium*, Publications of the Research Institute of the Abð

Akademi Foundation, no 78, 277–89.
—— (1982b) 'Intonation and connectedness in discourse', in Ehlick, K. and van Riemsdijk, H. (eds), *Proceedings of a Symposium on Connectedness*, Tilburg, The Netherlands, 179–98.
—— (1983) 'Intonation and discourse: some principles and procedures', *Text* 3, 1, 139–56.
—— (1984a) 'Tag questions', *Discourse Analysis*, special issue of *Ilha do Desterro*, 11, 93–108.
—— (1984b) 'The intonation of sentences read aloud', in Gibbon, D. and Richter, H. (eds), *Pattern, Process and Function in Discourse Phonology*, Berlin: de Gruyter, 46–66.
—— (1985) *The Communicative Value of Intonation*, Discourse Analysis Monograph no. 8, University of Birmingham: ELR.
—— (1986a) 'Discourse intonation', in Morley, J. and Partington, A. (eds), *Laboratorio degli Studi Linguistici*, Camarino: Associazione Italiana di Anglisti, 35–45.
—— (1986b) 'Investigating the intonation of language learners', in Cling, M. and Humbley, J. (eds), *Hommage à A.C. Gimson*, Villetaneuse: CELDA, 121–39.
—— (1986c) 'Intonation and the study of dialect', *Annual Report of Dialectology* 29, Tokyo, 263–78.
—— (1987) 'Intonation and the grammar of speech', in Steele, R. and Threadgold, T. (eds), *Language Topics*, Amsterdam: John Benjamins, 145–59.
—— (1990) 'O what is that sound – an exercise in metrical analysis', in Yoshimura, K. (ed.), *Linguistic Fiesta: a Festschrift for Hisao Kahehi*, Tokyo: Kuroshio Publishers, 67–82.
—— (1992) *The Communicative Value of Intonation*, Discourse Analysis Monograph no. 8, 2nd edn, Birmingham: ELR.
—— and Coulthard, R. M. (forthcoming) *Discourse Intonation for the English Language Teacher*.
—— Coulthard, R.M. and Johns, C.M., (1980) *Discourse Intonation and Language Teaching*, London: Longman.
Bresnan, J.W. (1971) 'Sentence stress and syntactic transformations', *Language* 47, 257–81.
Brown, G., Currie, K. and Kenworthy, K. (1980) *Questions of Intonation*, London: Croom Helm.
Brown, P. and Levinson, S.C. (1978) 'Universals in language usage: politeness phenomena', in Goody, E.N. (ed.), *Questions and Politeness: Strategies in Social Interaction*, Cambridge: Cambridge University Press.
Brumfit, C.J. (1980) *Problems and Principles in English Teaching*, Oxford: Pergamon Press.
Burton, D. (1978) 'Towards an analysis of casual conversation', *Nottingham Linguistic Circular* 7, 2, 131–64.
—— (1980) *Dialogue and Discourse*, London: Routledge & Kegan Paul.
—— (1981) 'Analysing spoken discourse', in Coulthard, R.M. and Montgomery, M.M. (eds), *Studies in Discourse Analysis*, London: Routledge, 61–81.
Bygate, M. (1988) 'Linguistic and strategic features of the language of learners in oral communication exercises', unpublished PhD thesis, Institute of Education, University of London.
—— (1991) 'Towards a typology of oral tasks', talk given at IATEFL International Conference, 3–6 April, Exeter.
Caldas-Coulthard, C.R. (1987) 'Reporting speech', in Coulthard, R.M. (ed.), *Discussing Discourse*, Birmingham: ELR, 149–67.
Chafe, W. (1976) 'Givenness, contrastiveness, definiteness, subjects and topics', in Li, C.N. (ed.), *Subject and Topic*, London: Academic Press, 22–55.
Cheung, D.S.L. (1984) 'Analysing the discourse structure of small group inter

action', unpublished MA dissertation, University of Birmingham.

Chomsky, N. (1957) *Syntactic Structures*, The Hague: Mouton.

— (1965) *Aspects of the Theory of Syntax*, Cambridge, Mass.: MIT Press.

— (1972) *Studies on Semantics in Generative Grammar*, The Hague: Mouton.

— and Halle, M. (1968) *The Sound Pattern of English*, New York: Harper & Row.

Churchill, L. (1978) *Questioning Strategies in Sociolinguistics*, Rowley, Mass.: Newbury House.

Clear, J. (1987) 'A modest proposal', in Coulthard, R.M. (ed.) *Discussing Discourse*, Birmingham: ELR, 63–79.

Cook, V.J. (1982) 'Second language learning: a psycholinguistic perspective', in Kinsella, V. (ed.) *Surveys 1*, Cambridge: Cambridge University Press, 5–52.

Coulthard, R.M. (1977/1985) *An Introduction to Discourse Analysis*, London: Longman.

— (1981) 'Developing the description', in Coulthard, R.M. and Montgomery, M.M. (eds), *Studies in Discourse Analysis*, London: Routledge, 13–30.

— (ed.) (1986) *Talking about Text*, Birmingham: ELR.

— (ed.) (1987a) *Discussing Discourse*, Birmingham: ELR.

— (1987b) 'Intonation in discourse', in Coulthard, R.M. (ed.), *Discussing Discourse*, Birmingham: ELR, 44–62.

— and Ashby, M.C. (1976) 'A linguistic description of doctor–patient interviews', in Wadsworth, M. and Robinson, D. (eds), *Studies in Everyday Medical Life*, London: Martin Robertson, 72–86.

— and Brazil, D.C. (1979) *Exchange Structure*, Discourse Analysis Monograph no. 5, Birmingham: ELR.

— and Brazil, D.C. (1981) 'Exchange Structure' in Coulthard, R.M. and Montgomery, M.M. (eds), *Studies in Discourse Analysis*, London: Routledge, 82–106.

— and Brazil, D.C. (1982) 'The place of intonation in the description of discourse', in Tannen, D. (ed.), *Analysing Discourse: Text and Talk*, Washington: Georgetown University Press, 94–112.

— and Montgomery, M.M. (eds) (1981) *Studies in Discourse Analysis*, London: Routledge & Kegan Paul.

Crystal, D. (1969) *Prosodic Systems and Intonation in English*, Cambridge: Cambridge University Press.

— (1975) *The English Tone of Voice*, London: Edward Arnold.

— and Davy, D. (1969) *Investigating English Style*, London: Longman.

— and Davy, D. (1975) *Advanced Conversational English*, London: Longman.

Culicover, R.W. and Rochemont, M. (1983) 'Stress and focus in English', *Language* 59, 123–65.

Davis, C.W. (1987) 'An Examination of the Criteria for the Characterisation of Spoken Discourse in the English as a Second Language Classroom', unpublished PhD thesis, University of Singapore.

Davis, T. (1986) 'Forensic handwriting analysis', in Coulthard, R.M. (ed.), *Talking about Text*, Birmingham: ELR, 189–207.

Deyes, T. (1987) 'Reading intonation and the control of discourse', in Coulthard, R.M. (ed.), *Discussing Discourse*, Birmingham: ELR, 272–321.

Edmondson, W. (1981) *Spoken Discourse: A Model for Analysis*, London: Longman.

Ellis, R. (1984) *Classroom Second Language Development*, Pergamon Institute of English: Pergamon Press.

Firth, J.R. (1935) 'The technique of semantics' in *Papers in Linguistics (1934–1951)*, London: Oxford University Press (1957), 7–33.

Fonagy, I. (1978) 'A new method of investigating the perception of prosodic features', *Language and Speech* 21, 34–49.

Francis, G. and Hunston, S. (1987) 'Analysing everyday conversation', in Coulthard, R.M. (ed.), *Discussing Discourse*, Birmingham: ELR, 107–48.

Fries, C.C. (1952) *The Structure of English*, New York: Harcourt Brace.

Garfinkel, H. (1967) *Studies in Ethnomethodology*, Englewood Cliffs, NJ: Prentice-Hall.

Gaskill, W. (1980) 'Correction in native speaker/non-native speaker conversation', in Larsen-Freeman, D. (ed.), *Discourse Analysis in Second Language Research*, Rowley, Mass.: Newbury House, 125–37.

Gibbons, J. (ed.) (in press) *Language and the Law*, London: Longman.

Goffman, E. (1987) *Forms of Talk*, Oxford: Blackwell.

Goldman-Eisler, F. (1968) *Psycholinguistics: Experiments in Spontaneous Speech*, New York: Academic Press.

Gordon, D. and Lakoff, G. (1975) 'Conversational postulates', in Cole, P. and Morgan, J.L. (eds), *Syntax and Semantics III: Speech Acts*, New York: Academic Press, 83–106.

Grandcolas, B. (1987) 'Feedback in the foreign language classroom', in Coulthard, R.M. (ed.), *Discussing Discourse*, Birmingham: ELR, 213–20.

Grice, H.P. (1975) 'Logic and conversation', in Cole, P. and Morgan, J.L. (eds), *Syntax and Semantics III: Speech Acts*, New York: Academic Press, 41–58.

Grimes, J.E. (1975) *The Thread of Discourse*, The Hague: Mouton.

Halliday, M.A.K. (1961) 'Categories of the theory of grammar', *Word* 17, 3, 241–92.

—— (1967) *Intonation and Grammar in British English*, The Hague: Mouton.

—— (1970) *A Course in Spoken English: Intonation*, London: Oxford University Press.

—— (1973) *Explorations in the Functions of Language*, London: Edward Arnold.

—— (1978) *Language as Social Semiotic*, London: Edward Arnold.

—— (1985) *An Introduction to Functional Grammar*, London: Edward Arnold.

Hasan, R. (1984) 'The nursery tale as a genre', *Nottingham Linguistic Circular* 13.

Hatch, E. (1978) 'Discourse analysis and second language acquisition', in Hatch, E. (ed.), *Second Language Acquisition*, Rowley, Mass.: Newbury House.

Hazadiah, M.D. (1991) 'The structure of topic', PhD thesis, University of Birmingham.

Hewings, M.J. (1985) 'Teacher appraisal of learner utterances in the formal, elementary EFL classroom', unpublished MA thesis, University of Birmingham.

—— (1987) 'Intonation and feedback in the EFL classroom', in Coulthard, R.M. (ed.), *Discussing Discourse*, Birmingham: ELR, 221–35.

—— (ed.) (1990) *Papers in Discourse Intonation*, Birmingham: ELR.

Hjelmquist, E. (1984) 'Memory for conversations', *Discourse Processes* 7, 321–36.

—— and Gidlung, A. (1985) 'Free recall of conversations', *Text* 3, 169–86.

Hoey, M.P. (1979) *Signalling in Discourse*, Discourse Analysis Monograph no. 6, Birmingham: ELR.

Hollien, H. (1990) *The Acoustics of Crime*, London: Plenum.

Holmes, J. (1984) 'Modifying illocutionary force', *Journal of Pragmatics* 8, 345–65.

Horn, L. (1985) 'Metalinguistic negation and pragmatic ambiguity', *Language* 61, 121–74.

Huddleston, R. (1984) *Introduction to the Grammar of English*, Cambridge: Cambridge University Press.

Hudson, R.A. (1975) 'The meaning of questions', *Language* 51, 1–31.

Jakendoff, R. (1972) *Semantic Interpretation in Generative Grammar*, Cambridge, Mass.: MIT Press.

Jefferson, (1972) 'Side sequences', in Sudnow, D. (ed.), *Studies in Social Interaction*,

New York: The Free Press, 294–338.
—— (1978) 'Sequential aspects of storytelling in conversation', in Schenkein (ed.), *Studies in the Organisation of Conversational Interaction*, New York: Academic Press.
—— and Schenkein, (1978) 'Some sequential negotiations in conversation' in Schenkein (ed.), *Studies in the Organisation of Conversational Interaction*, New York: Academic Press, 153–72.
Jespersen, O. (1933) *Essentials of English Grammar*, London: Allen & Unwin.
Kasper, G. (1985) 'Repair in foreign language learning', *Studies in Second Language Acquisition* 7.
Katz, J. (1972) *Semantic Theory*, New York: Harper & Row.
—— (1977) *Propositional Structure and Illocutionary Force*, New York: Cromwell.
—— and Fodor, J. (1963) 'The structure of a semantic theory', *Language* 39, 170–210.
Katz, J.J. and Postal, P. (1964) *An Integrated Theory of Linguistic Description*, Cambridge, Mass.: MIT Press.
Kempson, R.M. (1977) *Semantic Theory*, Cambridge: Cambridge University Press.
Kendon, (1973) 'The role of visible behaviour in the organisation of face-to-face interaction' in von Cranach, M. and Vine, I. (eds), *Social Communication and Movement*, London: Academic Press, 29–74.
Kintsch, W. and van Dijk, T.A. (1978) 'Towards a model of text comprehension and production', *Psychological Review* 8, 363–94.
Kiparsky, P. and Kiparsky C. (1971) 'Fact', in Steinberg, D. and Jakobovits, L. (eds), *Semantics*, Cambridge: Cambridge University Press, 345–69.
Knowles, G. (1978) 'The nature of phonological variables in Scouse', in Trudgill, P. (ed.), *Sociolinguistic Patterns in British English*, London: Edward Arnold, 80–90.
Kunzel, H. (1987) *Sprechererkennung: Grudzuge Forensischer*, Heidelberg: Kriminalistik-Verlag.
Labov, W. (1970) 'The study of language in its social context', *Studium Generale* 23, 30–87.
—— (1972) 'Rules for ritual insults', in Sudnow, D. (ed.), *Studies in Social Interaction*, New York: Free Press, 120–69.
—— and Fanshel, D. (1977) *Therapeutic Discourse*, New York: Academic Press.
—— and Weletzky, J. (1966) 'Narrative analysis: oral versions of personal experience', in Helm, J. (ed.), *Essays on the Verbal and Visual Arts*, Seattle: University of Washington Press, 12–44.
Lackstrom, J., Selinker, L. and Trimble, L. (1973) 'Technical rhetorical principles and grammatical choice', *TESOL Quarterly* 7, 2, 127–36.
Lakoff, R. (1972) 'Language in context', *Language* 48, 4, 907–27.
Laver, J. (1970) 'The production of speech', in Lyons, J. (ed.), *New Horizons in Linguistics*, Harmondsworth: Penguin Books, 53–76.
Leech, B.N. (1977) *Language and Tact*, Paper no. 46, Linguistic Agency, University of Trier.
Leech, G. (1983) *Principles of Pragmatics*, London: Longman.
Levi, J.N. and Walker, A.G. (eds) (1990) *Language in the Judicial Process*, London: Plenum.
Levinson, S.C. (1979) 'Activity types and language', *Linguistics* 17, 5/6, 356–99.
—— (1981) 'The essential inadequacies of speech act models of dialogue', in Parret, H., Sbisa, M. and Verschueren, J. (eds), *Possibilities and Limitations of Pragmatics: Proceedings of the Conference on Pragmatics at Urbino*, July 8–14, 1979, 473–92.
—— (1983) *Pragmatics*, Cambridge: Cambridge University Press.
Lieberman, P. (1960) 'Some acoustic correlates of word stress in American English',

Journal of the Acoustical Society of America 32, 451–4.

Long, M. (1983) 'Native speaker/non-native speaker conversation and the negotiation of comprehensible input', *Applied Linguistics* 4, 126–41.

Long, M. H. (1979) 'Inside the black box: methodological issues in classroom research on language learning', unpublished paper presented at the 13th Annual TESOL Convention, Boston, Mass.

Lyons, J. (1977) *Semantics*, 2 vols, Cambridge: Cambridge University Press.

—— (1981) *Language and Linguistics*, Cambridge: Cambridge University Press.

McCarthy, M.J. (1987) 'Interactive lexis: prominence and paradigm', in Coulthard, R.M. (ed.), *Discussing Discourse*, Birmingham: ELR, 236–48.

—— (1988) 'Some vocabulary patterns in conversation', in Carter, R. and McCarthy, M.J. (eds), *Vocabulary in Language Learning*, London: Longman, 181–200.

McDonough, S. (1981) *Psychology in Foreign Language Teaching*, London: Allen & Unwin.

McTear, M.F. (1975) 'Structure and categories of foreign language teaching sequences', mimeo, University of Essex.

Milroy, L. (1980) *Language and Social Networks*, Oxford: Basil Blackwell.

Newman, S. (1946) 'On the stress system of English', *Word* 2, 171–87.

Nolan, F. (1983) *The Phonetic Bases of Speaker Recognition*, Cambridge: Cambridge University Press.

Oakeshott-Taylor, J. (1984) 'On the location of "tonic prominence" in English', *Linguistische Berichte* 91, 3–24.

O'Connor, J.D. and Arnold, G.F. (1973) *Intonation of Colloquial English*, 2nd edn, London: Longman.

O'Neill, R. *et al.* (1971) *Kernel Lessons Intermediate*, London: Longman.

Open University (1981) *Talk and Text*, Educational Studies Block 5.

Orton, H., Sanderson, S. and Widdowson, J. (eds) (1978) *The Linguistic Atlas of England*, London: Croom Helm.

Pagano, A. (1991) 'A pragmatic study of negatives in written text', unpublished MA dissertation, Universidade Federal de Santa Catarina.

Pearce, R.D. (1973) 'The structure of discourse in broadcast interviews', unpublished MA thesis, University of Birmingham.

Pike, K.L. (1945) *The Intonation of American English*, Ann Arbor: University of Michigan Press.

—— (1948) *Tone Languages*, Ann Arbor: University of Michigan Press.

Prabhu, N. (1987) *Second Language Pedagogy: a Perspective*, Oxford: Oxford University Press.

Quirk, R., Greenbaum, S., Leech, G. and Svartvik, J. (1972) *A Grammar of Contemporary English*, London: Longman.

—— Greenbaum S., Leech, G. and Svartvik, G. (1985) *A Comprehensive Grammar of the English Language*, London: Longman.

Richardson, K. (1978) 'Worthing Teachers Centre: A Case Study in Discourse Analysis', unpublished MA thesis, University of Birmingham.

—— (1981) 'Sentences in discourse', in Coulthard, R.M. and Montgomery, M.M. (eds), *Studies in Discourse Analysis*, London: Routledge, 51–60.

Sacks, H. (n.d.) 'Aspects of the sequential organization of conversation', unpublished MS.

—— (1972) 'On the analysability of stories by children', in Gumperz, J.J. and Hymes, D. (eds), *Directions in Sociolinguistics*, New York: Holt, Reinhart & Winston, 325–45.

Sadock, J. (1974) *Towards a Linguistic Theory of Speech Acts*, New York: Academic Press.

Schegloff, E.A. (1968) 'Sequencing in conversational openings', *American Anthropologist* 70, 6: 1075–95.

—— (1972) 'Notes on a conversational practice: formulating place', in Sudnow, D. (ed.), *Studies in Social Interaction*, New York: Free Press, 75–119.

—— and Sacks, H. (1973) 'Opening up closings', *Semiotica* 8, 4, 289–327.

Schenkein, J. (ed.) (1978) *Studies in the Organisation of Conversational Interaction*, New York: Academic Press.

Schmerling, S. (1976) *Aspects of English Sentence Stress*, London: University of Texas Press.

Searle, J.R. (1969) *Speech Acts*, Cambridge: Cambridge University Press.

—— (1975) 'Indirect speech acts', in Cole, P. and Morgan, J. (eds), *Syntax and Semantics III: Speech Acts*, New York: Academic Press, 59–82.

—— (1976) 'A classification of illocutionary acts', *Language and Society* 5, 1–23.

—— (1979) *Expression and Meaning*, Cambridge: Cambridge University Press.

Sinclair, J.McH. (1972) *A Course in Spoken English: Grammar*, London: Oxford University Press.

—— (1973) 'Linguistics in Colleges of Education', *Dudley Journal of Education* 3, 17–25.

—— (1980a) 'Discourse in relation to language structure and semiotics', in Greenbaum, S., Leech, G. and Svartvik, J. (eds), *Studies in English Linguistics*, London: Longman, 110–24.

—— (1980b) 'Applied discourse analysis: an introduction', *Applied Linguistics*, 1, 3, 1–10.

—— (1980c) 'Some implications of discourse analysis for ESP methodology', *Applied Linguistics*, 1, 3, 253–61.

—— (1981) 'Planes of discourse', in Ritzvi, S.N.A. (ed.), *The Twofold Voice: Essays in Honour of Ramesh Mohan*, Hyderabad: Pitamber Publishing, 70–91.

—— (1984) 'On the integration of linguistic description', in van Dijk, T.A. (ed.), *Handbook of Discourse Analysis*, vol. 2, London: Academic Press.

—— (1987) 'Classroom discourse: progress and prospects', *RELC Journal*, 18, 2.

—— (1990) *The Structure of Teacher Talk*, Birmingham: ELR.

—— (forthcoming) 'Trust the text', in Davies, M. and Ravelli, L. (eds), *Advances in Systemic Linguistics: Recent Theory and Practice*, London: Pinter.

—— and Brazil, D. C. (1982) *Teacher Talk*, London: Oxford University Press.

—— and Coulthard, R.M. (1975) *Towards an Analysis of Discourse: the English Used by Teachers and Pupils*, London: Oxford University Press.

—— Forsyth, I.M., Coulthard, R.M. and Ashby, M. (1972) *The English used by Teachers and Pupils*, final report to SSRC.

Stenström, A. (1984) *Questions and Answers in English Conversation*, Lund Studies in English, Malmö: Liber Forlag.

Stubbs, M. (1981) 'Motivating analyses of exchange structure', in Coulthard, R.M. and Montgomery, M.M. (eds), *Studies in Discourse Analysis*, London: Routledge, 107–19.

—— (1983) *Discourse Analysis*, Oxford: Basil Blackwell.

Sudnow, D. (ed.) (1972) *Studies in Social Interaction*, New York: Free Press.

Svartvik, J. and Quirk, R. (eds) (1980) *A Corpus of English Conversation*, Lund: Liberläromodel.

Sweet, H. (1875–6) 'Words, logic and grammar', *Transactions of the Philological Society*.

—— (1906) *A Primer of Phonetics*, London: Oxford University Press.

Taglicht, J. (1982) 'Intonation and the assessment of information', *Journal of Linguistics* 18, 213–30.

Trudgill, P. (1974) *The Social Differentiation of English in Norwich*, Cambridge: Cambridge University Press.

Tsui, B.M.A. (1986) 'A linguistic description of utterances in conversation', unpublished PhD thesis, University of Birmingham.

266   Bibliography

— (1987) 'On elicitations', in Coulthard, R.M. (ed.), *Discussing Discourse*, Birmingham: ELR, 80–106.
— (1989a) 'Beyond the "adjacency pair" ' *Language in Society* 18, 545–64.
— (1989b) 'Systemic choices and discourse processes', *Word* 40, 1–2, 163–88.
— (1991) 'Sequencing rules and coherence in discourse', *Journal of Pragmatics* 15, 111–29.
— (in press) 'The interpenetration of language as code and language as behaviour', in Ventola, E. (ed.), *Recent Systemic and other Functional Views on Language*.
— (in press) 'The description of utterances in conversation', in Verschueren, J. (ed.), *Proceedings of the 1987 International Pragmatics Conference*, Amsterdam: John Benjamins, 229–47.
van Lier, L. (1984) 'Discourse analysis and classroom research: a methodological perspective', *International Journal of the Sociology of Language*, 49, 111–33.
— (1988) *The Classroom and the Language Learner*, London: Longman.
Ventola, E. (1987) *The Structure of Social Interaction*, London: Pinter.
Wardhaugh, R. (1985) *How Conversation Works*, Oxford: Basil Blackwell.
Warren, M. (1985) 'Discourse analysis and English language teaching: a contrastive study of discourse-based and communicative activities', unpublished MA thesis, University of Birmingham.
— (1987) 'Communicative activities or discourse activities?', in Coulthard, R.M. (ed.), *Discussing Discourse*, Birmingham: ELR, 196–212.
— (forthcoming) unpublished research papers, University of Birmingham.
Wells, G., McClure, M., and Montgomery, M.M. (1981) 'Some Strategies for sustaining conversation', in Werth, P. (ed.) *Conversation and Discourse*, London: Croom Helm.
Wells, W.H.G. and Local, J.K. (1983) 'De-accenting and the structure of English intonation', *Linguistics* 21, 701–15.
Widdowson, H.G. (1980) 'Contrived and natural language', *EFL Bulletin* 4, Oxford: Oxford University Press.
Willis, J. (1981) 'Spoken discourse in the ELT classroom; a system of analysis and a description', unpublished MA thesis, University of Birmingham.
— (1987) 'Inner and outer: spoken discourse in the language classroom', in Coulthard, R.M. (ed.), *Discussing Discourse*, Birmingham: ELR, 1–19.
— and Willis, J.D. (1988–9) *The Collins Cobuild English Course, Levels 1, 2 and 3*, London: Collins.
Willis, J.D. (1981) 'Needs analysis and syllabus specification', *English Language Research Journal* 2, Birmingham: ELR.
— (1983) 'The implications of discourse analysis for the teaching of spoken English', unpublished PhD thesis, University of Birmingham.
— (1985) 'Theory and methodology: do we do what we are knowing?', in Das, B.K. (ed.), *Communicative Language Teaching*, Singapore: Singapore University Press.
— (1987) 'An analysis of directive exchanges', in Coulthard, R.M. (ed.), *Discussing Discourse*, Birmingham: ELR, 20–43.
— (1990) *The Lexical Syllabus*, London: Collins COBUILD.